The Premature Revolution

Literature and Society

General Editor: Herbert Tint

The Premature Revolution

Russian Literature and Society 1917–1946

Boris Thomson

Weidenfeld and Nicolson
5 Winsley Street London W1

ISBN 0 297 99450 6

Printed in Great Britain by
Willmer Brothers Limited, Birkenhead

Contents

Foreword

For the transliteration of Russian names and titles I have followed a simplified form of the system used by the *Slavonic and East European Review*. The 'soft sign' and the 'hard sign' have been ignored. Certain well-known names, however, such as Meierhold and Eisenstein, appear in their Western spelling, rather than in a strictly transliterated but less familiar version.

All translations are my own.

Russia continued to observe the Julian calendar until 1/14 February 1918. Since the greater part of this book takes place after 1918, in the interests of consistency and clarity all dates are given in the 'new style', i.e. according to the Western (Gregorian) calendar. But it is perhaps worth observing that although the Bolshevik Revolution of 25 October 1917 is nowadays commemorated in Russia on 7 November, it is still the month of October rather than November that possesses revolutionary connotations for Russian ears.

I am most grateful to Professor George Luckyj and Professor Gleb Zekulin of the University of Toronto for reading parts of the manuscript and for their helpful suggestions.

For permission to use copyrighted material acknowledgments are due to the following publishers and publications: for quotations from Boris Pasternak, SOCHINENIA, edited by Gleb Struve and Boris Filippov, Copyright © by The University of Michigan, 1961 to the University of Michigan Press, Ann Arbor; for quotations from Andrey Platonov's *Kotlovan* to the editors of *Grani*; for material from my article 'Blok and the October Revolution', published in *Coexistence*, to Pergamon Press Ltd; for material from my article 'Leonid Leonov' to the editors of *Forum for Modern Language Studies*. I have also made use of an article 'Leonid Leonov: Soviet Novelist' first published in *Kolokon*.

BORIS THOMSON

Toronto
September 1970

Part I

1917-28

I

Marxism and the Bolsheviks: The Premature Revolution

On 7 November 1917, the Acting Government of the largest country in the world was overthrown by a group of revolutionaries inspired by the ideas and ideals of Karl Marx. Within a few years the attempt of his Russian disciples to put his doctrines into practice had profoundly affected every corner of Soviet life. It is the aim of this book to examine the consequences for Russian culture, and particularly literature, during the first thirty years of Communist rule.

The subject of Marxism is by now almost limitless; not only does the thought of Karl Marx form a vast all-embracing system in itself, but it has profoundly influenced social, economic and political theory and practice throughout the entire world. Innumerable books have been devoted to the man and his works, his predecessors and his disciples, to confirmation or refutation of his theories, to the development or revision of his ideas. Here we are concerned only with those aspects of his thought that are of particular relevance to the development of modern Russia. This means that we shall be dealing with Marxism rather than with Marx, and in particular with the interpretation of Marx's thought as it has evolved in the Soviet Union.

The distinguishing feature of Marx's approach lies in his claim to have applied the techniques of the natural sciences to the study of human society. He rejected as unscientific all theories that were not firmly based on empirical evidence; 'metaphysics' and 'idealism' are therefore terms of disapproval in the writings of Marx and his followers. The starting-point for his work is the axiom that society is primarily concerned with its own perpetuation, in other words with the production and distribution of the necessities of life. These socio-economic forces dictate the structure of society and ultimately every aspect of social life, even man's interpretation of the world around him. In Marx's phrase: 'Social being determines consciousness.'[1]

In the primitive beginnings of human society, Marx believed, all members of the community were engaged in production; society was organised on a simple co-operative basis, in which all men were on an equal footing. The interests of each individual were identical with those of the group. This meant that society was perfectly integrated; its members were united by common interests and values, while their closeness to their work provided a visible and satisfying justification for their labour.

With the growing complexity of human society this happy homogeneity gradually disappeared. The urge to increase production led to specialisation and to division of labour; the requirements of organising labour and distributing its proceeds led to the appearance of middlemen. Although these measures increased the efficiency of work they had also the effect that society ceased to be homogeneous, as men began to be differentiated according to their place in the scale of production. In other words the developments in the mode of production had led to a change in the structure of society.

Where once the interests of society had been identical with those of each its members, the different strata now began to discover their own group-interests. The ruling class alone, however, had the power (by definition) to impose its wishes on the rest of the community, and it succeeded so well that even the oppressed classes were persuaded that the interests of the community or nation-state, as interpreted by their rulers, were identical with, or even took precedence over, their own. They were encouraged to regard the present state of affairs as divinely sanctioned and immutable; and this in turn served to perpetuate the power of the ruling classes.

But at the same time the natural development of technical innovations and the consequent pressures to evolve new forms of social organisation better adapted to their full exploitation, were creating strains and tensions in society. In Marxist terminology, the forms, or basis, of society were becoming increasingly ill-adapted to the developing superstructure of institutions and value systems. These tensions, by the nature of the case, could only intensify, until they eventually exploded in violent social upheavals, during which the previous ruling class would be displaced by a new one. This new class would in turn elevate its own group-interests into the status of a universal system. It would instinctively refashion the religion, the political and legal institutions, the cultural patterns, the whole system of values, to reinforce its dominance, until it in turn would be weakened and destroyed by the growing contradictions in its own position; whereupon the whole process would begin again.

The attractiveness of this theory derives from the fact that it provides an explanation for the growth and development of societies in scientific terms. Writing soon after Darwin had formulated his theory of evolution, Marx seemed to show that evolution applied to human society too. Whereas previous thinkers had tended to regard society as essentially static, and had accounted for change and development in terms of local conditions or the intervention of higher powers, Marx claimed that the mechanism of change was built into the very nature of society and kept it in a state of permanent flux.

This dynamic of contradictions is known as the dialectic – the term is taken from the Socratic 'dialogue', in which the disputants move towards the goal of absolute truth by a process of setting different opinions against one another, and combining the best elements of each to form a new definition – and dialectical materialism has been developed by Marxists into a technique for dealing with all processes of growth and evolution. As in the Socratic dialogue the clash of the two opposites leads not to the absorption of one by the other, nor to a mere quantitative combination, but to a qualitatively new synthesis. Each new synthesis in turn generates its own contradictions, and thus eventually contributes to a higher synthesis, and so on *ad infinitum*.

In the field of social development, however, Marx believed that the number and the order of the stages was strictly fixed. Special conditions might affect the length of time that a society might spend in any one stage, but these stages must follow in a certain order; there are no short cuts in the historical process. Accordingly, he declared that no social order can collapse until it has attained the maximum possible development of its productive potential. At this point the tensions within would begin to weaken it and bring it into a decline.

Bourgeois society seemed to Marx to have reached just such a culmination in the nineteenth century. The workers in industry now saw only a fraction of the processes of manufacture, and in many cases they were quite unable to enjoy the benefits of the finished article; the consumers, for their part, were as likely as not ignorant of the methods of production and of working-conditions. The result was that on both sides of society men were increasingly alienated from the actual creative work of production. For some life had become mere parasitism; for others it had become meaningless drudgery; for all it was fast losing any social or individual relevance.

The rapid development of science and technology, the bewildering diversification of social activities that this development had entailed, and the widening gulf between the privileged and the labouring classes might seem at this point to have consolidated the domination of the bourgeoisie in perpetuity. But in fact Marx was convinced that this society was not only doomed like its predecessors, but also that this doom was imminent; the conflicting tendencies within modern industrial society seemed to have reached extremes. With the vast increase in wealth that modern technology and commerce had brought, businesses were no longer confined to a single town or even country; they crossed the oceans in search of raw materials, cheap labour, and, eventually, new markets. Because the stakes were so high, commerce was becoming inextricably involved with militarism and imperialism (Lenin was later to demonstrate how events since Marx's death had confirmed these predictions).[2] But this fantastic outgrowth of the superstructure of society was coming progressively into conflict with the basis on which it all rested. Its seeming strength was merely an illusion, and revolutionary developments were at hand.

Once again society was being driven into dialectical polarisations. On the one hand, the capitalists were becoming more and more disunited by the savage struggle for survival at the top; on the other the workers were being welded by the disciplines of industrial labour and their common plight into a staunch solidarity. The numbers of the former were being visibly diminished, while their casualties went to swell the ranks of the proletariat. This numerical disproportion between the exploiters and the exploited was continually increasing, rendering society as a whole more and more unstable. Sooner or later the exploited masses would take the law into their own hands and overturn the entire system. The exploiters would be annihilated, and the instruments of their power would either disappear or pass under the control of the workers. A new society would have synthesised out of the contradictions of the old.

Marx believed that this, the proletarian revolution, would initiate the final stage of the development of society. All previous systems, he argued, had entailed the rule by a minority over a majority, and were therefore essentially unstable. The minority had extracted their profits from the labour of the majority; in other words, a worker received less for his work in producing a given article than he would pay for the same article in the shops. Under the capitalist system an army of shareholders, middlemen, distributors and retailers all exploited the workers' labour to their own profit. The inevitable sense of fear and guilt had led them into a vicious spiral of increasing oppression. The proletariat, on the other hand, was the lowest class in contemporary society; it had no privileges or even possessions to exploit, no subordinate class to fear; after the Revolution it would still continue to work, while for the first time actually enjoying the fruits of its labour. There was thus no cause for the proletariat to be corrupted by power. Indeed the very processes of industrialisation had given the worker a certain education and discipline, which fitted him for the refashioning of society in a more practical, as well as a more humane, manner.

It was also essential that the proletarian revolution should be an international movement. Marx's experience of the revolutions of 1848 and 1871 had convinced him that the bourgeoisie would unite and crush any genuinely proletarian movement, and that therefore a successful revolution was impossible unless it was organised on an international scale; only in this way could it be secure against bourgeois counter-revolution. In any case, by crossing national frontiers in search of profits, big business had set an example to the workers and shown that men were not united by such abstractions as nationality, but by their classes. By education and propaganda the workers could be made to see where their true interests lay; once this was achieved, the first proletarian uprising would lead spontaneously to mass risings in all countries of the world: 'Proletarians have nothing to lose but their chains. They have a world to win. Working-men of all lands, unite.'[3]

Marx realised that the final revolution could hardly usher in Communism instantaneously, and he envisaged a transition stage, which he called 'the dictatorship of the proletariat' (sometimes called socialism), a state in which the class-divisions of earlier societies would still exist, with the difference that the dominant class would now no longer be a minority group, but the majority; while not particularly admirable in itself, Marx maintained that such a society would still be infinitely more democratic than any of the Western democracies, which he regarded essentially as dictatorships of the bourgeoisie. The proletarian dictatorship would frankly recognise what had been obscured by earlier social systems, namely, that the dominant class inevitably imposes its own ideals, interests and values upon the other classes. But gradually as all members of society became absorbed into the labouring class, men would come to recognise their common interests, and the need for this dictatorship would vanish. The state, as the instrument of coercion by which the ruling class asserted its dictatorship, and defended its position, would no longer be required, and would wither away of its own accord. Society would be free to work for the millennium.

Unlike most socialists, who have been concerned with inequalities of distribution, Marx emphasised the primary importance of the processes of production. Once these were in the hands of society there would no longer be any need for the system of inflated prices, caused by each manufacturer's and middleman's need to make a profit; instead of making a profit in each separate sector society would only need to balance its books over the whole economy. In such a society there would be no economic crises and so no temptation to acquire any more than one actually needed. Marx, however, did not envisage a necessarily egalitarian, still less a regimented, uniform, society, but a community of individuals, with differing needs and abilities; but now, instead of frustrating one another, their aims and interests would be mutually compatible and harmonious. Hence to characterise the transition stage of socialism he coined the slogan: 'From each according to his ability, to each according to his capacity';[4] under Communism men would receive freely according to their needs.

The wheel would thus have come full circle; human society would once again be classless and homogeneous, but on a vastly higher plane of development. With the means of production placed at the service of society, the drudgery would be taken out of labour, and the whole of life would regain the meaning it once had; there would be no distinction felt between work and leisure. The antagonism between the individual and society would disappear. Human life could at last attain the potential that had hitherto only been dreamed of. Culture would flourish as never before. In Marx's phrase, human prehistory would have ended, and human history could now begin.

These prophecies may not all have been fulfilled; some of them have not been realised in the way that Marx foresaw; and this summary inevitably oversimplifies the weighty argumentation with which he supported his theories. In his lifetime, however, the contemporary evidence of the trend towards monopolies, the recurrence of economic crises, the growing dissatisfaction of the labouring classes, the latent militarism of the imperialist powers, all seemed to confirm his diagnosis of the malaise of bourgeois society, and so to give the ring of scientific objectivity and impregnability to his comments on the present and his predictions for the future. But Marx was not content merely to prove the inevitability of revolution; he wanted to hasten its coming. He declared: 'Philosophers have only interpreted the world; the point is to change it.'[5] For Marx, therefore, philosophical theory is always subordinate to practice. He was an active participant in the revolutions of 1848, and he was a founder-member of the first International of Workers. Even his journalism was aimed at educating people in the logic of history and so converting them to the revolutionary cause.

Thus there are two distinct but inseparable aspects to Marxism: the study of the laws of historical development, and the message that it is man's duty to accelerate the historical process. Man cannot hope to frustrate the workings of history, but by understanding them, he can learn to work with them; they can be controlled and harnessed for man's benefit like any other natural force. Man's consciousness can at last begin to transform his environment; Engels quoted with approval Hegel's remark: 'Freedom is the recognition of necessity.'[6]

Since the goal, the classless society, is both inevitable and desirable, any means are justified in its pursuit. The extent to which an action assists the coming of this Utopia thus becomes the only moral criterion in the Marxist system of values. To work with the historical process is the only rational and right thing to do; only in this way can man be free. To oppose history may be heroic, but it is also stupid and even immoral, in that it wastes valuable human energies on a hopeless cause. What assists the historical process is good; what obstructs it is bad.

The academic and the prophetic elements in Marx's teaching can be combined in an infinite number of different proportions, and since Marx's time a multitude of schools all claiming orthodoxy has arisen. These may be divided into two main groups. The socialist (or social-democratic) parties of Western Europe have accepted Marx's view of the ultimate end of the current historical process, but they have aimed at making the birth of the new order as painless as possible; they have on the whole tried to work within existing democratic institutions, and they have concentrated on such matters as improving workers' conditions, guaranteeing them their human rights, and so fitting them for the day when power falls into their hands. Opposed to them have been the apostles of revolution; these have aimed at overthrowing existing bourgeois society, and so thrusting humanity forcibly into the next stage of its development. This trend is exemplified above all by Lenin and the Bolshevik Party who successfully brought off just such a revolution. For this they were denounced by more orthodox Marxists and Social-Democrats; on the other hand orthodox Marxism has not yet achieved any revolutionary successes. To distinguish themselves from the more cautious socialist parties the Bolsheviks took the name 'Communist' in 1918 and this styling has since been adopted by like-minded Marxist parties outside the Soviet Union.

Marx's theories grew out of his experience of Western industrial society; he envisaged the proletarian revolution taking place in England, Germany or the United States, countries with a large urban working-class, disciplined by the requirements of modern industrial life, and so qualified to take control of it when the time should come. Russia, with its overwhelmingly rural population and embryonic industry, he regarded as backward and unripe for proletarian revolution. Towards the end of his life, however, Marx seems to have modified these views. He became disenchanted by the complacency of the Western proletariat (particularly in England) and he began to fear that it might be seduced from its revolutionary mission by such concessions on the part of the bourgeoisie as better pay and improved living standards. The catastrophic failure of the French Revolution of 1871 and the massacre of the Paris Commune seemed to him to have put back by decades the hopes of world revolution. On the other hand, Russia, though she was technically backward was undeniably in a potentially revolutionary situation. Marx, who felt himself often ignored in Western Europe, was flattered to discover that his works were eagerly read in certain sections of the radical intelligentsia of Russia. He began to feel that this revolutionary situation could be harnessed to the cause of the proletariat, and in his last years he took a close interest in developments within Russia;[7] but he made no attempt to reconcile his hopes of Russia with the logic of his economic theories.

There was indeed a vast revolutionary potential in Tsarist Russia. The political and cultural backwardness of the country were plain to all, but the autocracy's habit of treating reformers, critics and rebels alike as enemies of the State had the effect of driving most educated Russians into the extremes either of reaction or of revolution. Many of these men felt that Russia's backwardness was a result of the long centuries of Tartar domination which had isolated her from Western progress. They therefore looked to the political institutions, the cultural and technological achievements of Western Europe for guidance in the development and reorganisation of Russia, to enable her to catch up and occupy a worthy place among the nations of the world. Such men proved naturally responsive to Marx's teaching, which seemed to confirm their diagnosis that Russia needed a technological as well as a political revolution, if she was ever to compete with the Western nations on equal terms.

From a strict Marxist point of view, Russia did not present any prospect of a proletarian revolution; she could not be said even to have passed through the stage of bourgeois revolution, such as had characterised England in the seventeenth century and France in the eighteenth century. Thus, paradoxically, orthodox Marxists in Russia (such as the Mensheviks and their leader Plekhanov) were condemned to work for a bourgeois revolution as the only way of hastening the eventual victory of the proletariat. The more revolutionary Marxists, such as Lenin and the Bolsheviks, nourished the hope of somehow short-circuiting history; of exploiting the confusion of a revolutionary situation to snatch victory out of the hands of the bourgeoisie, and so lead society straight through into a proletarian dictatorship. Where Marx had envisaged that capitalism would be most vulnerable at the peak of its success, Lenin identified the revolutionary moment with its hour of greatest weakness.

The so-called Westernisers did not have a monopoly of the ideals of socialism and a classless society in Russia; some thinkers, the Slavophiles and their followers, claimed that there was no need for Russia to look to the West for a model. In the first place, Western civilisation had sacrificed its spiritual values to the cult of material progress and prosperity; in the second, socialist institutions in a primitive form could still be found among the Russian peasantry, and these could serve as the basis for the development of a socialist society. Thus, they maintained, there was no need for Russia to repeat the path trodden by the advanced Western countries; her very backwardness could enable her to shortcut the historical process and so blaze a path for the West to follow. Later in the century, when the prospects for a peaceful revolution in Russia were fading, they reminded their opponents that in Russian history it was traditionally the peasantry that had been the chief revolutionary force, and they would point to the risings of Stenka Razin and Yemelyan Pugachev in the seventeenth and eighteenth centuries. This train of thought emerged in the twentieth century as the ideology of the party of the Social-Revolutionaries.

The party of the Marxists, the Russian Social-Democratic Workers' Party, possessed only a limited appeal; its strength was concentrated in intellectual circles and in some important industries; during the 1905 Revolution, however, and the Great War it had managed to extend its influence considerably, and in the last months of Tsarism it gained wide support in the armed forces. But the Bolshevik leaders were usually abroad in exile, and so tended to lose touch with developments at home; they were taken unawares by the events of January 1905 and of February 1917. The Social Revolutionaries, on the other hand, were overwhelmingly strong in rural Russia, where the Social-Democrats had little or no appeal, and throughout 1917 they even controlled several important cities.

It was therefore essential for the Bolsheviks to increase their appeal to the peasantry. Lenin achieved this by adopting some of the Social-Revolutionaries' policies and slogans; he declared that in the unique conditions of Russia the peasantry were potentially as revolutionary as the proletariat. Hence the Bolsheviks took power in 1917 in the name of both these classes, and the flag of Soviet Russia bears to this day the twin emblems of the hammer and the sickle on the red background of revolution. Even though in 1918 the Bolsheviks were to break with the Social-Revolutionaries, and, under Stalin, to revert to a more orthodox Marxism in preferring the proletariat at the expense of the peasantry, the influence of the Slavophile mystique has penetrated Russian Marxism, progressively replacing the ideals of international solidarity with an increasingly nationalistic messianism.

The success of the Bolsheviks' coup in November 1917 effectively stood Marx's theories on their head. Marx had foretold that changes in society would eventually result in a political revolution; in fact the Bolsheviks' seizure of power had changed only the superstructure, not the underlying realities of society. The Russian Communists were, however, confident that they could implement the social revolution by political measures from above. Marx had advocated preparing for revolution, but he had never seriously envisaged the possibility of a premature proletarian revolution in a predominantly non-proletarian country. If in his youth he seems to have toyed with the possibility of a revolution carried out in the name of the masses, the disastrous outcome of the revolutions of 1848 had convinced him that power could be seized only *by* the proletariat. Unless the social structure was ripe for revolution, the attempt to destroy it could only lead to its restoration; the social and economic realities would not just go away in deference to the ambitions of revolutionaries. The subsequent history of the Bolshevik Revolution may best be understood in terms of the logic of the 'premature' revolution.

The instrument of Lenin's revolution was the Bolshevik Party, the most momentous of all his amendments to Marxism. Like other social-democratic parties, the Bolsheviks claimed to represent the interests of the proletariat; but because they identified these interests with revolution, the logic of the situation actually cut them off from the proletariat. The movement was based in exile abroad, and it was led by intellectuals of middle-class extraction. Even abroad the ubiquitous Tsarist secret police forced a conspiratorial mode of existence upon the Bolsheviks. Decisions, taken in secrecy by a small inner elite, were enforced with rigid discipline on all members. When eventually the Bolsheviks came to power in 1917, the assumptions and practices of the underground years – the discipline, the secrecy, the sense of the Party as the elite rather than the servant of the proletariat – had acquired a momentum of their own, and could not be abandoned so easily.

The success of the Bolshevik Revolution raised a question which the Party has never honestly faced: if the Party's *raison d'être* was the engineering of a successful revolution on behalf of the proletariat, what is the justification for its continued existence after that revolution? Here the elitist, authoritarian character of the Party has surfaced from the underground. It was perhaps only natural that the Bolsheviks should continue to govern in the name of the proletariat for some time after the Revolution; they were assuming the burden of power only to hasten the day when there would be no further need for it. But, having seized power, the Party became increasingly reluctant to surrender it. It now sought to justify its dictatorship not by its dedication to the cause of the proletariat, but by its success in bringing off a Marxist revolution. The interpretation of the writings of Marx (and later of Lenin) became by implication its special prerogative. Inevitably it began to select and manipulate these writings so as to justify its actions and legitimise its retention of power. In so doing it shifted its own *raison d'être* from the future to the past. The result was a travesty of the principle of the dialectic. Instead of the truth painfully synthesising out of the imperfect and conflicting elements of contemporary reality, issues were decided in terms of the crudest black and white, and the solutions justified by quotations from the works of men long since dead and buried. Marx's prophecies of the dangers of the premature revolution were beginning to work themselves out. Imperceptibly, but inexorably, the revolutionary gospel of Marx ossified into Marxism, the essentially conservative ideology of an established ruling elite.

Equally far-reaching has been the profound effect exerted

by the success of the premature revolution on the psychology and attitudes of the Bolshevik leaders. Marx had believed that history developed according to natural laws. The Bolsheviks, however, had brought off their revolution against all the odds, and in defiance of all historical 'laws'. As a result they had far less respect for nature; their own experience had convinced them that organisation and will-power were far more effective in triggering revolutions than the spontaneous, but unpredictable, movements of the masses or the slow mechanisms of the historical process. It is, therefore, understandable, why it is the Party and not the proletariat that should stand in the centre of Russian Communist thinking. And just as the Bolsheviks seized power prematurely in 1917, so they have ever since been acutely conscious that the revolution might after all be snatched out of their hands, despite all the assurances of the Marxism that they profess. In confronting the problems that were a direct consequence of the premature revolution, the cultural and industrial backwardness of the country, the threat posed by the existence of a vast unsocialised peasantry, the failure of the international revolution to materialise, the Bolsheviks' natural reaction has never been to allow the historical process to run its course, or even to trust it to do so, but to tackle the problem by the application of brute force and concentrated will-power.

In the practice of Soviet Communism there are thus two main strands. From Marx comes the idea of the all-embracing system; the Party is not just the arbiter of political, social and economic matters, it is concerned with the minutest, even the most intimate, details of man's personal, cultural and spiritual existence. Also from Marx comes the intolerance of any dissent; his heavy sarcasm reappeared as vicious invective in Lenin, and eventually in Stalin's physical liquidation of all opponents, real or imagined. From Lenin comes the idea of the Party, the insistence on discipline, the obsession with security, and the belief in the power of the human will; in a word, the paradox of the premature revolution.

2

The Other Tradition: Two Writers

Marxism represents only one strand in the complex mythology of modern Russia. Equally strong in the Russian cultural tradition is an abiding sense of the insufficiency of rationalism, a near-mystical faith in the validity of permanent values, moral, spiritual and aesthetic, and above all in the mysterious destiny of human life. This tradition too flared into brilliant life in the first years of the Bolshevik Revolution: notably in Zamyatin's novel *We* (*My*, 1921) and in the tragic history of Aleksandr Blok, Russia's greatest poet of the twentieth century.

We

Marx had envisaged a world rationalised, industrialised and urbanised to the highest degree. The advance of technology would remove the drudgery, danger and dehumanisation from man's labour. With the advent of a life of purely creative work and ample leisure-time, human culture would be free to flourish as never before. Instead of the isolation of the talented individual there would now be every opportunity for him to find fulfilment within the community. The traditional conflict between the individual and society would have disappeared.

The ideal is undeniably attractive, but the opponents of this collective, rationalistic Utopia have also exerted a profound influence on the climate of Russian thought. They argued (notably Dostoyevsky) that the belief in the fundamentally social and rational nature of man leaves no room for the moral, spiritual and aesthetic dimensions of human life, and ultimately denies the existence of free will, for a rational man is not free to choose any but the most rational course of action. Accordingly, the attempt to solve the difficulties of humanity by reason alone could only lead to the destruction of the individual. It might make men happy, but only at the expense of their freedom, the very basis of their humanity. The traditional form of the novel, with its theme of the individual in society, and the abiding interest of the artist in special cases is ideally suited for countering the abstractions and generalisations of the philosophers.

In the nineteenth century the novelists were confronted only by the theoretical possibility of Utopia; but after 1917, when the Communists seemed all set to put their blueprints into action, the problem became very much more urgent. Yevgeniy Zamyatin had been a Bolshevik in his youth, but paradoxically it was his devotion to the dialectic that made him a Soviet heretic, for he argued that, by providing a challenge to established opinion, the heretic creates the possibility of further development. His novel *We* is the first and greatest of the anti-Utopian novels.

The 'We' of his title indicates the final triumph of the collective; the first person singular has almost ceased to exist; the separate human beings are not names but numbers. Arithmetic now provides the basis for all values, moral and aesthetic. In the name of mathematical efficiency and economy, the citizens wear identical clothes, live in identical apartments, with identical furniture arranged in identical positions. Happiness is guaranteed; it is: 'mathematically infallible';[1] beauty is thought to be contained in:

> . . . absolute aesthetic subordination to an ideal non-freedom.[2]

Every element of unpredictability or freedom is to be eliminated in the name of the happiness of society. Outside this arithmetic there are chaos, crime and misery, the consequences of human individualism.

The action takes place in a vast city, built entirely of glass, a symbol of the light of order and reason, but also of sterility, inhumanity and the lack of privacy. The world of nature (even the weather) is kept out by a vast glass dome, through which the inhabitants can observe the green chaotic world outside. The citizen belongs entirely to the community (or the State, for the two are now indistinguishable); he is required to repeat to the authorities all his private thoughts and dreams, even any words and actions of his friends that might fall outside the limits decreed by the State in its infallible wisdom. Science and the arts have been purged of any hint of irrationality or questioning of established truths; they are now devoted entirely to the perpetuation of the reign of reason, and the glorification of the Benefactor's dictatorship. All possibility of heresy or change seems to have been removed.

Thus the creation of the Single State has led to a series of contradictions; words have lost their meanings. The State is devoted to the collective, yet it is ruled by a dictator, the Benefactor. In spite of his name, the Benefactor is a figure of terror; his police are known as the Guardians. The prime social duty is that of informing on one's neighbour, and so in place of any real community there are only isolated individuals, fearful and distrustful of communicating their true thoughts and feelings to one another. Society is orientated to the future to the point of obsession; the past has been destroyed, turned into myth or caricatured as a time of senseless chaos; and yet in the place of progress there is only stagnation. Culture is theoretically universal; in practice it is dead. Happiness seems no nearer for all the loss of freedom.

The amazing feature of Zamyatin's novel is that, though many of these paradoxes were to become the commonplaces of life under Stalin, this vision was based not on the brutal abuses of power by the Communist Party, but on an imaginative thinking-out of the most admired aspects of the systems of Marx and Lenin. For example, the Single State of Zamyatin's novel has achieved the goal of Communism: 'From each according to his ability, to each according to his needs'; and so everyone's needs, nutritional, cultural and sexual, are all individually calculated and satisfied to exactly the right degree.

Zamyatin formulates his objections to this systematised rationalism through the non-materialistic worlds of the arts, the feelings and morality: his characters fall in love; they rediscover the arts of the past; they come to trust their own impulses; finally even the Glass Wall between the State and the world of nature is breached. Above all it is the reader's natural reaction of moral and aesthetic horror that confirms his case. But it is no less characteristic of Zamyatin that he takes his illustrations from arithmetic and the sciences. He ridicules the assumption that there can be a 'last' revolution – how can there be a last number? (here indeed Zamyatin would seem to be closer to the spirit of the dialectic than the Communists); he denounces the sterile rationalism of the Glass City – the irrational, indeed meaningless $\sqrt{-1}$ is still of practical value in engineering (it is significant that D.503, the hero of *We*, is an engineer like his creator). The indestructible link of the present with the past is symbolized by the hairy hands of D.503, that distinguish him from his fellow-citizens – in the 1930's and 1940's the science of genetics in Russia was to be stamped out by Stalin.

But the heart of Zamyatin's novel lies in the use of a first-person narrator. The collective society of *We* is described by an individual 'I', and the whole novel springs from this paradox; D.503 discovers his identity in the process of contemplating the 'We' society; even in taking up his pen on the first page ('*ya*', 'I', is the first word of his text) he is unknowingly but inexorably distinguishing between the singular and the plural; the evolution of this 'I' out of the 'we', its protest against the stagnant conformity of society is built into the very structure of the novel. The mathematical symbol for $\sqrt{-1}$ is 'i'. The girl D.503 falls in love with, and who later leads the rebellion is I.330. In the literature of socialist realism, the device of the first-person narrator was to disappear almost entirely.

There is of course no final answer in this debate. Both Marx and Zamyatin have given us statements of faith, based on differing views of man and society, and consistently worked out from their original premises. The appearance of D.503 in the controlled society of the Single State is a rejection of the theory that environment determines consciousness; but then Marx and Lenin, the prophets of the proletárian revolution, had appeared out of the bosom of the bourgeoisie. The Marxists look to a man-made Utopia; Zamyatin denies that it can exist independently of the world of nature. Where the Communists set their sights single-mindedly on the future, and regard the past merely as a tool for achieving it, Zamyatin asserted the organic unity of all human experience: without the past, the future can only stagnate. To those who, sincerely or opportunistically, demanded the creation of a totally new culture, Zamyatin replied:

> Russian literature has only one future: her past.[3]

The words are both a warning and an affirmation.

Even though *We* has never been allowed to appear in the Soviet Union, the theme of D.503 and the world of unplanned and unplannable life runs subterraneanly through Soviet literature, surfacing occasionally in such diverse works as Olesha's *Envy*, Mayakovsky's *The Bedbug*, Leonov's *The Russian Forest* and the works of Solzhenitsyn. In the days when the writer was required to be an 'engineer of human souls' the novel of the engineer Zamyatin served to keep the dialectic alive.

Aleksandr Blok

The views argued by Zamyatin in the pages of *We* were illustrated in contemporary Russia by the life and art of the poet Aleksandr Blok.

By birth, upbringing and temperament, Blok belonged to the class of the Russian gentry. By his education and natural sensitivity he was a typical member of the liberal intelligentsia. His was a profoundly contradictory character; he was at one and the same time an analytical and sceptical intellectual and an impulsive, at times ecstatic, dreamer. Little in his early work gave any hint of the extraordinary change that was to come over him in November 1917, and find expression in his final masterpiece *The Twelve* (*Dvenadtsat*, 1918).

In his youth Blok had been very much of a poet's poet. He wrote for a small circle of friends, and it was they who arranged the first publications of his poems and persuaded him to bring out his first book, *Poems about a Beautiful Lady* (*Stikhi o Prekrasnoy Dame*, 1905). The archaic Dantean associations of this title conjure up a timeless world of mystery and legend, hardly ever troubled by contemporary reality; the setting is usually the halflight of evening or early morning, and the prevailing atmosphere one of mysterious expectancy. The red glow of the sun beneath the horizon seems to promise an imminent revelation. Blok himself appears as a knight wooing his lady, a monk praying before the altar, a disciple waiting for the sign. The *Poems about a Beautiful Lady* are not just love-poems addressed to a woman of flesh and blood (Lyubov Mendeleyeva, later to become his wife), but invocations to a Muse, prayers to some virginal deity, or, in the light of Blok's later development, hymns to the spirit of Russia.

The turning-point in Blok's poetic development was the abortive revolution of 1905; he actually carried a red flag in one of the many processions of that year. But of no less significance for Blok himself was an obscure but haunting dream on the night of 16 November 1905, later described in the poem *The Night-violet* (*Nochnaya fialka,* 1906). These two apparently unrelated experiences seemed to Blok to be different aspects of the same deeper reality, and they confirmed his sense of his own poetic mission. He was now convinced that the inner world of the poet corresponded in some mysterious way to the physical reality around him. Poetic inspiration was simply an individual faculty by which the poet recorded the pressures and shifts in the cosmic order of things. But the poet should not allow his peculiar gifts to isolate him from his fellows; the insights which he gained were of universal concern. It was not enough merely to contemplate the world; the poet must participate actively in preparing it for change.

The poems of this new phase of Blok's development, 1905–08, form the second book of his collected verse; here he tries to adapt his earlier mannerisms to the new poetic mission that had been revealed to him. The ecstatic rhythms vividly convey the inspirational origins of his poetry; the combination of realistic detail with blurred imagery suggests the difficulty of translating this inspiration into words; while the sensuous music of his lines casts an unearthly glow over the bald civic message that he now sought to express. Blok had started on the long road that was to lead him to *The Twelve.*

The atmosphere of lyric contemplation now gives place to passionate involvement in contemporary affairs. He openly mocked his former ideals in the satirical plays *The Puppet-show* (*Balaganchik,* 1906) and *The Unknown Lady* (*Neznakomka,* 1906); he indicated his hatred of the contemporary urban scene in the cycle of poems *The City* (*Gorod*), his disgust with the Russian bourgeoisie in the poem *The Fat* (*Sytyye*); later his travels abroad in Western Europe convinced him that something was rotten not just in Russia, but in the whole state of European civilisation. Blok was determined to break out of the narrow circle imposed by the very nature of his lyrical gift. In the hope of reaching a wider audience he turned to the theatre; he took to writing popular articles, in which he discussed the aims and significance of the various literary trends of the day.

This new attitude of Blok's can be seen best in a group of three works, which all treat the same ideas, and even employ some of the same images: the play *The Song of Fate* (*Pesnya sudby*, 1908), the cycle of five poems, *On the Field of Kulikovo* (*Na pole Kulikovom*, 1908), and the article *The People and the Intelligentsia* (*Narod i intelligentsiya*, 1908). Three titles, three different literary forms, but a single theme. As the third of these titles suggests, Blok was concerned with the relationship between the common people and the intelligentsia (it was typical of him to put them in this order). This had been a perennial theme of Russian literature throughout the nineteenth century, but Blok believed that the gulf between them was widening, and for this he blamed the intelligentsia. Their privileged positions and superior education imposed certain responsibilities upon them, but they were unwilling or unable to do anything but talk and write and split up into an innumerable host of warring factions. Against them Blok saw the vast mass of the Russian people like a sleeping volcano, which must sooner or later erupt and sweep them all away. He reminded his readers of the Battle of Kulikovo (1380) in which the Russians had gained their first major victory over the Tartars, and taken their first steps towards establishing their independence. The battle he interpreted as a 'symbolic' prophecy of the eventual overthrow of the Westernised, rootless intelligentsia by the Russian people.

Perhaps Blok was influenced by the revolutionary theories which were then so fashionable in Russia, but it was characteristic of him to see this great catastrophe as a cosmic event, which would be produced not so much by economic or political factors, as by an elemental explosion, affecting every aspect of human life. The comparison of the people to a sleeping volcano was not mere poetic licence; in 1909 he welcomed the earthquake at Messina as confirmation of his theories, and he could scarcely restrain his excitement at the sinking of the *Titanic* in 1913. Throughout his life Blok saw nothing incongruous in making such interrelationships; great natural catastrophes, passion for a current mistress, social upheavals, the experience of poetic inspiration, were for him equally manifestations of the same cosmic power at work. In his poetry they are often expressed by the symbol of the Russian blizzard, a blind elemental force that can sweep a man off his feet, destroy his sense of direction, and bring him face to face with the inconceivable.

But though Blok's vision is apocalyptic it is not hopeless; in *The Song of Fate* he represents his vision of a pure uncorrupted Russia in the figure of a wild and primitive gypsy-girl, Faina, whom the poet follows in blind adoration. Together they reject the world of nineteenth-century materialism and commerce in the search for some higher ideal; but this is not realised in the play itself. It ends with Faina leaving the poet alone in the plains of Russia in a whirling snowstorm, telling him to wait for her return.

Blok's hopes and aspirations of these years collapsed in ruins. In 1907 his wife had left him for an actor; when she returned she was pregnant. When the baby died only eight days after birth, Blok was deeply shaken, and the poem *For the Death of a Child* (*Na smert mladentsa*, 1908) records his sense of spiritual devastation.

This personal tragedy was reflected externally in a growing sense that all his extra-literary activity had failed to get his urgent message across; the people that he was writing for did not read the periodicals to which he contributed. The mockery and hostility of the intellectuals to his methods and views was almost universal. They were prepared to accept him as a poet, but not as a serious thinker about society; in this they had some justification, for his ideas were hardly practicable, or even logically coherent. Blok, however, made little distinction between his poetry and his journalism, and he regarded the incomprehension of his former friends as wilful, ostrich-like blindness to the facts of the case. Finally, *The Song of Fate*, on which he had placed great hopes, failed to find a producer; Stanislavsky was interested in the play but could never take the plunge; after blowing hot and cold for some months he finally turned it down.

Blok's attempt to get across to the Russian people by a direct head-on assault had collapsed in humiliating failure, personal, social and artistic. From the ruins of these hopes he returned to the lyric forms with which he had made his name. The resulting poetry went to form the third volume of his poetry, and corresponds to the third stage of his development. By common consent, it contains his greatest lyric poetry, although Blok himself, aware of the mental and psychological states that had produced it, always preferred his first book, the *Poems about a Beautiful Lady*.

The first section of this book, *The Terrible World* (*Strashnyy mir*), is haunted by the sense of imminent catastrophe: the world is rotten and past saving; even the most personal poems suggest not just the degradation of an individual life, but of a whole civilisation. Though the poems are set in the modern city, it is not just St Petersburg, but a universal phenomenon, a state of the soul, a vision of Hell on earth. Black is the dominating colour; day and night, life and death are deliberately confused. Even the elemental power of art seems impotent and irrelevant:

Как тяжело ходить среди людей
И притворяться непогибшим,
И об игре трагической страстей
Повествовать еще не жившим.

И вглядываясь в свой ночной кошмар,
Строй находить в нестройном вихре чувства,
Чтобы по бледным заревам искусства
Узнали жизни гибельный пожар!*4

The red glow on the horizon of the early poetry has now, by a bitter irony, become an image of ruin, not hope; the poet is powerless to do anything but turn his powerlessness into poetry. His very success in creating a work of art out of his situation only serves to perpetuate the curse on him and his age.

But if Blok's third volume opens with the hopeless visions of *The Terrible World*, it ends on a more hopeful note with the cycle *My Country* (*Rodina*). Here Blok tries to see Russia from the angle of the people, not from that of the urban intelligentsia. He still retains his faith in the Messianic destiny of the Russian people, but it is now expressed more soberly, in terms of everyday reality, and less in the language of mysticism or eschatology.

Blok no longer idealises his people. He does not regard the peasants, or even the Russian character as saintly or redemptive. At times his horror of the Russian bourgeois mentality becomes

* How hard it is to live among people/And to keep up the pretence of not being dead,/And to chronicle for those who have not yet lived/The tragic game of passions./And, gazing into one's nightly nightmare,/To seek for order in the disordered whirl of feeling,/So that in the pale, reflected glow of art/Men might discern the blazing ruin of a life!

as uncontrollable as the feelings in *The Terrible World.* In the poem *To sin shamelessly ...* (*Greshit besstydno ...* 1914) he describes a day in the life of a Russian bourgeois, its moral squalor, inhumanity and hypocrisy, only to end with the astonishing lines:

Да, и такой, моя Россия,
Ты всех краев дороже мне.*[5]

Ironically, it was this return to lyric poetry that made Blok famous. From 1910 onwards he became a national figure. His works were passionately read and memorised, and the agonies and frustrations of his poetry seemed perfectly attuned to the unstable and expectant atmosphere of the times. People from all walks of life, budding poets, schoolchildren, even peasants wrote to him, asking for advice on literary matters, personal problems, philosophical and social questions. Blok answered all these letters conscientiously, but the achievement of his ambitions gave him little satisfaction; he remained tragically isolated, with only a handful of close friends. At times he even considered abandoning lyric poetry altogether.

In 1915 he was called up, and worked as a medical orderly, but he deserted in the first months of 1917 and made his way back to Petrograd. He was at first enthusiastic about the February Revolution, and especially impressed by the calm and good order with which people reacted to events. He was given a job on a commission, investigating the crimes of the former Tsarist ministers and officials. But he gradually came to feel dissatisfied with this secretarial work. He noticed with mounting concern the reintroduction of the old Tsarist policies, the decision to resume hostilities with Germany, the re-introduction of the death penalty, and the growing stagnation of life under the Provisional Government. This was not after all the Revolution of which he had dreamed. From the summer of 1917, he began to complain of the 'stifling atmosphere'[6] and to look to the Bolsheviks for some way out of the impasse which Russia seemed to have reached.

We have no direct evidence of Blok's immediate reactions to the Bolshevik coup, because he later destroyed his diaries for the period. But the poem *The Twelve* (written in January 1918) is conclusive enough. It was composed in two bursts of inspiration,

* Yes, even like that, my Russia,/You are dearer to me than all other countries.

bordering on ecstasy – on completing the poem, Blok wrote in his notebook: '*Today I am a genius*'.[7] It is set in Petrograd in January 1918, immediately after the dispersal of the Constituent Assembly. It is dominated by Blok's most characteristic images – the raging blizzard from the end of *The Song of Fate* (and elsewhere) – while the red glow of the lyric poems now comes into the foreground as the blood and fire of revolution. Twelve drunken Bolshevik soldiers are roaming the streets of Petrograd, robbing, raping and shooting on impulse, until, finally, in the closing lines of the poem, the twelve soldiers glimpse the shadowy figure of Christ at their head, and the title reminds us of the twelve disciples.

The ending to this poem is the most controversial point in the whole of Blok's work. Except for the final lines the tone is deliberately unpoetic, all the more unexpected for being so at odds with Blok's usual manner: snatches of popular speech, street songs, captions from contemporary posters, parodies of sentimental ditties and the rattle of machine guns jostle side by side with one another, and their disjointed, disordered juxtaposition creates a deliberately chaotic impression. The emergence of Christ from such a background comes as an outrageous shock. Nor is it to be explained by Blok's religious beliefs; he professed himself an atheist, and said of this ending:

> Я иногда сам ненавижу этот женственный призрак.*[8]

If the figure of Christ is to be taken simply as a symbol of a new and better world to spring from the ruins of the old, then it is decidedly arbitrary. But in the context of the poem itself and the great climax which explodes only in the final line, this figure is identified with the forces of destruction; by linking the theme of catastrophe with the Coming of Christ, Blok inevitably reminds us of the Day of Judgement, an idea frequently suggested by the poems of his third book. At the same time the almost excessively musical rhymes and rhythms of these closing lines do indeed conjure up that 'effeminate figure' that Blok resisted. In this extraordinary synthesis Blok created a world of conflicting hopes and fears.

The shock of this poem can be felt even today. At the time Blok's former friends cut him in the street. The idea that the

* I myself sometimes hate this effeminate apparition.

revolutionaries could be compared to Christ and the disciples has embarrassed *émigré* critics ever since. Some have claimed that the Red soldiers were really chasing out Christ; others have defended the poem on the grounds that Blok's infatuation with the Bolsheviks was only shortlived; yet others have declared that it is just a bad poem. On the other hand, Soviet critics have been no less embarrassed by the figure of Christ, and have tried to explain it away as some kind of Utopian symbol. None of these oversimplifications, however, can disguise the sheer drive and power of the poem, which in its grandeur and complexity has been justly compared to Pushkin's *The Bronze Horseman.* It is one of the few works of modern Russian literature which is accepted as a masterpiece both inside and outside the Soviet Union.

Blok lived for another three and a half years after completing the poem, and the story of his closing years is almost as controversial as the poem itself. Those who met him in this last period have often been influenced by political considerations in penning their memoirs: *émigré* Russians have tended to emphasise his growing disillusionment and exhaustion, while Soviet Russians have preferred to stress his continuing devotion to the Bolshevik cause. But most writers are agreed in testifying to Blok's sense of isolation in these years, and his tragic awareness of his loss of inspiration since the composition of *The Twelve*.

Blok's poem and his unconcealed Bolshevism in the early months of Soviet power had alienated many of his former friends. He was the chief support of his mother and aunt, both seriously unbalanced by the chaos of the times; and for much of the time he was more or less estranged from his wife. On the other hand, he received few privileges from the new rulers. He was conscripted into the Red Army, and only exempted after appeals had been made at a very high level. On 15 February 1919, his flat was searched, and he himself arrested, in connection with the campaign against the Left Social-Revolutionaries (he was released unharmed two days later). In the summer and autumn of the same year, he was threatened with eviction from his rooms to make way for a sailor and his family. After time-consuming appeals he was eventually reprieved; but at the beginning of 1920, after the death of his stepfather he decided to move out anyway into his mother's small flat.

His public activities during these years were various and demanding; he seems to have performed them all conscientiously. The most important projects with which he was concerned under the Bolsheviks were his work in Gorky's publishing-house, World Literature, from December 1918, where he was responsible for the German section; his Presidency of the Union of Poets; and his Chairmanship of the Governing Body of the Bolshoy (now the Gorky) theatre in Petrograd, from April 1919. But in all these fields he experienced increasing frustration and discontent, both personally and in his official capacity.

There was, however, a deeper reason why these activities could not satisfy Blok. For many years he had been oppressed by the vast gulf between the intelligentsia and the mass of the Russian people. He now reproached himself that he was still privileged because of his education and talents, and he began to wonder whether there was any difference between the intelligentsia and the bourgeoisie. Even during the summer of 1917 he was writing:

Буржуем называется всякий, кто накопил какие бы то ни было ценности, хотя бы и духовные. Накопление духовных ценностей предполагает предшествующее ему накопление матерьяльных.*[9]

At first, therefore, he was prepared to look tolerantly on the excesses of the early days of the Revolution. Even in July 1919 surveying the filth and bloody-mindedness of the new Soviet officials, he wrote:

Никто ничего не хочет делать. Прежде миллионы из-под палки работали на тысячи. Вот вся разгадка. Но почему миллионам хотеть работать? И откуда им понимать коммунизм иначе, чем — как грабеж и картеж?†[10]

But this tolerance did not come easily. He was particularly distressed by the destruction of his family home by rioting

* A bourgeois is anyone who has accumulated valuables of any description, even spiritual ones. The accumulation of spiritual valuables presupposes the previous accumulation of material ones.

† Nobody wants to do anything. In the old days millions of them were driven to work for a few thousand. There's the answer. Why should these millions want to work? And how are they to understand Communism except as robbery and gambling?

peasants at the beginning of 1918. He was shaken, not only by the loss of his library – as Mayakovsky records[11] – but also by the desecration of a place that had always seemed to him quintessentially Russian. He was often to wake up in tears after dreaming about the house that had been burnt and pillaged. At the end of December he wrote:

Жизнь становится чудовищной, уродливой, бессмысленной. Менделеевская квартира с передвижническим архивом, по-видимому пропадет . . . .*[12]

Blok found himself reduced to the same vandalism in the struggle for existence. He was forced to sell his books for food, and to chop up the family furniture for firewood.

All his life Blok had been prone to interpret the present and to foretell the future in terms of historical precedents. Thus he had called the battle of Kulikovo a symbolic event, and in *The Twelve* he had identified the revolutionaries with the first disciples. But *The Twelve* was written in the comparatively heady days of January 1918; the Civil War had not yet begun, and the real difficulties of the Revolution still lay in the future. A few months later Blok returned to the central image of the poem. In his essay *Catiline* (*Katilina*) Blok recounts the history of the famous conspiracy, and then moves on to the theory that Catullus in his ode 'Attis' was somehow referring to its failure. The interrelation of poetic inspiration and social revolution at once recalls the creation of *The Twelve*. But the real meaning of the essay lies in the frequent parallels between the situation of pre-Christian Rome and post-Revolutionary Russia.

The equation between the coming of Christianity and the Bolshevik Revolution has thus undergone a significant change in the three months since the composition of *The Twelve*. There Christ had placed himself at the head of the twelve Red soldiers; but the Catiline conspiracy is not directly linked to the coming of Christ; it is merely symptomatic of a greater revolution in the air. In other words, it is now not the Bolshevik Revolution which is being compared to the coming of Christianity, but the situation of which it is a symptom to the situation of the Western world before the birth of Christ. The Bolshevik Revolution is

* Life is becoming monstrous, hideous, senseless. The Mendeleyev flat with its *peredvizhnik* archive will evidently be lost. . . .

not, after all, the last word; it is simply the antithesis of the corrupt old world, which Blok hated with all his heart. Out of this opposition there should spring a synthesis, as Christianity had sprung out of the instability of the Roman Empire.

This transition from interpreting the Revolution as a final chapter to the idea that it was only a temporary stage necessary for a higher synthesis was naturally a slow and painful one. In *Catiline* Blok was himself perhaps unaware of where his ideas were leading him. But in a letter to Mayakovsky, drafted at the end of 1918 (though probably never sent), he states the synthesis principle quite clearly:

> Не меньше, чем Вы, ненавижу Зимний дворец и музеи. Но разрушение так же старо, как строительство, и так же *традиционно* как оно . . . Разрушая мы все те же рабы старого мира: нарушение традиций — та же традиция . . . Одни будут строить, другие разрушать, ибо "всему свое время под солнцем", но все будут рабами, пока не явится третье, равно не похожее на строительство и на разрушение.*[13]

Behind all Blok's activities and attitudes there lies the question of his own art. He had, in fact written little poetry since the end of 1915, apart from the brief outburst that produced *The Twelve*. He was to write virtually no more poetry in the remaining years of his life. His many commitments, and the appalling conditions of the time were of course hardly conducive to artistic creation, least of all the kind associated with Blok's name before the Revolution. But the fact remains that many other poets did contrive to write poetry at this time, and not a few of them produced their finest work during these very years. Blok was bitterly aware that apart from his revolutionary poem, his work in general was not of much interest or relevance at the present. His notebooks laconically record the rejection of his poems by newspapers and magazines: 'not suitable for the workers'. When Korney Chukovsky, later a prominent Soviet writer, asked him why he had written no new poetry, Blok

* I hate the Winter Palace and museums just as much as you do. But destruction is just as old as construction and just as traditional too . . . When we destroy we are still slaves of the old world: the breaking of traditions is itself a tradition . . . Some people will build and others destroy, for 'there is a time for all things under the sun', but we shall all be slaves until a third force appears, as different from mere construction as it is from mere destruction.

replied that the source of his inspiration, his music, had gone dead:

Все звуки прекратились. Разве вы не слышите, что никаких звуков нет?*[14]

Publication in the few remaining private presses helped to bring in some money during these years. So also did the public recital; but the poems that he read on these occasions were always old, well-known ones, and he never read *The Twelve* in public. One of his friends, Nadezhda Pavlovich, recently recalled that in these readings even:

строчка: "Узнаю тебя, жизнь, принимаю" — прозвучала не радостно и открыто, а как-то горько и хрипло.†[15]

Blok's last book of poems, *The Grey-haired Morning* (*Sedoye utro*), came out in 1920. The very title is expressive of age and weariness, though perhaps of hope too; but in February 1921, Blok carried the idea to its unambiguous conclusion:

Следующий сборник стихов, если будет: "Черный день".‡[16]

Blok's last major work was his Pushkin speech of February 1921, on the eighty-fourth anniversary of the poet's death. In view of his fondness for symbolic history, it is hardly to be doubted that he was speaking of himself as much as of Pushkin; in any case there are several turns of phrase that make the parallel quite plain. The poet, according to Blok, is necessarily a tragic figure, fated to be persecuted by the mob. Who are the mob?

... уже на глазах Пушкина место родовой знати занимала бюрократия. Эти чиновники и суть наша чернь: чернь вчерашнего и сегодняшнего дня. §[17]

How far will they go in their campaign against the artist?

* All the sounds have stopped. Can't you hear, there are no sounds?

† the line 'I recognise you, life, and accept you' sounded not joyous and open, but somehow bitter and hoarse.

‡ My next book of poems, if there is one: 'Black Day'.

§ In Pushkin's own time the place of the hereditary aristocracy was being taken by the bureaucracy. These bureaucrats are our mob: the mob of yesterday and today.

. . . они могли бы изыскать средства для замутнения самых источников гармонии: что их удерживает — недогадливость, робость или совесть — неизвестно. А может быть, такие средства уже изыскиваются?*[18]

Blok went on to make these Zamyatin-like warnings even more explicit, pointing to the dangers of a new authoritarianism of the Left, in the form of an alliance between Nicholas I's police-chief, Benkendorf, who had acted as Pushkin's personal censor, and the socialist utilitarian critics like Belinsky, who had exploited the poet's life and work for political ends:

Над смертным одром Пушкина раздавался младенческий лепет Белинского. Этот лепет казался нам совершенно противоположным, совершенно враждебным вежливому голосу графа Бенкендорфа. Он кажется нам таковым и до сих пор. Было бы слишком больно всем нам, если бы оказалось, что это — не так. И если это даже не совсем так, будем все-таки думать, что это совсем не так . . . И Пушкина тоже убила вовсе не пуля Дантеса. Его убило отсутствие воздуха. . . . Пускай же остерегутся от худшей клички те чиновники, которые собираются направлять поэзию по каким-то собственным руслам, посягая на ее тайную свободу, и препятствуя ей выполнять ее таинственное назначение.†[19]

Blok's prophecy of the fate of Russian literature was to be tragically confirmed by events. The first victim was Blok himself. His last illness is shrouded in mystery. In April 1921, he first began to complain of pains in his legs. From here his condition rapidly deteriorated. In the stifling summer of 1921 he was confined to his room in Petrograd; he could not get out of town to the fresh air of the country or seaside:

* They could well work out techniques for muddying the very sources of harmony. What is stopping them – lack of intelligence, timidity, or conscience? Who knows? Or perhaps these techniques are being worked out even today?

† The childish prattle of Belinsky could be heard over Pushkin's death-bed. This prattle always seemed to us utterly opposed, utterly hostile to the polite voice of Count Benkendorf. It seems so to us even today. It would be too painful for all of us, if it were to prove that this is not so. And even if it should prove to be not quite so, let us believe all the same that they are not one and the same. . . . Pushkin was killed not by D'Anthes' bullet, but by the lack of air . . . Let those bureaucrats beware of an even worse title, when they try to direct poetry down their own channels, violating its inner freedom, and preventing it from fulfilling its mysterious mission.

Делать я ничего не могу, потому что температура редко нормальная, все болит, трудно писать, дышать и т. д.*[20]

The last entry in his diary to deal with his health reads:

Мне трудно дышать, сердце заняло полгруди.†[21]

Rumours circulated that in the final weeks Blok had renounced *The Twelve*, even that he had gone mad. Gorky tried to obtain permission for him to travel to a sanatorium in Finland, but after delays and mistakes this came through only on 3 August. It was too late. Blok could not be moved, and he died four days later, at the age of forty. Yuriy Annenkov's portrait of the dead poet is a terrible revelation of his condition.

What Blok regarded as the failure of the Revolution was undoubtedly a prime cause of his eventual breakdown. This disenchantment was expressed unmistakably in the same image of 'suffocation' which he had associated with the dying Pushkin, and which he himself had experienced in the summer of 1917. His last illness and death were brought on and accelerated less by the privations of revolutionary Petrograd than by the loss of any desire to live. But to be fair, the mystical hopes and expectations which he had placed on the Bolshevik Revolution in 1917–18 were no more capable of realisation than those associated with the 'Beautiful Lady' at the very beginning of his career twenty years earlier.

If this tale of an idealist disillusioned were all, Blok's significance would remain only marginal. But in Blok's poetry the private miseries and ecstatic visions of an individual are miraculously fused with the inarticulate feelings of an entire generation in the unmistakable and unique tones of a great poet. In the irrational nature of his genius, the near-prophetic quality of his utterances, and his conviction of the supreme significance of art in the destiny of the world, Blok is the very antithesis of the aggressive, materialist, utilitarian gospel of Marx.

For every literate Russian, whatever his political views, the new age of Communism is darkened by the corpse of Blok lying across its threshold.

* I can't do anything, because my temperature is seldom normal, everything aches. It's hard to write, breathe, etc.

† It's hard to breathe. My heart takes up half my chest.

3

Political and Social History

The problems that brought down Tsar Nicholas II in March 1917 were to prove even more intractable for his successors. The war with Germany was going disastrously; there were serious food-shortages in the big cities, and there was widespread discontent in the countryside. These problems required a decisive and courageous government for their successful solution. In the event power was fatally divided between the two chief contestants, the Provisional Government and the Soviets.

The Provisional Government was composed of the more liberal members of the last Imperial Duma. Its legitimacy was based on the principle of constitutional continuity, and it saw its function in clearing the ring for elections in November to a fully representative Constituent Assembly. The Soviets were a much more radical proletarian movement. They had first appeared during the 1905 Revolution and had unexpectedly revived again at the beginning of 1917. They originated in the factories and workshops, spread from there to army units, thence to whole towns and cities, and finally to the villages. Thus their very origins determined their working-class orientation. Their legitimacy was based simply and conclusively on the evidence of the popular will expressed through them. The Soviets were arranged in a hierarchical order, the delegates at each level combining to elect delegates to represent them at the next level, and so on up to the top, the Soviet of Workers' and Soldiers' Deputies. Elected delegates could be challenged and replaced at any time, so that the Soviets provided a genuine reflection of the popular mood and of the relative strengths of the various parties. But by the same token they were unstable, and quite unsuited for the taking of painful or far-sighted decisions.

There was naturally tension between the two authorities from the start. It was effectively the workers and soldiers of Petrograd that had brought down the Tsar; the subsequent assumption of power by the Provisional Government seemed a classic example of the technique of a bourgeois revolution, leaving the poor to do the dirty work, and then running in to claim the credit. In fact the Provisional Government was guilty not so much of abusing its power, as of an excess of constitutional scruple; all knotty problems were postponed for a properly elected government to deal with. This, however, did nothing to lessen the suspicions of the Soviets. Between the two Russia slid inexorably into ever deeper chaos.

For the revolutionary groups the fall of the autocracy presented something of a dilemma. It was natural to interpret it as a bourgeois revolution, but it was not clear what the correct attitude of the workers' parties should be. Should they work for the bourgeoisie to hasten its maturity and so bring nearer the day of the proletariat? or should they obstruct the Provisional Government, and force it into a more left-wing position? This course carried the risk of prompting a right-wing reaction, and so of delaying the coming of socialism. Not surprisingly, the socialists, notably the Mensheviks and the Social-Revolutionaries, who had played a major role in the March events, plumped for caution; they felt themselves in a strong position, and did not want to risk losing the power and authority that they had gained.

The Bolsheviks, who had taken a comparatively minor part in the actual revolution, because their leaders were in exile or in emigration and their rank-and-file members not too numerous, at first tended to follow this moderate line. It was only when Lenin returned to Russia in April that they shifted to a more aggressive strategy. Lenin saw clearly the instability of the political situation and that a determined blow might bring the Bolsheviks to power. He took up the theory of the 'permanent revolution',[1] first mooted by Trotsky in 1906, as a possible way of exploiting a revolutionary situation to short-circuit the course of history and extend the limited bourgeois revolution into an international and proletarian one.

The success of the 'permanent revolution' depended on the continuation of the present unstable situation, and Bolshevik propaganda was therefore devoted to this end. This was not difficult to do. At the front German superiority, revolutionary propaganda and the democratic election of commanders had resulted in the collapse of military discipline and mass-desertions. In the countryside, peasants who had at first looked forward to possessing the land among themselves began to be disillusioned; rioting and attacks on the landowners began to increase in frequency. The instability of food-supplies to the big cities led to rapid inflation, and this naturally further intensified the dissatisfaction of the workers and their distrust of the new government.

In this situation the Bolshevik slogans 'Bread, Peace, Land' were hardly practical policies, but they appealed strongly to all three groups, the urban proletariat, the soldiers at the front and the peasantry. In the volatile atmosphere of 1917 the Bolsheviks' popularity rose rapidly, only to subside in July when they allowed themselves to be carried away into an unsuccessful bid for power. But when in the following month General Kornilov tried to use the army to overthrow the Government from the Right, the Provisional Government was forced to appeal to the Bolshevik Red Guards for support, and the Bolsheviks' stock soared again.

The rise in the Bolsheviks' fortunes was reflected in their growing power in the Soviets. Their call for 'All power to the Soviets' had originated as a slogan to embarrass the Provisional Government; with the rising power of the Soviets it was quietly dropped, however, so long as the Bolsheviks were in a minority. Now it was revived once again. When the Bolsheviks finally struck on 7 November, they were able to confirm their coup by a resolution of the Congress of Soviets within a few hours. Their triumph was assisted by the fact that the Mensheviks and Social Revolutionaries boycotted the Congress in protest at the Bolsheviks' undemocratic way of jumping the gun.

Even so it was widely believed at the time that the Bolsheviks had overreached themselves, and that their government could only last a few days or weeks. The intelligentsia was overwhelmingly opposed to the coup; the existing government bureaucracy at first refused to co-operate; even some of the leading trades unions struck in protest. The Bolsheviks' support in the country was confined to a somewhat unreliable majority in the Soviets of the big cities; in the countryside the peasants were solidly for the Social Revolutionaries. With the elections to the Constituent Assembly imminent the weakness of the Bolshevik position was likely to be exposed publicly.

As expected, the elections to the Constituent Assembly gave the Bolsheviks only a quarter of the seats, but the voting revealed that they held a majority in the Army and the big cities. This proved to be sufficient. When, at the first session, the Assembly refused to approve the overthrow of the Provisional Government, the Bolsheviks walked out; they then used the Red Guards to disperse the delegates, and to prevent them from reassembling. A few days later the Bolshevik-controlled Soviets, whose authority had, strictly speaking, been superseded by the Constituent Assembly, formally approved the Bolshevik measures. The Bolsheviks and the Soviets were now in command.

The Bolshevik leaders were, however, well aware of their precarious position. The chaos which they had fostered up to November 1917 was now in danger of engulfing them too. They pinned their hopes, therefore, on the spread of revolution to Western Europe. At the front they encouraged fraternisation with the enemy but this did not lead to any revolutionary outbreaks. The German High Command was interested in winding up the Russian campaign as soon as possible so as to free its troops for the Western front. The Germans resumed the offensive, and forced the Russians to sue for peace.

The issue of peace confronted the Bolshevik leaders with their first major crisis. For most Russian Marxists the only hope of preserving the Revolution in Russia was the successful outbreak of proletarian revolutions elsewhere. Almost alone among the Bolshevik leaders Lenin saw that the real alternatives were the total extinction of the Russian Revolution, or the chance of a short breathing-space. He was therefore prepared to accept any peace-terms available, but his proposals were at first flatly rejected by his less flexible colleagues. They were finally forced to yield by the continuing advance of the Germans into Russian territory. Under the terms of the treaty of Brest-Litovsk Russia was condemned to lose large areas of the former Tsarist Empire in Eastern Europe; Poland, Finland and the Baltic States, and, worst of all, the Ukraine with its industrial and agricultural wealth. After the defeat of Germany, however, the Russians were able to repudiate this unequal treaty, thus justifying Lenin's decision.

Russia had scarcely extricated herself from the Great War when the Civil War broke out. Almost the whole of the territory of Russia now became a battlefield between the Red Army and its various enemies. On the face of it the Communists were in a hopeless position. The White Armies under Yudenich (in the North), Kolchak (in the East), Denikin, and later Vrangel (in the South) were better trained, and, with their predominantly officer composition, seemed militarily and psychologically better equipped than their untrained, though admittedly numerically superior, opponents. They were supported by the intervention of the Western Allies, who provided them with men and munitions.

Why then did the Whites lose? In the first place, they failed to co-ordinate their tactics, their policies and their objectives; some were fighting for a restoration of the monarchy, others for a constitutional democracy, yet others for personal aggrandisement. In the event of a Red defeat, the various White armies might well have turned on one another. Secondly, the Whites failed to convince the local populations of their cause. Their propaganda was patronising, and often blind to the hopes and fears of those for whom it was intended. Thirdly, the involvement of the Western Allies of their side proved to be a liability; it served to alienate uncommitted Russians from the anti-Bolshevik cause, without producing any visible military advantages.

For all this, the achievement of the Red Army was remarkable, and the credit for this must go primarily to Trotsky. In a few months he had re-imposed military discipline, and created a fighting army out of a demoralised rabble. The strength of the Communists was based on the major cities of Western Russia, which stood at the centre of the administrative and communications systems. This proved decisive in the critical autumn of 1919 when the Bolsheviks were surrounded by a ring of enemies advancing from all directions. The deeper the Bolsheviks retreated, the more solid their support, and the greater the difficulties of the Whites. At this crucial moment the Whites failed to co-ordinate their strategy, and within a few weeks the Reds had broken out of the ring. After that, the final issue was never in doubt again.

But the Bolsheviks were not secure even in the cities. Petrograd was close to the front line, and vulnerable to a German attack – hence the removal, early in 1918, of the seat of government to Moscow. But there was an even more serious enemy, the internal one; the unpopularity of the Bolsheviks was considerable. Intellectual and liberal opinion was overwhelmingly against them. The press had remained hostile to the Bolsheviks throughout 1917, and most opposition papers were closed down soon after they came to power. The only non-Bolshevik paper tolerated, Gorky's *Novaya zhizn* (*New Life*), maintained a constant barrage of outspoken criticism. The effect was all the greater for the fact that Gorky had been on friendly terms with many of the Bolshevik leaders. In spite of official disapproval and obstruction, the paper continued to come out until July 1918, when it was finally closed down. It was the last legal opposition paper in Soviet history. But the effect of driving dissent underground was to inflame the suspicions of the Communists still further, and to inspire even more savage repressions. From 1918 until 1921 martial law reigned in the cities, and this period is generally known as that of 'War Communism'.

But the political confusion was nothing to the deepening chaos in which Russia was engulfed. Since the autumn of 1916 basic foodstuffs had been scarce, and prices had been rising steeply; with the outbreak of Civil War, this situation could only worsen. In the winters of 1918–19 and 1919–20 the hardships of the civilian population were appalling: the cold was intense, and there was little food or fuel; people tore down fences, chopped up furniture, and even burnt their libraries in a vain attempt to warm themselves. The lack of food and the breakdown of sanitation led to uncontrollable epidemics of typhus and cholera; even minor cuts took weeks to heal.

The two years of the Civil War have left deep traces in Soviet mythology. The terrible dilemmas confronted by every citizen of a nation bitterly divided against itself, the appalling cruelties perpetrated by each side, could not be lightly forgotten or forgiven once the war was over. The intervention of the Allies and their financial and material support for the Whites only served to confirm the Bolsheviks' argument that international capitalism would stop at nothing in its attempts to stamp out the proletarian revolution. Hence the victory of the Reds over these apparently overwhelming odds gave the Russians a new pride in themselves after the humiliations of the Great War, and did something to reconcile even the sceptical to the continuance of Communist power. It was the heroic age of the Revolution.

The experience of the Civil War has coloured Russian thinking, language and behaviour throughout the Soviet period. The sense of Russia as a beleaguered fortress threatened by foreign enemies, the awareness of non-sympathisers even in the Communist-held areas is natural enough for a nation that was born in these circumstances, but it has also been exploited by the Communists for their own purposes in the form of war-scares, spy-mania, and sometimes crude xenophobia. The language of conflict has extended to all the problems that have confronted the country, mass-epidemics, famine and a shattered economy, not merely in the conventional terms of struggle and strategy, but even in such words as shock-tactics, brigades, heroes, deserters and traitors.

If in 1917 the Bolsheviks had seriously believed in the possibility of a short-cut into Communism, in 1921 they were faced with a very different prospect. The greater part of Marxist theory had been constructed around the hypothesis of a proletarian revolution occurring as a more or less natural explosion; the resulting political system and state organisation would be purely temporary phenomena, awaiting the outbreak of proletarian revolutions on an international scale, and the establishment of a classless and truly co-operative society. The premature birth of the proletarian revolution in Russia and the non-occurrence of the international revolution indicated that the process of transition would be rather longer and more complex than had been foreseen.

In the first place the Soviets proved to be quite inadequate as an organ of power or administration. Faithfully reflecting every changing current of opinion, as they did, they could not provide a reliable political base for the Bolsheviks. The system was a hindrance to efficiency too. Frequent elections and interminable meetings (early Soviet literature is full of meetings) prevented the taking of urgent or practicable measures. The elected representatives often had very little idea of administration; in many factories the Soviets simply used up existing stocks and then allowed the works to close down. The Party was forced to intervene, and the first years of Communist power witnessed a steady diminution of the power of the Soviets.

On the other hand the Bolsheviks owed much of their success to their slogan 'All power to the Soviets', and they could not simply discard it now. The hierarchy of Soviets provided an admirable democratic framework, and theoretically all power belonged to these elected bodies. Even today the Supreme Soviet is technically the country's highest legislative body. In practice the hierarchy of Soviets is paralleled by the Party's own organisation, whose senior organ is the Central Committee, and its inner Cabinet – the Politburo (or Praesidium); it is these that control the real levers of power. The Supreme Soviet meets for only a few days in the year, for the formality of rubber-stamping decisions already taken by the Party leaders. The ideal of a democracy of Soviets still survives, however, and is considered important enough to be incorporated into the title of the Union of Soviet Socialist Republics; the reality is suggested by the technical error, made by Russians as well as Westerners, of using the word 'Soviet' as a synonym for Communist or Russian; the word has lost its meaning.

As revolutionaries the Bolsheviks had naturally underestimated the difficulties of administering a modern State. They had imagined that any conscientious and literate citizen would be adequate. An immediate consequence of the premature revolution, however, was a desperate shortage of qualified and reliable personnel. They were forced to turn to the defeated bourgeoisie to help them out. Trotsky's achievements with the Red Army would have been impossible without the recruitment of some 40,000 officers from the old Imperial Army. The re-establishing of order in the cities, which had relapsed into near anarchy, and the activities of anti-Bolshevik groups, naturally necessitated the recreation of the police force. Faced with the evidence of the administrative and industrial breakdowns, with the urgent problems of supplying and administering a large army, of organising a system of food-rationing, and of making the first plans for the creation of the new social order, the Communists needed trained civil servants. Even in industry, the scheme of giving all power to the workers had backfired, and the Communists were forced to reinstate the former managerial class. From the first the Bolsheviks had to co-exist with survivals from the old regime.

Naturally, the Communists did not trust their bourgeois colleagues, and they kept an eye open for treason and sabotage through the appointment of political representatives and commissars in industry, the bureaucracy and the Army, who had to approve and countersign all their measures, orders and decisions. If these precautions were understandable in the circumstances, they were not calculated to raise efficiency, and frequently led to friction. But this system of dual authority increasingly commended itself to the Communists as a method by which the Party could keep itself closely informed in every sphere. In this way the Party inevitably began to take a hand in the organisation of matters hitherto reserved for other bodies, and so to extend the limits of its power still further.

Slightly different was the case of the secret police. On the day after taking power the Bolsheviks had abolished capital punishment, but before the year was out they had authorised the establishment of a secret police force, the Cheka (from Ch.K., an acronym for the Extraordinary Commission [for the Suppression of Counterrevolution and Sabotage]). At first its chief weapon was the confiscation of work-permits (since these served also as ration cards, the measure was a drastic one). Even this proved insufficient, however, and the Cheka soon acquired virtually unlimited powers of arrest and execution. In August 1918 the head of the Petrograd Cheka, Uritsky, was assassinated, and a few days later there was an attempt on Lenin's life. The Cheka responded with indiscriminate and arbitrary arrests, and the execution of hundreds of hostages, a use of terror that was to set a grisly precedent. For both Lenin and Trotsky, capital punishment rapidly became a panacea for curing all kinds of social unrest, and even plain inefficiency.

The most far-reaching consequences of the premature revolution concerned the rule of law. Lenin, following Marx, had assumed that bourgeois legality was simply another instrument of bourgeois repression, which would be rendered unnecessary by the proletarian revolution; once the last throes of the class struggle had died down there would be no class conflicts and therefore no need for laws to regulate them. Accordingly, the Bolsheviks abolished the existing legal system, and during the period of War Communism summary justice was dealt out unceremoniously by revolutionary tribunals. Armed with the dialectic of Marx for the changing course of history, the Party had no need to establish fixed and absolute laws. In its self-appointed role of spearhead of the working-class it made the laws, interpreted them and carried out the sentences. The Party itself was above the law, as it supposed the bourgeoisie to be in other Western countries. This removal of all legal checks and balances on the exercise of power was to have unforeseen consequences in the future, when Soviet law was to be used increasingly against the proletariat, and ultimately against the Party too.

The NEP Period

The end of the Civil War confronted the Communists with evidence of a vast gap between theory and practice. They had successfully defended the Revolution against all enemies, but they had not created a proletarian dictatorship, only a dictatorship in the name of the proletariat; Russia still remained overwhelmingly a peasant country. The industrial base had been almost destroyed and would have to be rebuilt from scratch. The masses were largely illiterate, and would have to be educated and trained before Communism in any sense of the word could be attained. Meanwhile, the State had shown no sign of withering away; on the contrary the speed and thoroughness of Russia's recovery depended largely on the initiative of the central authority. Seven years of war had left the country exhausted. The nation's industry and transport were at a standstill. With the demobilisation of the Red Army the problems of unemployment were added. Inflation was catastrophic: when the currency was finally stabilised one new ruble was exchanged for 500,000,000 old rubles.[2] Meanwhile the peasantry had been alienated by the compulsory grain requisitions of the Civil War years; they were concealing their produce and slaughtering their livestock rather than surrendering it to the cities, thus raising the spectre of famine.

The country had been reduced to beggary; and yet this was the nation that had aspired to set the whole world ablaze with proletarian revolution. The gap between its present state and its ambitions seemed unbridgeable. It could not even offer work to its own workers. If the example of the revolution had not infected the rest of the world already, then the spectacle of post-revolutionary Russia could hardly strengthen its appeal. Far from having improved the situation the Communists seemed to have worsened it irreparably. Even among the industrial workers their popularity had ebbed dangerously.

The more articulate workers, who had traditionally made up the core of Bolshevik supporters, had observed with some concern the growing subjection of their organisations, the Trades Unions and the Soviets, to the needs and wishes of the Party. The Workers' Opposition, headed by Shlyapnikov, an old Bolshevik, tried to resist the Party's monopolisation of power from within the Party machine, but events tore the initiative out of their hands. A wave of strikes hit Petrograd, and in March 1921 the naval garrison at Kronstadt, the Bolsheviks' trump-card in 1917, mutinied. Their demands were no different from the workers' demands in 1917, but the Communists were now on the side of law and order; the mutiny was put down brutally. The question of the primacy of the proletariat or the Party claiming to speak in its name had been finally settled.

In the political sphere the suppression of the Kronstadt rising was paralleled by the outlawing of all opposition: the Menshevik leaders were expelled from the country in 1921, and in 1922 a group of prominent Social Revolutionaries were put on trial and sentenced to death. This trial bore all the features of the later show trials; the accused were condemned in the Press even before the trial had begun; the defence was not allowed to put its case. But in response to outraged socialist opinion in the West, the sentences were commuted to imprisonment and before long the condemned men were expelled from the country. Even inside the Party opposition was now forbidden; once a decision had been reached at the top level, no Communists had the right to question it. The effect of this measure was to weaken the power of the Central Committee, and increase that of the Politburo still further. Under Stalin the charge of 'factionalism' was to be used with a total lack of scruple in the destruction of his rivals.

But there were also concessions: chief of these was the introduction of the New Economic Policy (the NEP). The ideal of total nationalisation, advocated in the early years of the Revolution, was temporarily abandoned; it was a tacit admission that the Revolution had not after all been a proletarian one (Lenin described the NEP as 'State capitalism').[3] Peasants, traders, technicians were now allowed to set up their own enterprises, and to make their profits. The Party recognised that this concession to man's acquisitive instincts was more likely to salvage the country's economy quickly than ideological propaganda or world revolution. Private enterprise was, however, tolerated only on a small scale; the large industries, the 'commanding heights' (in Lenin's phrase), remained firmly under State control. But in many spheres the State enterprises were forced into direct competition with private businesses, and this led to the reappearance of advertising. State lotteries were instituted with large, but very few, prizes; they were plugged by naked appeals to get rich quick. The whole country had reverted to a frankly bourgeois ethos.

At first, however, progress was minimal; continuous breakdowns and shortages hamstrung even those sectors that were producing results. But from 1924 onwards the economy was running normally, and by 1928 Russia had attained the industrial and economic level of 1913. In this respect the NEP had succeeded, and it had laid a solid foundation for the vast and rapid expansion of the period of the Five-year Plans. But it was also a perplexed and paradoxical period.

For the workers the first two years of the NEP brought even further depressed conditions, long hours and poor rewards. Yet at the same time they could see the peasantry and small traders making quick and substantial profits. For many Communists too the introduction of the NEP was a painful shock. It was not only doctrinaire Marxists who considered that the theory had been cynically abandoned; even loyal moderates felt that the Communist Party had betrayed its fundamental ideals. In Soviet literature of the 1920s the case of the disillusioned Communist was to become one of the most popular as well as one of the most poignant themes.

The temptations of wealth and luxury, however, proved irresistible for some Party members. In the early days, they had been paid on the same scales as other workers, but they now came to feel that their heavy responsibilities and onerous duties and their past services entitled them to some perks. As a way of rewarding them and singling them out from ordinary citizens, special stores were reserved for their exclusive use. Inevitably as the privileges of the Party multiplied, so its ranks began to swell, no longer with revolutionary zealots, but with ambitious careerists.

The introduction of the NEP led too to a shift in Russia's international posture. Ever since 1917 the Bolsheviks had lived in hope of proletarian revolutions in Europe coming to their support. The revolutions in Germany, Austria and Hungary, and the appearance of Soviets in several European cities in 1918 all seemed to presage a wider conflagration. In 1920 Lenin advocated the invasion of Poland in the hope of sparking off a revolution in Germany. But with the failure of all these ventures, the Russian Communists came to realise that they might have to go it alone for some years to come. Since there was no immediate prospect of overthrowing the bourgeois regimes of the West, the Communists could not afford to antagonise them; the only rational alternative was to exploit their wealth and expertise.

This too was a natural consequence of the premature revolution. Russia could not reconstruct her industry without foreign goods and capital, and without industrialisation she could hardly claim to be blazing the trail for the world proletariat. From 1921 onwards the Communists began to explore the possibilities of restoring diplomatic relations and raising foreign loans. The Western powers were at first suspicious of dealing with a government openly dedicated to the cause of world revolution, and the first foreign country to recognise Soviet Russia was Germany, the other outcast of the European community. Marx's high opinion of the revolutionary potential of Germany, and the first sparks of proletarian revolution there, were additional arguments in favour of this fateful alliance. At Rapallo in 1922 the two governments concluded a political and commercial alliance, with secret clauses on military co-operation.

Loans of foreign capital proved harder to acquire; the Bolsheviks had repudiated all the foreign debts of the previous Russian governments and the Western capitalists were understandably chary of investing any more money in a country that was still threatening them with revolution. Trade, however, was a different matter, and several Western countries soon followed the German example by concluding trade agreements, and later establishing full diplomatic relations. The Communist International (or Comintern) dedicated to the cause of world revolution was not actually renounced, but it was subordinated increasingly to the interests of the Russian Communist Party. Communist parties in the West were now advised to abandon their former hard-line tactics, and to co-operate for the time being with the moderate socialist parties. Indeed, it often proved harder to explain to loyal Communists that the policy of negotiating with the capitalists was not incompatible with the aims of world revolution than to persuade the suspicious capitalists that the Russians were no longer aiming at subversion and revolution.

No less symptomatic of the increasingly Russian orientation of the international movement was the solution to the problem of the national minorities bequeathed by the Empire. The Russian revolutionary movements had always attracted a high proportion of non-Russians, particularly Jews, Balts and Caucasians. For them the rights of their oppressed peoples were inseparable from the internationalist ambitions of the Revolution. Hence one of the first acts of the new Republic was to proclaim the right of secession to all non-Russian nationalities; Lenin even went so far as to consider renouncing the 'unequal treaties' imposed upon China. Several nationalities availed themselves of this offer, including Finland, Poland and the Baltic states. The loss of the Ukraine was confirmed by the advance of the Germany army and the installation of a puppet government. During the Civil War many areas of the Caucasus and Central Asia openly supported the Bolsheviks' enemies.

But there were strong arguments in favour of reuniting the former Tsarist Empire. In the first place, the rich lands of the Ukraine and the Caucasus were essential to the economy of

Russia and could not be abandoned so lightly. Secondly, the tight centralised control, characteristic of Bolshevik Party organisation, was not compatible with the ideal of a loose, voluntary federation of socialist states. In this collision the interests of the Russian Communist Party and of Russia came first. It was argued (by Stalin) that self-determination was meaningless unless it was granted to the proletariats of these countries, and the Russian Communist Party was, of course, the best judge of that. For all Lenin's warnings against the excesses of 'great power chauvinism', attempts to recover the lost territories were inevitable. In 1918 the Russians tried unsuccessfully to engineer a revolution in Finland; in 1920 they invaded Poland with no more success; but the Ukraine was reincorporated in 1921, and the Baltic states were returned to Russian ownership by Hitler in 1940.

The crucial issue, however, was the secession of Georgia, where a Menshevik government had been elected. Although the Russians had formally recognised its independence and sovereignty in 1920, this did not deter them from instigating a rebellion there in the following year, as a pretext for sending in the Red Army, and setting up a Bolshevik government. Three years later, a new rising in Georgia was brutally put down. Ironically enough Stalin, the man responsible for these measures, was not only a Georgian himself, but also the man who had originally given the Finns their liberty in 1917. His policies in Georgia in these years were to lead to Lenin's accusations of 'great power chauvinism' and a deepening chasm between the two men.

Yet it should also be recognised that the Bolsheviks often acted promptly and generously towards the national minorities, especially the more backward ones. The local languages were officially given equal status with Russian in both cultural and administrative matters; in some cases Soviet scholars even had to create new alphabets. Schools were set up, and practical schemes for irrigation and power stations were instituted.

The NEP period has a unique flavour in Soviet history. Set between the ordeals of the Civil War and the First Five-year Plan, it has acquired an aura of security and well-being that it never actually possessed. It is a period full of contradictions; on the one hand, massive unemployment and poverty, on the other the reappearance of ostentatious wealth and luxury. If, politically, it witnessed the gradual extinction of the original revolutionary enthusiasm, and the rise of the Party functionary and the shameless careerist, culturally, the first decade of Soviet power was richly imaginative and creative. Its bright colours were set off, rather than dimmed, by the darkening shadows of 1927–8.

It was the most cosmopolitan period of Soviet history. The close contacts between Russia and the West before 1914 were renewed after 1921. Families divided by emigration continued to correspond across the frontiers; even emigration was not difficult up to 1924. Some individuals, like Erenburg and Gorky, contrived to lead an extended semi-*émigré* existence before finally plumping for life in the Soviet Union. Mayakovsky's annual tours abroad were given official backing; Soviet writers frequently travelled to Italy to visit Maksim Gorky. In these years the Russian Communists still felt that they had everything to gain from these contacts; it was rather the Western governments that were worried.

The regularisation of relations with Germany had important consequences. In the early 1920s, after the catastrophic inflation, Germany was a cheap place to live in; accordingly Berlin became the first centre of the Russian emigration, and hopes of re-establishing contact between the two Russias ran high. In particular the movement *Smena vekh* (Change of Landmarks) set out to explore the possibilities of building bridges to a Russia apparently normalised by the NEP. Its membership consisted largely of intellectuals who felt that they still had much to give their country, and, like most Russians, they felt ill at ease in Europe once the initial charm had worn off. For all the hopes of the *émigrés*, however, the *Smena vekh* movement had only a minimal effect on the Soviet intelligentsia, and by 1923 it was clear that the Soviet authorities were not interested.

The Bolshevik Government had torn up the international agreements accepted by its predecessors, and in several cases it was vulnerable to countermeasures. Berlin offered a convenient way round these difficulties. For example, by repudiating the international copyright conventions, Russia was enabled to pirate literature from the West. In the 1920s translations from Joyce, Kafka and Proust, and many others subsequently rejected by Soviet criticism, helped to keep Russian readers abreast of Western cultural developments. On the other hand, the existence of Russian publishing houses in Berlin enabled Soviet writers to protect their works against Western retaliatory piracy; it was a common practice therefore for the better known writers to publish their works simultaneously in Russia and in Germany. This practice continued throughout the 1920s, gradually declining with the growing isolation of Soviet Russia from the mainstream of European development, until the notorious case of Zamyatin and Pilnyak in 1929 finally put an end to this convenient system once and for all.

But the most typical feature of the 1920s was the emergence of the characteristic Soviet attitude of love-hatred towards the USA. On the one hand America stood for everything that was most hateful to the Marxist; it was a successful capitalist country, and unashamed of it. Yet the Russians could not help admiring many features of American business: its energy, its technology, its efficiency. The techniques of cost efficiency and time and motion studies were eagerly introduced into Russian industry, in the hope of capturing the capitalist secret; the very word 'americanisation' was often used to justify acts of heartlessness, both institutional and individual. As the Communist dream of world revolution began to fade, the Russians began to see the future increasingly in terms of a contest between the two nations, whose outcome would finally demonstrate the superiority of Marxism. They began to collect and compare industrial statistics, percentages, rates of growth, as evidence that capitalism was sooner or later doomed. Indeed Communist materialism, since the NEP, with its emphasis on figures and results and its contempt for failures is not so different from the capitalist ethos after all.

The New Life

The Bolshevik Revolution is, however, to be judged not so much by the internal politics of its leaders or by its international posturings, as by its success in creating a new and better society, whether socialist or not. That was after all the chief justification for the Revolution in the eyes of most Russians.

The end of the Civil War revealed the full extent of the

social upheaval that had taken place in revolutionary Russia. The social structure had collapsed; former landowners now found themselves struggling for survival, while former peasant lads and street urchins had graduated through the Red Army and the Party into positions of authority. But the new situation had not yet had time to solidify; for all, except the former 'exploiting' classes, the prospects were richly fluid.

At the same time seven years of war, and the accompanying epidemics and famines had created vast and urgent social problems. It is estimated that in this period Russia must have lost about thirteen million men. Families had been broken up, dispersed, bereaved or orphaned. Hundreds of thousands of homeless children (*besprizornyye*) roamed the country in bands, making a living by begging, stealing and the black market. At the same time, the traditional problems of the demobilised serviceman struck Russia with particular violence. There were far too few jobs for them, and the habit of living by the gun tempted many men into the criminal underworld. There was a dangerous sense of anti-climax and disillusionment in the air.

The Communists succeeded in diverting much of this dissatisfaction on to the former middle classes; the word 'bourgeois' sounds particularly repulsive in Russian, and they served as convenient scapegoats for the old aristocracy and capitalists who had mostly fled or been arrested. In the cities they were compelled to share their apartments with working-class families, who had moved into the former 'smart' areas; in some cases they were simply evicted. The rationing system was weighted in such a way that non-manual workers, except in approved professions, were classified as 'non-labouring elements' and so received the lowest rations of all. At the same time they were liable for service as nightwatchmen, snow-shovellers or trench-diggers, without any compensation. Although the terrorist attacks on the Bolsheviks could usually be traced to the Social-Revolutionaries the reprisals were aimed at the middle class generally. They were held as hostages and frequently executed. Under the Constitution of 1918 democratic rights, such as the vote, higher education, freedom of speech and assembly were promised specifically only to the working class. The problem of the *lishentsy* (the deprived ones), children of the former 'exploiting' classes, was to haunt Russian life long after this form of social discrimination was officially abolished by the Stalin Constitution of 1936. They were still regarded with suspicion, and were immediate targets for arrest or administrative exile, whenever there was a new wave of repressions. Rarely mentioned in Soviet literature of the time, the fate of the *lishentsy* does, however, play an important part in Leonov's *The Russian Forest,* (*Russkiy les*) 1953.

At the same time other members of the former bourgeoisie, the *spetsy* (specialists), whose expertise in industry or administration made them indispensable to the new Government, enjoyed favoured treatment. They received high wages, far in excess of the standard rates laid down for the proletariat and Party members; they were well-housed, and they were given access to the special shops. The reappearance of these officials was particularly intolerable, since they often made little attempt to adapt their previous manners and attitudes to the changed situation. Ordinary Russians, whose standard of living had dropped catastrophically, felt increasingly frustrated as they saw the good things of life falling once again into the hands of people whom the Revolution had set out to overthrow. The resentment felt by the former bourgeoisie, and the distrust felt by the masses, were to run deep in Soviet society for many years. By the end of the Civil War the tensions and antagonisms within Soviet Russia were even more intense than they had been at its beginning.

At first the family too was regarded as a quintessentially bourgeois social unit, and a dangerously infectious environment for the heirs of the Revolution. Since full-time institutions would have to be created anyway for the *besprizornyye* it seemed logical to extend the system; it would rescue children from the reactionary influences of their homes, and, in the case of proletarian households, release another pair of hands for work. But the problem of the *besprizornyye* was not to be solved until the 1930s, and by then the establishment of part-time crêches, and the rediscovery of the rather older institution of grandmothers, had set up a new tradition for working families that it was not worth breaking.

In the same way the institution of marriage was fundamentally revised. The radical intelligentsia of pre-revolutionary Russia had always despised it; indeed, they had made their common-law marriages almost a matter of principle. This was partly a protest against the hypocrisy of the Church and State ceremonies, partly a gesture of support for the ideal of feminine emancipation. These traditions were inherited by the Bolsheviks. One of the first revolutionary decrees declared that the mere fact of cohabitation, whether registered or not with the State authorities, was equivalent to marriage; thus any distinction between legitimate and illegitimate children was automatically abolished. Divorce was open to either partner equally informally. Abortion was readily available and inexpensive.

Many Communists, notably Aleksandra Kollontay in her book *The Love of the Working Bees* (*Lyubov pchel trudovykh*, 1924), advocated the complete abolition of marriage, with its implications of one human being 'owning' another; instead they advocated and practised free love, explaining that the sexual instinct was no different from other physiological needs: 'If I am thirsty I drink a glass of water. . . .' In many cases, particularly among the Komsomol, this soon degenerated into promiscuity, recorded in such 'shocking' novels as Malashkin's *Moon on the Right* (*Luna s pravoy storony,* 1926). Later, however, with the stabilisation of life, and the need to prop up the sagging birthrate – venereal disease was rampant, and many children were born physically or mentally deficient – abortion was made illegal, illegitimacy penalised, and the virtues of respectable married life advocated once again.

It was only natural too that a party of Marxists should be utterly opposed to the system of inheritance, by which a social group manages to preserve wealth and privileges, merely by right of birth. These rights were abolished in 1918. But, in practice, even convinced Communists found it hard to relinquish them; the one reward that they asked for their service to the Party was that their children should be better off as a result. During the NEP period it was only consistent to relax these regulations, but these concessions have now long outlived the NEP period, growing more rather than less generous.[4] In Soviet literature, however, the accumulation of private possessions has always been a standard image for bourgeois and individualistic tendencies.

The creation of a workers' welfare state naturally involved the workers in some new responsibilities. The penalties for absenteeism were high; in the Civil War period a man could be reported to the Cheka for three days' absence from work without leave; in the NEP period heavy fines acted as a severe deterrent. So long as private enterprise was tolerated, strikes could hardly be forbidden, but in the case of the nationalised industries the Trades Unions were persuaded that their duty lay with the Party and only secondarily with their workers. In many instances this led to considerable dissatisfaction among the workers. They worked long hours (often eleven or twelve hours a day); they had little security, and travel to and from work was slow and inconvenient. There were frequent delays in the payment of wages, and then they were in the form of goods or vouchers, which had to be exchanged in yet another locality. On top of all this the workers could see the growing prosperity of conspicuously non-proletarian sections of the population.

Realisation of the goals of the Revolution was now seen to be a slow process. It was, therefore, only natural that the Communists should wish to mark, at least symbolically, the great changes that had not yet materialised. Like the French Revolutionaries, they tried to leave their mark on the calendar; on 14 February 1918 the Russian style of dating was finally brought into line with the Western Gregorian calendar. (The Russian Orthodox Church, however, still retains the Julian calendar, thirteen days behind.) An unofficial attempt to renumber the years from the Revolution, however, seems to have got no further than the year 4. The anniversary of the Revolution (7 November) and International Labour Day (1 May) were naturally made public holidays; in the early years the anniversary of the founding of the Paris Commune (which had given its name to Communism) was celebrated as a holiday too. But Mayakovsky's suggestion that workers should celebrate 'festivals of labour' by putting in an extra unpaid day's work at weekends does not seem to have caught on. One of the most sensible reforms affected the alphabet: orthography was simplified and three letters were scrapped; the resulting economy of space has been estimated at 8 per cent, and though it offended the older generation, it simplified reading and writing for children and the newly literate.[5] This reform has been followed by most (though not all) *émigré* writers and publishers. In 1923 Soviet Russia switched to the metric system.

Other attempts to leave permanent traces of the Revolution affected the changing of place names. This trend had been started by the renaming of St Petersburg as Petrograd in 1914, as a gesture to the anti-Germanic passions of the time. In 1918 the Palace Square in Petrograd was renamed Uritsky Square after the murdered Chief of Police, and the famous Nevsky Prospekt – 25 October Prospekt. Within a few days of the death of Lenin, Petrograd, where the Revolution had broken out, was renamed Leningrad. Strangely, some of the earliest examples such as Uritsky Square and 25 October Prospekt soon reverted to their original names, and a large number of streets and squares in Leningrad today retain their pre-revolutionary designations. (Moscow, on the other hand, whose idiosyncratic street names mostly survived until the Second World War, underwent drastic transformation in the last years of Stalin; today few of the original street names survive and they are dwindling.)

It was only natural that such institutions as theatres, which bore the name of members of the royal family or of the owner, should be given more democratic or descriptive titles. Men seized the opportunity to change their surnames, if these were felt to be unworthy or in some way associated with the old regime, to a more contemporary styling: Novyy (New), Partizanov, Stolyarov (Carpenter).[6] In place of the traditional saints' or old Slavic names, loyal Communists frequently gave their children such names as Vil (from Lenin's initials), Vladlen, Ninel (Lenin backwards) or such revolutionary names as Barrikada, Antikhrist, Elektrifikatsiya and Diamata.[7] The bestowing of such names was of course a solemn affair, and in place of the old christening ceremony (*krestiny*) a new *oktyabriny* ritual was devised. There was even an attempt to abolish the traditional Russian form of address by name and patronymic as a bourgeois relic; non-Communists were addressed as *grazhdanin* (citizen, an echo of the French Revolution); Communists (and occasionally non-Communists too, as a mark of respect or favour) were addressed as *tovarishch* (comrade). By now the more exotic first names have largely disappeared; the traditional forms of address still survive alongside the innovations of the Soviet period.

The social and structural upheavals of the Revolution

naturally left their mark on the Russian language. The most characteristic feature of Soviet neologisms is their combination of bureaucratic circumlocution with military abbreviation, a curiously expressive reflection of the spirit of the early years of Soviet rule: *likbez* (for liquidation of illiteracy), *prodmag* (for food-store), *kolkhoz* (for collective farm); some like 'Smersh' and 'OGPU' have now passed into universal currency.

Simultaneously, a new code of behaviour was emerging. Differentiation between the social classes by styles of clothing had always been a feature of the Russian class system, and this tradition, suitably transformed, continued to play an important part after the Revolution. Veterans of the Civil War naturally clung to their military apparel; in fact the leather jacket of the commissar soon became a shorthand character description in the literature of the period. Loyal Communists now defiantly asserted their proletarian origins by sporting the traditional cloth cap of the Russian worker, a style affected by Lenin himself; to wear a tie was regarded as clear evidence of bourgeois propensities. When dealing with foreigners, however, the Bolshevik leaders often made concessions to bourgeois standards. If, at the Brest-Litovsk negotiations, they had dressed provocatively informally, by the time of Rapallo they were prepared to wear morning dress and top hats, though not without some protests from old-fashioned Bolsheviks at home. The NEP period brought with it a certain hankering after Western fashions. In 1927, the magazine *Ekran* (Screen) published the results of a questionnaire on clothing and advocated the reintroduction of such formalities as evening dress; but the reaffirmation of proletarian values that accompanied the First Five-year Plan effectively put an end to that. The conductors of Soviet orchestras, however, continue to wear the formal dress of their Western colleagues.

The gradual retreat from the experimental, even revolutionary social innovations of the first years of Soviet power was an inevitable trend. After the cataclysmic changes of the previous decade, people naturally yearned for some visible signs of stability, and they instinctively reverted to many of the principles and values of pre-revolutionary society, adapted or transformed where necessary. Even so, the extent of the reaction was still overcompensatory. The reasons for this are to be found in the changing political climate, the decline of the flamboyant revolutionary generation, and the emergence of the impersonal Party bureaucrat and the new ethos of conservatism, paternalism and secrecy; in a word, in the rise of Stalin.

From Lenin to Stalin

Under Lenin the problem of leadership had never really arisen. His seniority among the Bolsheviks, his authority as the chief architect of the Revolution, and his personal magnetism made any threat to his primacy unthinkable; without Lenin there could hardly have been Bolshevism. His comparative tolerance of those who had once disagreed with him, even in the crucial months of 1917, enabled him to form a government including several gifted, even brilliant men. He presided over them as the first among equals – his only formal post in the Government was that of Chairman of the Council of People's Commissars (or ministers). His attractive human qualities, his gifts as an orator, his simple style of life, his ability to communicate easily with all types and classes of people made him a genuinely popular leader; though popular feeling was also influenced by hatred and fear of most of his colleagues.

Lenin suffered his first stroke in May 1922; from March 1923 he was totally incapacitated, and he finally died in January 1924. His last months were spent in isolation, but this was only partly due to his physical condition; the other Bolshevik leaders were united in their desire to prevent him from returning to political life. He alone had the authority to question the powers which they had accumulated under him, and they had good reason to fear his recovery. In his Testament of 1923, Lenin had left certain recommendations for the succession, but these were phrased so negatively – Stalin was judged particularly harshly – as virtually to disqualify all the candidates. The leading contenders for power were all willing to hush up this document to protect their own chances – it could always be produced to embarrass the successful one later. Meanwhile, Lenin was surrounded by nurses and secretaries, mostly selected by Stalin; his wife Krupskaya and the few family members admitted were all subject to pressure from the Party organs. One indication of his isolation is the general sense of shock and surprise at the announcement of his death (well attested in contemporary literature). His successors had been ruling in his name so skilfully that his absence had not been noticed.

Lenin dead, however, was quite a different matter. At his funeral the leaders vied with one another in claiming the succession. Zinovyev recalled his long personal association with the dead leader; Stalin posed as the one true disciple. He undertook in the name of the Party and the Russian people to remain true to the wishes of Lenin. The solemnity of his words, the use of archaisms and religious terminology prepared the way for the subsequent deification of Lenin, and the resulting sanctification of his closest disciples. A brisk industry in Leniniana now started up: his body was embalmed and displayed in a mausoleum in Red Square; his head began to figure on Soviet postage-stamps; commemorative mugs, table-cloths, cigarette cases, busts and portraits began to appear like mushrooms. Lenin himself had disliked such manifestations, and many loyal Communists, headed by his widow, opposed the campaign; a projected editorial in *LEF* denounced the growing cult.[8] But the popular need was undoubtedly there, and it took the place of the portraits of the Tsar and the banners of Church processions before 1917. In both the popular and the official mind the figure of Lenin increasingly obscured that of Karl Marx.

For the Communist Party the cult of Lenin was even more useful. Although it was proclaimed that 'Lenin is alive, Lenin is with us', it was Leninism rather than Lenin that was required, a body of scriptures, equal in authority and flexibility to the texts of Marx and Engels. This trend was already apparent in the Russian Communists' reverential attitude to Marx, but now aphorisms and opinions coined by the two men for special situations in the remote past were taken out of context and applied as universal laws. The guardianship of these texts and their interpretation became the preserve of the Communist Party and of its current leaders; even power struggles were formulated as disputations over rival texts or rival interpretations of one and the same text, rather than their truth or applicability to the present. The dialectic of change and evolution rapidly withered into the barren scholasticism of manipulating the scriptures.

Finally, the cult of Lenin opened the way not only to the cult of his successor, but of countless minor Communist demigods, whose names are immortalised in libraries, hospitals, subways, even breweries. A few days after his death the city of Petrograd was renamed Leningrad. A few months later the city of Yelizavetgrad was renamed Zinovyevsk. This, the first city to be named after a living Bolshevik, was to set a melancholy precedent, for the fall of Zinovyev followed soon afterwards; it was later renamed Kirovo and then Kirovgrad, after his equally ill-fated successor in the Leningrad Party organisation. In 1925 Tsaritsyn, scene of Stalin's first public clash with Trotsky in the Civil War, was awarded the name Stalingrad, and by 1953 over a hundred towns and villages had been renamed to include Stalin in one form or another; all were to be renamed again in the decade following his death.

At first power was exercised by a triumvirate, Zinovyev, Kamenev and Stalin. On paper they formed a powerful group; the first two controlled the organisations of Leningrad and Moscow, while Stalin who lacked, apparently, their personal following, was indispensable for his organisational experience and his control of the Party Secretariat. The triumvirate was motivated primarily by fear of Trotsky's brilliance, his oratorical gifts, and his control of the Red Army. Parallels with the French Revolution suggested the danger of the emergence of another Napoleon, a role to which only Trotsky could have laid claim at that time. In point of fact, none of the Bolshevik leaders was so obsessed with these parallels as Trotsky himself, and his actions were actually designed to discountenance any such analogy. In the event it was Trotsky's unwillingness to bid for power as much as Stalin's ambition that was to dictate the future course of Russian history.

At this time, Stalin, the General Secretary, was little known or feared. He worked behind the scenes, and his name appeared in the press comparatively seldom. He was considered a valuable organisation man, but intellectually no match for the other Bolshevik leaders. In his later struggles with his rivals for the succession his reticence on the major issues of the day – industrialisation, the peasantry, the dilemmas of foreign policy

– was to prove an invaluable asset. He was not publicly committed one way or the other, and this enabled him to affect a 'moderate' position from which he could discredit the views of his garrulous rivals as 'extremist'. But through his control of the Secretariat, the bureaucracy within the Party, he was accumulating vast powers. The Secretariat had grown in numbers and influence even more rapidly than the Party itself. The Secretariat was responsible for the selection and appointment of Party and State officials; it determined the agenda of Party meetings at even the highest level. It controlled censorship, thus enabling Stalin to suppress or distort the opinions of his rivals. Most important of all it gave him the Secret Police. Thus piecemeal and unobtrusively Stalin had acquired vast powers. He could remove unwanted men, and replace them with his own. He could control the flow of information and the circulation of ideas; and in the police he had the means to drive home these advantages. The fact that this is obvious in retrospect makes it difficult to appreciate that it was not perceived at the time; but in fact Stalin's work in destroying the democratic function of most Soviet institutions and turning them into one-way channels of commands from the top had been approved by most of his colleagues, not least Lenin. By the time his rivals had come to appreciate the powers they had put into Stalin's hands it was too late.

For Trotsky Stalin felt a violent personal resentment. Like many other old Bolsheviks he regarded Trotsky as an upstart, who had joined the Party only a few months before the Revolution and had now run off with half the credit. Trotsky was undeniably arrogant, and his high-handed behaviour during the Civil War had alienated many of his colleagues. Yet he still commanded considerable support in the Army, and in the more intellectual and internationalist sections of the Party. It was therefore advisable to discredit him before attempting to remove him from power altogether.

To some extent Trotsky co-operated in his own downfall. He handled such explosive issues as Lenin's Testament with extraordinary clumsiness, and this enabled Stalin to turn this embarrassing document into a trump card – a demonstration of Trotsky's bad faith.[9] Stalin now began to decry Trotsky's role in the Civil War, his chief and till then unquestioned claim to the Party's gratitude. In the spring of 1924 he set about weakening Trotsky's position in the Army by appointing one of his own men to be his deputy. Still Trotsky did not protest. By the time that he finally realised the extent of Stalin's ambitions he had lost control of the forces that might have enabled him to mount a counterattack. He could only belatedly look for support among the other weakened leaders, like himself now cut off from any real sources of power.

Stalin now began to move more openly, and his real bid for power came when he publicly challenged Trotsky's theory of 'permanent revolution' with his own 'socialism in one country'.

Ever since the Revolution the Communist leaders had paid lip-service to the inevitability of an international proletarian revolution, which would enable the proletariat of the West to come to the aid of Russia's backward industry and hasten her path to socialism. The failure of the European revolutions had deeply disappointed them. Even so, the idea of the international revolution was so embedded in their thinking that few Bolsheviks ever thought of questioning its importance. Stalin's innovation consisted in recognising this changed situation and calling for the consolidation of 'socialism in one country'. He was careful to explain that this did not alter the goal of eventual world revolution, but declared that events had turned it into a long-term objective, and it was of course easy for him to illustrate the Leninist precedents, Brest-Litovsk, the NEP, the dealings with the bourgeois states, for this apparent change of line.

If this amendment to Marxist doctrine was no more than a recognition of the facts, it enabled Stalin to present himself as a moderate and to stigmatise the 'world-revolutionaries' as irresponsible doctrinaires who were willing to jeopardise the success of the Bolshevik Revolution, and so of world socialism, out of a blind adherence to the letter of the theory; had not Marx himself always stressed that practice was the touchstone of theory? Thus with this doctrinal utterance, Stalin finally vindicated his claim to be a Marxist philosopher, and so a fit ruler for a Communist State. Marxism-Leninism could now be extended into Marxism-Leninism-Stalinism.

The immense success of the cult of Lenin and the doctrine

of 'socialism in one country' suggest that they answered a genuine popular need; they gave the Soviet republic a mythology of its own. In the early days, the Bolshevik leaders, and indeed, the artistic world too, had searched for historical precedents and parallels. The French Revolution and the Paris Commune were natural models; in the early years the *Marseillaise* enjoyed an equal status with the *Internationale*. (The Bolsheviks' enemies more often recalled the Time of Troubles that preceded the accession of the Romanov dynasty.) But now Russia had at last acquired her own mythology; it was a gesture not only of political self-sufficiency, but of psychological independence.

The policy of 'socialism in one country' naturally identified the interests of socialism with those of the new Russian state. In foreign policy this led to paradoxical results. The Communist International, the prophet and would-be instigator of world revolution, gradually gave ground to the diplomats of the Commissariat of Foreign Affairs. Not only were the Bolshevik leaders now prepared to sit down at conference tables with the representatives of the bourgeois countries, but they were even ready to sacrifice foreign Communist Parties when the interests of Russia required it. But the first attempts to realise this policy were not a success. The clumsy attempts to interfere in the British General Strike of 1926, and the disastrous advice to the Chinese Communists to join Chiang Kai-shek backfired catastrophically. They seriously discredited Stalin's new line, and provided his rivals with ammunition for a real challenge. But Stalin's control of the levers of power enabled him to ride the storm. When on the tenth anniversary of the Revolution Trotsky and Zinovyev tried to stage an anti-Stalin demonstration in Leningrad it was easily broken up, and at the end of the year they and seventy-five other members of the 'left' opposition were expelled from the Party. Trotsky, who refused to recant, was exiled to Central Asia and in 1929 he was deported to Turkey.

The criticisms made by Zinovyev and Trotsky still remained valid, however, and with their disgrace Stalin felt free to adopt many of their ideas. This led in turn to the break with Bukharin, hitherto his closest ally. The pretext was the grain shortage at the beginning of 1928, which Stalin used to discredit Bukharin's policy (and his own) of concessions to the peasantry. Bukharin too was now accused of the crime of opposition. Once again the defeated rivals tried to unite their forces against their common enemy, but their previous disputes now made them appear not only as unprincipled conspirators, but ridiculous as well. Although Zinovyev and Bukharin, and Stalin's other opponents continued to play some part in Soviet politics, their authority and power had been effectively eroded; they were all to be liquidated in the great purges of 1936–8.

By the end of the decade Stalin was firmly in the saddle. On the occasion of his fiftieth birthday in December 1929 tributes were loyally sent in from every corner of the Soviet Union. The cities and public places were adorned with portraits, busts, and statues of the new leader alongside those of Lenin; he was hailed as the 'Lenin of today'.[10]

The transition period was over. The NEP period was wound up, and the country launched on the strenuous ordeals of the Five-year Plans and mass-collectivisation. The pattern of Stalinism had been established.

4

Intellectual Life

When the Bolsheviks came to power they were confident that they had successfully mastered and applied the Marxist laws of historical development. The success of the Revolution seemed to have vindicated the scientific claims of Marxism; and if history was on their side, the Communists could have nothing to fear from the truths of science. Indeed it was science that would prove the instrument for creating Communism. Technology would create the basis for universal prosperity; the superiority of materialism as a philosophy would be evident to all, thus increasing the intellectual and spiritual health of mankind; the organisation and rational planning of Soviet science would provide a far sounder and broader coverage than the disorganised individualist research of bourgeois science, shackled and restricted by commercial pressures. The changing policies of the Communist Party towards the intellectuals of the Soviet Union reflect this initial assurance and gradual disillusionment in nearly all intellectual spheres.

Believing that natural science and Marxism were inseparable allies, the Bolsheviks from the first encouraged the sciences, even during the critical years of the Civil War. They supported the work of Pavlov (1849–1936), the first Russian ever to win a Nobel prize, and they set up an Institute of Genetics under Vavilov, to name only the most celebrated cases. The majority of Russian scientists, however, remained hostile: many simply emigrated; Pavlov continued to voice his criticism into the 1930s. Only Timiryazev, the botanist, among leading scientists, accepted the Bolsheviks. The climate of the Civil War years, the ferocious anti-intellectualism of the workers and Red soldiers, the appalling living conditions – many scholars died during these years – further alienated them; they identified the new Government not with a new and progressive science policy, but with the forces of chaos that had made scholarly life impossible.

The Bolsheviks at first interpreted these disagreements as temporary misunderstandings. Little attempt was made to pressurise the scholars into ideological conformity. Provided they got on with their work and did not engage in anti-Soviet activities they were left in peace. The Communist leaders observed repeatedly that the furthering of science could only help to strengthen the socialist revolution, even though the scientists themselves might not be consciously working to that end. The majority of scientists were happy to accept these terms. Indeed many former Mensheviks and Social-Revolutionaries managed to find scholarly work, long after they had been purged from other walks of life. The Communists recognised that not only was their scientific work indispensable, but also their services as teachers for training the new generation of Soviet scientists. Once that had been achieved, the scientists would surely have come to recognise the superiority of the socialist system. If not, the Communists would then be able to replace them by loyal and reliable scholars. It was consistent with the logic of the premature revolution that the Party should allow for the possibility that history might not fulfil her mission.

The Party was, therefore, keen to start training the new generation of scientists as soon as possible. In rivalry to the (formerly Imperial) Academy of Sciences, it established its own Socialist (later Communist) Academy, staffed largely by Party members. Several Communist universities were set up, and during the 1920s a network of Party schools was extended throughout the country. In 1921, the traditional universities were required to set up *rabfaki* (abbreviation for 'workers' faculties') or crashcourses for potential students of peasant or proletarian origin. But an attempt to deprive the universities of the right to select their own staff and students was forestalled by a university strike. (The statute, however, was not formally repealed, and it was successfully reimposed in 1929.) In fact, academically speaking, the experiments had only a limited success. The Communist institutions, which claimed some of the best brains in the Party, were superior in the social sciences, notably in economics and history, but the older institutions remained unchallenged in the natural sciences and the humanities.

The tragic history of Russian intellectual life under Stalin springs from a fundamental ambiguity in the early Bolsheviks' view of science. According to Marxist theory, the natural sciences present us with a view of the external world which is unavoidably distorted, partly because of the physical limitations of our senses; but chiefly because of the distortions imposed by the class system; our consciousness is determined by our social being. (Lenin's word '*partiynyy*', later to become of central importance in the history of Soviet culture, can indicate both conscious and unconscious adherence to the party of one's class.) These imperfections can never be entirely eliminated, but they are continually being reduced both by the dialectical processes of science and the steady evolution of society towards a classless Communism.

The problem thus arises: is Marxism itself one of the sciences coloured by the class origins of its creator? or is it a science of a higher order than the other sciences, the 'science of the sciences', as it is sometimes called in the Soviet Union? These are not just academic questions, for the Party's answers to them were to dictate the theory and practice of Soviet science. In the 1920s passionate debates raged on the subject, for the early Soviet theoreticians were not agreed among themselves on the issue.

At the centre of the debate lay the issue of the nature of dialectical materialism, the whole philosophical basis on which the Bolshevik Revolution and the Soviet State stand. Which was the dominant element in this expression? Was it materialism, the assumption that all phenomena have a material basis which can be discovered by empirical investigation? Or was it the dialectic, the belief that truth was attainable only through the clash of contradictions? The natural scientists, not surprisingly, held that if the dialectic was indeed the method by which nature worked, then the scientists could be trusted to confirm the truth of the dialectic by their own scientific methods; as yet Marxism was no more than the science of history, and any attempt to elevate it into anything more grandiose was simply metaphysics; the adherents of this school of thought were dubbed 'mechanists'. Party theorists, on the other hand, led by Deborin, the senior Marxist philosopher in Russia, argued that it was the method of the dialectic that distinguished socialist from bourgeois science; Soviet scientists should therefore first master the dialectic, and then apply it to their scientific work. The Communist leaders for the most part remained neutral in this dispute. As a result, in the early 1920s the mechanists were in the ascendant, and the scientists were reasonably free of political pressures, provided that they paid at least lip-service to the supremacy of dialectical materialism.

But the dialectic was always a slippery weapon, for the central concept of the 'contradiction' was never clearly defined. It could be interpreted in several different ways,[1] and turned to different ends by different disputants. Although this clash of opinions might seem a model dialectical process, it was clearly difficult for the Party to accept, once the dialectic had become enshrined as a State ideology. It cast doubt on the infallibility of the dialectic as a method, and this in turn undermined the doctrinal foundations of the Soviet State. Furthermore, it reduced the Party to the status of a bystander. Philosophy and science were thus too important to be left to the philosophers and scientists. Inevitably, the role of interpreting the dialectic was increasingly assumed by the Party, which had applied it so successfully in 1917; indeed it may be said that this function is now the chief element in the legitimacy of the Communist Party's retention of power.

In the case of the social sciences, economics, historiography, jurisprudence and sociology, the topics, methods and findings of research are of course likely to be affected by the assumptions and sympathies of the investigator. Thus there was little sociology in the Soviet Union, because the Russian leaders were confident that the subject was covered by the Marxist conception of history; now that the laws of social development had been discovered and applied, there was really little need to study the subject further. Historiography was frankly tendentious. The leading historian of the period, Pokrovsky, reexamined the past, especially the Russian past, from the standpoint of the dictatorship of the proletariat. The Tsars, and such former heroes as generals and explorers were now castigated as exploiters, profiteers or imperialists, or at least as the lackeys of such.

The results were more interesting in the field of law. The Marxists believed that crime was the natural consequence of an unhealthy social environment. With the creation of a socialist state and a classless society, it was envisaged that crime would gradually die out, and with it all necessity for a system of law. Meanwhile the law aimed at providing social remedies rather than punishment; even the sentences of hard labour were officially entitled 'corrective' labour. The prisoners were treated with considerable humanity; they enjoyed generous privileges, received wages, and instruction in a trade. The sentence varied not according to the crime, but according to the social origins of the offender; the bourgeois were regarded as less redeemable, and political offences were, partly for this reason, treated with much less sympathy and consideration.

In the same way, the regime recognised the central importance of education. There were two important roles that education was called upon to play – one was the training of a new generation in socialist ways of thought and behaviour, off-setting the bourgeois influences in the child's home; secondly, to lay the foundations for a new socialist culture in the arts and sciences. A mass campaign to abolish illiteracy throughout the entire population, the *likbez* (acronym for 'liquidation of illiteracy'), was initiated in 1919. In the schools the most progressive methods were adopted. The early ideal was on practical education, to train children for life in an industrial society; the accent was on learning by doing rather than on classroom instruction; visits to factories, libraries and museums became an integral part of the curriculum. Traditional school discipline was revolutionised. Marks, exams, corporal punishment were all abolished; the pupils were treated as equals with their teachers, and students' committees played an important part in the running of the schools; pupils were even encouraged to report on the social and political loyalties of their teachers. The atmosphere of these early Soviet schools is brilliantly recreated in N. Ognev's novel *The Diary of Kostya Ryabtsev* (*Dnevnik Kosti Ryabtseva*, 1926–7).

The Church posed a rather more complex problem. Like most Russian intellectuals of the Left, the Bolsheviks were militant atheists. Before 1917 their hostility had been directed at the Church as an institution closely identified with the autocracy, rather than at religion as such. Religious beliefs seemed so absurd in their eyes that ignorance and skilful propaganda were the only possible explanations for its survival. In a democratic and enlightened state, they felt that religion would fade away painlessly for want of support. However, once they had come to power the Communists were forced to take it rather more seriously.

They could not simply wait for religion to wither away, as they had predicted. One of the consequences of the 'premature revolution' was that the mass of the population was not yet ready to abandon its old beliefs. Meanwhile, religion asserted a system of absolute values which frequently opposed those propagated by the Marxists. It too claimed an authority over men's minds and souls. It too claimed to be supranational; indeed it had been rather more successful in this respect than the Comintern. In all these respects the Church seemed to the Communists to represent a continuing threat to the monopoly of authority by the new State. Here too they tried to force history's hand. Many churches were demolished or desecrated; in some cases they were turned into social clubs. The use of Church bells was forbidden; the famous chimes on the Spassky tower of the Kremlin were reset to play the *Internationale* at midnight. Believers often found themselves being asked to work on Sundays. But for all this persecution the appeal of religion has strengthened rather than weakened over the years.

In the fields of the social sciences, the Marxists and the liberal intelligentsia saw roughly eye to eye. In the natural sciences, however, the Marxist line was the subject of passionate controversy. In the first half of the 1920s, the trend was towards a thorough-going materialism. Philosophy – even indeed the claims of dialectical materialism to be the 'science of the sciences' – was dismissed as contemptuously as religion; science seemed to have all the answers. Pavlov's rejection of the idealist overtones of the word 'psychology' in favour of the more materialistic 'physiology' set the keynote of the age. His work on conditioned reflexes was extolled as a model of the Marxist method; the reaction of the nervous system to external stimuli was taken as an ideal illustration of the dialectic at work in nature, and therefore as confirmation of the universality of the Marxist method. Yet it was also possible in these years for Soviet psychologists to follow the work of Freud, even though his concept of the unconscious might seem perilously non-materialist.

There are many cases, however, where specific scientific issues on the frontiers of knowledge have far-reaching philosophical implications. Such questions leave plenty of scope for disagreement, since the answers, in the absence of any conclusive evidence one way or the other, are inevitably influenced by personal preferences. Such cases sometimes seem to suggest, at least to Soviet scientists, that there really is a distinction between bourgeois and socialist science. On the other hand, some of the new scientific concepts of the twentieth century – relativity, the quantum theory and modern genetics – all of which have important practical applications for industrial and military purposes, seem to conflict in several important respects with the tenets of dialectical materialism.

Einstein's theory of Relativity was from the first the subject of passionate controversy in the Soviet Union. The extension of the familiar ideas of relativity in space to our thinking about time has important philosophical consequences: if 'before' and 'after' are as relative as 'behind' and 'in front of', then it follows that not only is ultimate reality unknowable by human beings, who cannot possibly transcend the limitations of time and space, but also the crucial scientific concept of causality is inadequate. These consequences are obviously of profound significance for modern philosophy and science, but they are not in themselves irreconcilable with dialectical materialism; indeed Einstein's theory is a product of the same 'relativism' that had produced Marxism. But the growing arrogance of the Russian Communist Party in all theoretical matters, and its deepening reluctance to admit the relativism of its own position, forced it to be suspicious of any theories that were independent. The specific Soviet objections to relativity are based on misunderstandings and distortions, and represent attempts to rationalise prejudice against its consequences, rather than a serious challenge to its arguments.[2]

Some Soviet scientists, such as the Bolshevik botanist Timiryazev, remained irreconcilably hostile to Einstein's theories; others, like Deborin, claimed them as triumphant vindications of the dialectical method. Lenin simply advised a pragmatic approach to the problem: Soviet scientists should take what was philosophically and practically acceptable, but ignore the philosophical conclusions drawn by bourgeois interpreters. Rice's *Theory of Relativity* was translated into Russian in the mid-1920s, but it was promptly banned; the editor who had commissioned the translation was sacked.[3] Practising scientists found it best therefore to ignore the doctrinal disputes and to pursue their work as unobtrusively as possible. Three decades of controversy were finally resolved in 1951 by the device of assigning all previous Soviet objections to 'Western pseudo-scientists'.

The quantum theory presents a rather more serious challenge to Marxist thought. Dialectical materialism assumes the complete objective reality of the external world independently of the existence of any observer. In the field of atomic and subatomic physics, however, the very processes and techniques of observation can affect the behaviour of what is being investigated, leading to apparent violations of the laws of cause and effect. Matter at this level cannot be satisfactorily interpreted in terms of either particles or wave-movements, but as a seemingly self-contradictory combination of the two. The behaviour of any one particle or wave can only be predicted on a statistical basis.

These features of quantum mechanics cannot easily be reconciled with traditional dialectical materialism. The suggestions that mere observation can affect the behaviour of matter and that causality can be no more than a statistical probability, both seem to undermine the basis of strict materialism. The paradoxes of quantum mechanics have long been accepted in the West, and philosophers have adapted their positions accordingly; but in the Soviet Union, with the establishment of dialectical materialism as an official creed, the adjustment has been more painful. The applications of the theory, however, notably in the exploitation of atomic power, have become increasingly important; for practical purposes, therefore, the Soviet Union has been forced to recognise the value of the new physics; the philosophical implications have, however, been discouraged.

The limitations of dialectical materialism (at least as interpreted by the Russian Communist Party) were to have far-reaching consequences in the field of genetic biology, one of the fields in which Russian scientists had made an outstanding contribution to modern knowledge. Geneticists hold that the gene reproduces itself virtually unchanged from generation to generation, except for occasional mutations. Some Soviet scientists, however, distrusted the theory and the science built upon it; it seemed to deny the possibility of evolution, and it therefore seemed irreconcilable with the principle of the dialectic (in fact, the theory of mutations does manage to account for evolution). Instead, they preferred to interpret evolution in terms of adaptation to the environment and the hereditary transmission of the characteristics thus acquired, an idea generally associated with the pre-Darwinian philosopher Lamarck, but long since discredited in scientific circles. The mechanists believed that the interaction of environment and species, and the emergence of new species from this 'contradiction' was an obvious example of the dialectic in nature, and based their arguments accordingly. Their beliefs had political implications because the Communists claimed to have established a new type of social environment, and a new socialist man should therefore emerge from it. In this debate, the geneticists, led by Vavilov, could only point to the facts.[4]

In the 1920s the authority of Vavilov and his fellow-geneticists was so great that no serious challenge was mounted. The hankering of the Soviet leaders after a more promising programme for quick and effective social changes was shown, however, by the case of the German biologist Kammerer, one of the last Western exponents of the Lamarck position, who was offered a post at Moscow University. However, shortly before his planned departure, his experiments were shown to have been crudely faked, and he committed suicide. In the Soviet Union he was promptly portrayed as a martyr to bourgeois obscurantism, and he was even commemorated in a film *The Salamander*. It was thus not altogether coincidental that in 1928 a young man, Trofim Lysenko, who was to elaborate Lamarck's and Kammerer's theories, first appeared on the scene.

In spite of such difficulties, however, science flourished under the conditions of the NEP. It was an attractive vocation: scientists were still confident that science was the chief instrument for bettering life. Political and nationalistic considerations did not yet seriously interfere with their work. Russian scientists enjoyed free access to Western publications, and were allowed to travel to international conferences, even in some cases to pursue their studies abroad, notably Petr Kapitsa at Cambridge, and Vavilov in building up his unique plant collection. Foreign scientists too were welcomed in the Soviet Union.

Even so there were certain ominous clouds on the horizon. If the centralisation of scientific work brought certain advantages in the co-ordination and rationalisation of research and the establishment of priorities, there was also the danger of concentrating on too narrow a front at the expense of other fields of research. Since all research was financed by the State it was inevitable that the Party should wish to have a say in the topics to be researched, their priorities, the methods that should be employed, and even the results that would be desirable. In the 1920s however, these pressures were not irresistible, and Soviet science achieved many successes.

A more sinister feature of the controversies of the 1920s was their extreme bitterness. Each side denounced its opponents as un-Marxist, and called for their removal from all teaching and research posts, and even the suppression of their work. Each seemed to regard ideological orthodoxy as a stronger buttress to its case than mere empirical facts. The consequence was a serious weakening of the autonomy of Soviet scientists; if they were to justify their work on ideological rather than on scientific grounds, they were vulnerable to the judgements of the Party, whose chief *raison d'être* was the interpretation of doctrine. But at the time most scientists were unaware of this erosion of their position from within.

The Party at first took a neutral position in these controversies, and individual Communists were free to choose sides. This impartiality was characteristic of the early years of the regime; it was prompted to some extent by a sense that these things could safely be left to sort themselves out naturally; but partly too by the Party's own lack of expertise in these complex and abstruse matters. The situation began to change after the death of Lenin. With the rapid growth of the Party in the next two years and the graduation of the first fruits of the Party colleges, the Party was enabled to take a stronger and more sophisticated line in scientific affairs. If in the early 1920s the mechanists, with their advocacy of a science independent of ideological preconceptions, had been dominant, from 1926 the balance began to shift towards the Deborinites. Their rise paralleled the emergence of the new Party line along the whole cultural front.

The Party was now becoming more openly impatient for some signs of an emerging Soviet intelligentsia. Communist trained students were still few, and were still outnumbered by specialists of bourgeois origin. By 1928 less than 6 per cent of all scientific workers were members of the Communist Union of Scientific Workers (VARNITSO); the Communist Academy was still a small and uninfluential body, numbered in a few hundreds. The Academy of Sciences, still the most distinguished academic institution in the country, did not include a single Party cell.[5] Admittedly, the Communist Party did not then recruit from the kind of intellectual of which Academicians are made, but the Academy too was resistant to the appearance of any kind of Trojan Horse within its walls. The Party was becoming increasingly dissatisfied with the scientists' inclination towards research rather than application, their political indifference instead of activism, and above all with the prestige and power that their intellectual independence attracted.

Communist example and competition had manifestly not succeeded in turning the sceptical intellectuals into loyal supporters of the regime. With the number of qualified Communists still a small minority, the Party saw itself faced by the prospect of a bourgeois intellectual elite perpetuating itself for another generation. Even the programme for industrialisation now seemed threatened by the shortage of new and reliable technicians and scientists. In 1928 the Party began to move against the autonomy of the intellectuals.

By the end of 1929 the statements of the Party leadership began to acquire increasing authority in scientific matters. Stalin himself was being hailed as a genius in every branch of learning.

5

The Literary Scene

For the Marxist the arts might seem to be a typical expression, alongside morality, philosophy and religion, of the interests and values of the ruling class, and so of no relevance to a society at a different stage of development. Even though, in the conditions of the premature revolution, it was hardly possible to hope for the immediate flowering of a socialist, or even a proletarian, culture, it was still difficult to see any reason for preserving the arts of previous societies into the new age. Although, as will be seen, some of the artistic movements of the early Soviet period did follow Marxism to this logical conclusion, most Communists boggled at the idea.

They had received a conventional middle-class upbringing, they had been taught to respect the arts as some rather ill-definedly admirable cause, and they were, of course, aware of the important part played by Russian literature in the moulding of liberal opinion in the nineteenth century. It was therefore natural that they should envisage art in terms of the conservation of the past, rather than of creating a new culture. Lenin simply lumped the arts in with the sciences when he declared that the new age must master the entire culture of the past:

> Пролетарская культура должна явиться закономерным развитием тех запасов знания, которые человечество выработало под гнетом капиталистического общества, помещичьего общества, чиновничьего общества . . . Коммунистом стать можно лишь тогда, когда обогатишь свою память знанием всех тех богатств, которые выработало человечество.*[1]

* Proletarian culture must be the logical development of those reserves of knowledge, which humanity has created under the oppression of capitalist society, landowners' society, bureaucratic society . . . You can become a Communist only when you have enriched your memory with the knowledge of all the riches which humanity has created.

In practice, of course, Soviet theorists and censors found themselves forced to be rather more selective. But the paradox remains: the central problem of Soviet art has been not the problem of creating a new culture for a new society, so much as that of trying to find a place for the arts of the past.

The confusion goes back to Marx himself. Marx had no time for bourgeois ethics, bourgeois religion, or bourgeois philosophy; but he was susceptible to the arts, and was prepared to make some kind of an exception in their case. After demonstrating the differences between the classical Greek poets, Shakespeare, and contemporary writers, in terms of their economic and technological presuppositions, he went on to ask why Greek art should:

> 'still constitute with us a source of aesthetic enjoyment, and in certain respects prevail as the standard and model beyond attainment.'[2]

To this fundamental question he could give only an uncharacteristically sentimental answer:

> 'Why should the social childhood of mankind, where it had obtained its most beautiful development, not exert an eternal charm as an age that will never return? . . . The Greeks were normal children. The charm their art has for us does not conflict with the primitive character of the social order from which it had sprung. It is rather the product of the latter, and is rather due to the fact that the unripe social conditions under which the art arose and under which alone it could appear, could never return.'[3]

These nostalgic tributes to the 'charm' of 'the childhood of mankind', 'an age that can never return', hardly constitute an argument for the eternal value or relevance[4] (as opposed to the 'eternal charm') of art, that is not also applicable to, say, Greek religion. Curiously, this idea of art as an innocent 'opiate', uniquely exempt from the rigorous dialectic of historical materialism, was later echoed by Lenin, who is said to have opined that it alone could take the place of religion.[5] The contradictions in the Soviet attitude to art thus spring from inconsistencies in Marx's thought. With the added inconsistencies of Lenin's few utterances on the subject, it has proved possible to justify almost any policy towards the arts, past or present, as Marxist or Leninist.

The appointment of Anatoliy Lunacharsky, however, as Commissar for Enlightenment (this included both education and the arts) seemed on the face of it a promising start. He was a close friend of many intellectuals, and he displayed a certain discrimination in the arts; he was himself a competent, though hardly inspired, dramatist and literary critic. In the early years his fellow commissars were faced with more immediately pressing crises than the problems of the arts, and so he was left effectively a free hand. Immensely conscious of his responsibility for the future of Russian, and indeed universal, culture, Lunacharsky attempted to encourage artists of every school, provided they were not openly anti-Communist. But, like the other leaders, he did not really feel that the arts were more than a frill on a civilised life, and certainly not yet a suitable occupation for a Party member:

> Несмотря на все мое огромное уважение к искусству, я могу сказать, что в нынешнее время коммунист должен еще доказать, что ничем лучшим не может заняться как искусством, а искусство, конечно, дело важное и нужное, но этому делу могут себя посвящать и некоммунисты.*[6]

Lunacharsky's judgements were therefore based on his natural mildness and tolerance rather than on burning convictions or artistic insight, and this very mildness inevitably attracted bitter criticism from those with clearer and stronger ideas on the subject of art under the dictatorship of the proletariat. It is the story of these conflicting ideas that forms the subject of this chapter.

The Transition

The social and political revolutions that shook Russian society in 1917 had been preceded by equally drastic revolutions in Russian literature and the arts generally. Ever since the beginnings of Russian symbolism in the 1890s, the literary world

* For all my colossal respect for art, I can say that at the present time a Communist should still have to show that he cannot spend his time on anything better than art; art of course is a necessary and important business, but it is something to which non-Communists too can devote themselves.

had been in ferment. Symbolism had given place to Acmeism and Futurism, and each of these schools had given several major poets to Russian literature. In prose not only was there a revival of traditional genres in the work of Chekhov, Gorky and Kuprin, but Andrey Belyy and Aleksey Remizov seemed to be opening up altogether new possibilities for the medium. In criticism too new directions had been pointed by the Opoyaz (the Society for the Study of Poetic Language), later the Formalist school. The early years of the Soviet period thus witnessed not so much the beginnings as the extension of a revolution already in full flood.

Even so the cultural scene underwent a marked change in the first few months of Soviet rule. Like the majority of Russian intellectuals the artists were overwhelmingly hostile to the Bolshevik's unceremonious seizure of power. At first they believed that the Bolshevik Government could only be short-lived, because of the hostility to it both at home and abroad. When, in December 1917, Lunacharsky issued invitations to one hundred and twenty prominent figures in the art world to discuss with him the possibilities of co-operation with the Bolsheviks, only five turned up, – Blok, Mayakovsky, Meierhold, Natan Altman and Ryurik Ivnev. Even when the Bolsheviks seemed to be firmly in the saddle, many of the most famous writers of the time refused to come to terms. Merezhkovsky and his wife Zinaida Gippius, Marina Tsvetayeva, Bunin, Kuprin, and Andreyev simply emigrated. The poet Gumilev may or may not have taken part in an anti-Soviet conspiracy; he was at any rate accused of it and executed. Artists with the international reputation of Dyagilev and Stravinsky, who were already abroad, preferred not to return; Prokofyev emigrated as early as he could (although he was to return finally in 1934). Even such writers as Maksim Gorky, Ilya Erenburg and Aleksey Tolstoy, later to become pillars of the Soviet literary establishment, all emigrated for shorter or longer periods in these years. Other writers were unwilling to emigrate, but could not accept the new government; they chose instead to remain silent rather than compromise their gifts or invite repression from the authorities; these writers are sometimes known as internal *émigrés*. Of this group Anna Akhmatova produced two notable volumes of poetry in the early Soviet period, *Wayside Flowers*

(*Podorozhnik*, 1921) and *Anno Domini* (1922), but she was to publish virtually nothing more for the next eighteen years. Other poets such as Maksimilian Voloshin, Mikhail Kuzmin and Fedor Sologub continued to write, though with little hope of publication, and died in obscurity. Andrey Belyy, surprisingly enough, continued to publish his novels and critical works throughout the 1920s and early 1930s, in spite of intense opposition to his methods, style and philosophy.

Within the Soviet Union, however, these names were soon overshadowed by those of the men who did throw in their lot with the Bolsheviks. The most notable of these was, of course, Aleksandr Blok but his highly personal road to Bolshevism could hardly serve as a path for others to follow. Of the other Symbolists, the only one to accept the new regime was Valeriy Bryusov, who joined the Party in 1918; but this gesture was regarded by his former associates, as well as by many Communists, as unscrupulously opportunistic; he was never accepted in his life-time as a true proletarian writer, and he produced little original work in the remaining six years of his life. It was only after his death that his political conversion was allowed to outweigh his earlier 'decadence'. Mayakovsky and the Cubo-Futurists accepted the Revolution almost to a man, and the organisation LEF which sprang from them was to make an original contribution to Soviet literary theory, which will be discussed in its place. The remaining Futurists split up into purely literary groups, such as the Imaginists, with only a brief moment of fame.

The most important literary figure of the immediate post-revolutionary years was undoubtedly Maksim Gorky. Having stoutly resisted the Bolsheviks in his newspaper *Novaya zhizn* (*New Life*) until it was closed down in July 1918, he then seems to have decided that he could best serve Russian culture by co-operating with the new rulers. He was uniquely fitted for this role. His friendship with Lenin and other leading Bolsheviks enabled him to bypass the usual bureaucratic channels and go straight to the centres of power. His wide range of acquaintances among the different social and intellectual strata of pre-revolutionary Russia made him a plausible and effective go-between; while his international reputation enabled him to appeal directly to the United States and the Western powers during the famine years. He used his influence unsparingly in the name of Russian culture, and that so much survived the years 1917–21 is largely due to his efforts.

The Russian intelligentsia were notoriously ill-equipped for coping with life even in easier times, and they were particularly hard hit by the breakdown of law and order, the lack of food and fuel, and the requisitioning of private homes and property. They were an easy target for the spite and anarchism of the mob, partly because they were associated with the Provisional Government, but above all because their appearance and manner of living seemed in these times to be intolerably bourgeois.

Gorky did what he could to protect them from the rigours of the time. He founded such institutions as the *Dom Iskusstv* (House of Arts) and the publishing house *Vsemirnaya literatura* (World Literature). The former provided intellectuals with premises for sleeping, eating and finding work. The latter, a grandiose project for translating into Russian the world's classics from the epic of *Gilgamesh* down to the French Symbolists secured a living for any intellectual who possessed the slightest qualifications and was willing to work. Besides translations there were lecture tours, poetry readings and scholarly work to enable the hapless intellectuals to feel that, in spite of everything, they were still contributing something to the cultural life of the country. On many occasions Gorky interceded for the lives of men under sentence of death or held as hostages. He found relief for scientists who were prevented from pursuing their work, or were in danger of perishing in the cold and famine of the Petrograd winters. A list of the scholars and artists who worked with Gorky in these years is largely a catalogue of men and women who disappeared under Stalin. As a result there are few books on this period that are acceptable to the Soviet authorities even today.

Nobody would claim that Gorky was successful in all these undertakings. The execution of Nikolay Gumilev and the death of Blok were two of his most serious setbacks; but these were only a fraction of his total work. The nervous and emotional strain on top of the physical hardships of these years began to tax his health; inevitably too his frequent intercessions on behalf of men and institutions considered un-Soviet or bourgeois began to weary and irritate the already overworked leaders. His relations became particularly strained with Zinovyev, Lenin's deputy in Petrograd, and in October 1921, he was persuaded by Lenin to go abroad and restore his health. Even then, from outside the country, he still tried to keep in touch with and assist the cultural development of Soviet Russia.[7]

The hardships and shortages of the first years of Soviet power naturally made normal literary life impossible; few non-Communist books or journals were published[8] as the limited supplies of paper were mostly requisitioned by the Party for its own purposes. Thanks, however, to the ingenuity of publishers in pulping down old newspapers and wrapping-paper, some purely literary works did appear. Zinaida Gippius and Marina Tsvetayeva even contrived to publish some defiantly anti-Soviet poetry before emigrating. But the commonest form of communication between author and audience was the public recital, sometimes in spacious halls, more often on the floors of the small cafes that mushroomed at this time in Moscow and Petrograd; indeed these years have sometimes been dubbed the 'cafe-period' of Russian literature. But the writers from the older generation were soon to emigrate or to fall silent, and the stage was increasingly occupied by young men in their teens and twenties, most of whom had never appeared in print before.

The Proletkult

During the Civil War the only literary group to receive official support was the movement for proletarian culture, or Proletkult. This organisation had been founded in 1909 by Bogdanov, Lunacharsky and Maksim Gorky, but it had soon fallen foul of Lenin and had indeed been effectively sabotaged by him. The first practical steps towards setting it up in Revolutionary Russia were taken in the summer of 1917; it was put under the Commissariat of Enlightenment in the Provisional Government. It retained this position under the Bolsheviks too.

Bogdanov, the chief theoretician of the movement, believed that the revolution should proceed along three main fronts, the social, the economic and the cultural. The first two were the concern of the politicians, the third of the Proletkult. In campaigning for his brainchild with the Bolshevik leaders Bogdanov was shrewd enough to stress the political advantages of his plan. It was difficult, he argued, to expect the working-class to digest an unrelieved diet of political and economic facts and theories; the forbidding jargon and intellectual complexity of the arguments were beyond them. But the message could be put across clearly, effectively and even attractively by using the resources of imaginative literature and the arts. Bogdanov got his way. The Proletkult was recognised as a semi-autonomous institution, and a network of studios was set up throughout the country; at the peak of the movement some 400,000 workers were undergoing instruction in these schools.

The Proletkult saw itself as the artistic movement corresponding to the period of the 'dictatorship of the proletariat', and proletarian origins were always more highly valued than ideological orthodoxy or even Party membership. Most of the proletarian artists were convinced that in order to contribute anything of value to the present age one had to be a proletarian oneself. Even the distinguished literary figures who lectured in the Proletkult schools seemed utterly anachronistic. They had been educated and formed by a bourgeois society. What could they say that would be of any relevance to the proletariat? Perhaps even the culture that they represented was not just irrelevant, but actually harmful? It seemed far better for the proletarian artists to rely on their own talents than to risk contamination by ideological aliens. This led them to reject the arts of the past *in toto*. In the words of Vladimir Kirillov, one of the leaders of the movement:

> Во имя нашего Завтра — сожжем Рафаэля,
> Разрушим музеи, растопчем искусства цветы.*[9]

Quite naturally, therefore, the Proletkult students felt it was their job not to learn but to instruct. Even Bogdanov, one of the few Bolsheviks with any feeling for the arts, could not conceive of any function for the dead cultures of history, other than that of serving as useful text-books, 'do-it-yourself' guides for impatient proletarians. Once their lessons had been learnt, they would presumably become obsolete.

* Let us set fire to Raphael in the name of our To-morrow,/Destroy the museums, trample underfoot the flowers of art.

The subject matter of the new culture was of course to be the interests and aspirations of the international working-class. All aspects of proletarian life now became the object of glorification: the metals, especially iron and steel, were transformed into Muses. Gerasimov, in his *Song of Iron* (*Pesn o zheleze*, 1917), pillories the bourgeois use of iron for fetters, and bullets; now the proletariat had put it to peaceful ends, and it is 'tender, glowing with love'; it even 'trills like a flute'.[10] The proletarian writers found new significance too in the colour 'red'; where more conventional poets had seen only the blood and fire of battle and revolution, they discerned the new buildings of red brick and the glow of factory furnaces. Standardisation and synchronisation became the supreme virtues. The poet Aleksandr Gastev wrote a book of prose-poems, *Shock-work Poetry* (*Poeziya rabochego udara*, 1918) in their honour. Here is one of his poems, *Factory-Hooters* (*Gudki*):

Когда гудят утренние гудки на рабочих окраинах, это вовсе не призыв к неволе. Это песня будущего.
Мы когда-то работали в убогих мастерских и начинали работать по утрам в разное время.
А теперь, утром, в восемь часов, кричат гудки для целого миллиона.
Теперь мы минута в минуту начинаем вместе.
Целый миллион берет молот в одно и то же мгновение.
Первые наши удары гремят вместе.
О чем же поют гудки?
-Это утренний гимн единства! *[11]

Logically enough, Gastev soon gave up literature altogether to apply himself to the scientific organisation of labour.

The chief weakness of the proletarian poets lay undoubtedly in the field of form. They felt that a new age had dawned, but they could only find old ways of saying so. In their glorification of the proletariat and their industrial mystique, they had to fall

* When the factory-hooters sound in the workers' districts of a morning, this is no summons to slavery. It is the song of the future. Once upon a time we all worked in dismal workshops and started our work at different times in the morning. But now each morning at eight o'clock the hooters call to a whole million of us. Now we all begin together at the identical minute. A whole million of us take our hammers at the identical second. Our first hammer-blows resound in unison. What do the hooters sing of? It is our morning hymn to unity.

back on the aesthetic and even the religious terminology of the classes they abhorred, the bourgeois Symbolists, or even the American Walt Whitman. They could not create new images of beauty out of nothing; inevitably they had recourse to the perennial tropes common to all previous cultures. A labourer heaving a brick on to his shoulder is compared to the sunrise; a chisel becomes a swan, and the wood-shavings from it remind the carpenter of the curls of his beloved. It was almost a convention in this literature to talk of the factory in terms of the church which it was thought to have superseded. Kirillov even wrote a poem – or rather a hymn – to the 'Iron Messiah'.

The literature of the Proletkult may be imitative and immature, but it is spontaneous and bursting with enthusiasm. Perhaps the movement produced only one poet with a genuine lyric strain, Vasily Kazin; his poem, *My father is a simple pipe-layer* (*Moy otets prostoy vodoprovodchik*) is a good example of his talent – and his limitations. In comparing himself to his father, Kazin refrains from the usual Proletkult clichés; for example, he doesn't boast of his proletarian origins, or suggest that these have qualified him as a poet of the dictatorship of the proletariat. On the contrary, he is rather on the defensive, feeling, and suspecting that his readers also feel, that poetry is a bit of a come-down after pipe-laying. Nor again does he assert his proletarian soul by describing the craft of poetry in the same terms as plumbing. He simply comes back to the same ideals of craftsmanship which had distinguished his father's work. Their jobs are different but equally valuable; he can, after all, bear comparison with his father. This summary indicates the limitations of even the best Proletkult literature; even though the rhythmical eccentricity and the freshness of the language give the poem a quirky charm, it is content to aspire to craftsmanship rather than to art.

The years 1918–20 were the great years of the Proletkult. Officially sponsored by the new regime, and yet administratively independent, it enjoyed a virtual monopoly of the literary scene. But it had undoubtedly abused its position; it had asserted its autonomy in cultural matters aggressively, and its fanatical insistence that proletarian origins were a prerequisite for a proletarian artist had naturally irritated those Party members who had not been born with a wooden spoon in their mouths.

In October 1920 its autonomy was drastically curtailed, and it was placed once and for all under the control of the Ministry of Enlightenment; it was reminded that the control of cultural matters lay with the Party leaders and not with the proletariat, which was not yet mature enough to guide itself. It was never to regain its privileged position and it soon lost its impetus. It broke up into a number of splinter groups, of which only *Kuznitsa* (The Smithy) was to remain faithful to the original ideals; as a literary movement it ceased to play a dominant role. Those writers from the Proletkult, however, who went over to the Party organisation VAPP (All-Union Association of Proletarian Writers) continued to be influential in Soviet literary politics and so in the eventual control of literature by the Party.

Some of the 'Smithy' writers turned to prose in the early 1920s; their best-known productions are Lyashko's *Blast Furnace* (*Domennayapech*, 1924) and Gladkov's *Cement* (*Tsement,* 1925). Both novels are concerned with the restoration of factories that have fallen into disrepair and decay after the wartime years of neglect. The heroes are ordinary workmen, and the villains the bureaucrats; whether Party members or not, they are all bourgeois. The conflicts are intensified by the marriages of the protagonists. In Lyashko's novel, the hero's bourgeois wife obstinately obstructs her husband's plans, and he is finally forced to leave her and the children. In *Cement*, the problem is more complex: the hero returns from the Civil War to discover that his wife has been educated by the Communists, and that he is now the inferior partner; he has to learn that the old system of exploitation of the wife by the husband will no longer be possible. In the original version Gladkov had the honesty to leave this problem unresolved, but the novel has since been bowdlerised and the ideological heresies corrected. The last Proletkult work to create any stir was Mosolov's industrial ballet *Iron Foundries* (*Stal*, 1926), with its stylised imitation of the noise of machinery.

It was not merely coincidence that the downfall of the Proletkult followed so soon after the end of the Civil War. During these years, few people had the chance of reading, let alone composing, literature. Except at the front, life was largely taken up in queuing for food or scrounging fuel. It was really the proletariat who, with their basic requirements already guaranteed, were best placed for literary pursuits. Once the fighting was over, a more conventional reading public soon established itself. It could hardly be expected to stomach the productions of the Proletkult, which offered little in the way of escapism or relaxation. Indeed from the rapid disintegration of the movement after 1920, it would seem that even proletarian readers were not particularly interested in spending their little leisure time in reading of the experiences of other proletarians. The NEP was predictably a bitter blow to the Proletkult, and many of its members, including the leaders, Kirillov and Gerasimov, left the Party in protest.

There was another reason for the downfall too. So long as the outcome of the Civil War was in doubt, the Party had had little attention to spare for literary matters. The virtual monopoly of the supply of paper by the Proletkult at least prevented it from falling into the hands of those whose loyalty was less assured. But once the Whites had been effectively crushed, the Party was free to assert its authority over the Proletkult, and remind it that class origins were no substitute for correct ideology. The more stubborn Proletkult members refused to accept this decision; they came under increasing pressures from the Party, and they were finally liquidated in the purges of 1937–8. Discussion of the aims and achievements of the Proletkult has, until quite recently, not been possible in the Soviet Union; their works are published, if at all, in small and unrepresentative selections. Their influence survives only in the lip-service paid by the Communists to 'proletarian culture', and, perhaps, in Stalin's description of writers as the 'Engineers of human souls'.

Krasnaya nov *and the* poputchiki

Gradually the paper situation improved, and, with the introduction of the NEP, private publishing houses sprang up alongside the State-owned ones. As readers and writers returned from the front with a vast stock of new experiences, there developed something like a free market on the literary scene, a situation that was to hold for most of the decade.

There was, of course, censorship. At first, it was exercised by the State Publishing House; but with the reappearance of private publishing, this was obviously impracticable. A new body was at once set up, *Glavlit* (abbreviation for Chief Department for Literary Matters), to direct and co-ordinate censorship; similar bodies were instituted for the other arts too. In the early years censorship was discreet and concerned only with outright opposition (such as Zamyatin's *We*). During the 1920s however, *Glavlit* was drawn increasingly into the orbit of the Commissariat for Internal Affairs. As a result, by the end of the decade, it had become effectively a department of the security police; it has remained so ever since.

The rise of the censorship was paralleled by the decline of *Red Virgin Soil*, (*Krasnaya nov*) Soviet Russia's first and greatest literary periodical. *Krasnaya nov* was set up by the Party in 1921 under the editorship of Aleksandr Voronsky, hitherto an obscure Party member. (Gorky was officially joint editor, but his role was largely honorary since he emigrated during the first year of publication.) It was modelled on the famous Russian 'thick' journals of the nineteenth century with their characteristic emphasis on belles-lettres and social and political commentary. But its primary aim was to develop a generation of Communist writers, who, like the Communist scientists, would lay the foundations for the new culture.

The word 'red' in the title suggested revolutionary loyalties, the 'virgin soil' youth and fertility, and these promises at least were largely fulfilled. Few of the older generation appeared in its pages, while practically every important young author of the period contributed something. Most of them had fought in the Red Army or the partisans during the Civil War, and so, even if they might not be Party members, their political allegiance was hardly in doubt. To distinguish them, however, from writers who had thrown in their lot with the Communists unreservedly, they were dubbed '*poputchiki*' (fellow-travellers) by Trotsky. Although the word has since been discredited, and official histories of Soviet literature tend to treat them as inexperienced young men who were only saved from appalling heresies and potential counter-revolution by the wise and sensitive handling of the Party, the *poputchiki* were in most cases completely loyal to the new regime.

There was a wide range of political and literary attitudes among them. At the extreme revolutionary wing stood

Mayakovsky and the LEF group; the extreme 'right' was generally associated with Zamyatin (his novel *We* was well-known in literary circles) and such ex- or semi-*émigrés* as Count Aleksey Tolstoy and Ilya Erenburg. Accordingly the *poputchiki* had no common programme; they did not think of themselves as forming a school; they were just writers. Many of them indeed felt closer ties with the proletarians or Party writers than with some of their fellow *poputchiki*. They mostly belonged to the *Soyuz pisateley* (Writers' Union), a loose association, which required nothing of its members but literary qualifications. This lack of discrimination tended to frighten off more committed writers, and so the Writers' Union remained largely a *poputchik* organisation, thus giving an impression of greater homogeneity and unity than actually existed.

The most famous of the *poputchik* groups was the 'Serapion Brotherhood', a band of twelve young writers in their late teens and early twenties, who had come together in Petrograd in 1921. (They took their name from E. T. A. Hoffmann's hermit story-teller and the literary society gathered around him in the name of artistic freedom.) Their wit and irreverence, their formal and stylistic originality, and their refusal to identify literature with propaganda, made them suspect to Party critics, but, oddly enough, apart from the most brilliant of them all, Lev Lunts, who died when he was only twenty-three, most of the others, Tikhonov, Fedin, Kaverin and Vsevolod Ivanov survived into the Khrushchev era as pillars of the Soviet literary establishment.

The subject-matter to which the majority of the fellow-travellers turned was the Civil War. Here the fantastic variety of location, situation, and especially the frequency of guerrilla operations provided an inexhaustible fund of material. Yet the very intensity of these experiences, their revelations of human endurance, heroism, or even bestiality, were so searing that few writers had the stamina to sustain works at such a pitch for more than a few pages. Events were still too close to be judged objectively or placed in perspective, and while authors were aware that the battles they described in such lurid detail were often only incidental to a larger campaign, they had insufficient experience to create larger canvases. The short story, brought to an extraordinary degree of compression by Babel in his *Red*

Cavalry (*Konarmiya*, 1926), was the dominant form of the early 1920s. The extreme situations of the Civil War, the immense responsibilities often thrown on to the shoulders of unprepared individuals, the habit of bloodshed, were subjects that had not been treated in such detail before in Russian literature. At the same time, and here they were in line with pre-revolutionary tradition, the *poputchiki* were often less interested in the scenes of battle and adventure *per se*, than in the effects they had on the minds and characters of their heroes. The Civil War was a sort of vast laboratory, in which innumerable experiments were ceaselessly being conducted on men and women under extreme stress, whether of fear, hunger, lust or plain exhaustion. Man, stripped of all the trappings of culture, man as he really was, this seemed to be one of the secrets that the Civil War could unlock.

The official myth of the Civil War as a struggle of the progressive Reds versus the reactionary Whites, or of the united working-class and peasantry against the bourgeoisie and the monarchy is seldom echoed in these works. Man against man, man against his best friend, even against his own brother, man against nature, man against the mob, the tragedy of the intellectual in an age of violence; these are some of the conflicts that these writers depict. When they do turn to a social struggle, the interpretation is often far from Marxist. In Leonov's *The Badgers* (*Barsuki*, 1923–4) two villages have been feuding for a hundred years over a disputed piece of land. When the Bolsheviks award the meadow to one of them, both sides are equally indignant:

Сто лет спорим, сколько голов пробили . . . А ты пришел да тяп одним почерком пера. Люди, смотри-ка, осудят.*[12]

The Revolution is seen as only incidental to – perhaps even a distraction from – the feuds and resentments that make up the real history of Russia. Another writer, Pilnyak, saw the Revolution in almost Blok-ian terms as an elemental explosion of the anarchic Asiatic spirit of Russia against the reason and order of the West. In his famous novel *The Naked Year* (*Golyy god*, 1922), he hinted that the foreign Marxist creed too would soon be

* We've been squabbling for a hundred years, and how many skulls we've broken in that time. And then you come along and slash! with a stroke of a pen. I'm warning you, people won't like it.

rejected like all the other Western systems that had been foisted upon Russia since the time of Peter the Great.

This tendency of the *poputchiki* to trust their own experience and judgement, and their failure to appreciate the guiding role of the Communist Party in all these matters, was to become the main charge against them at the end of the decade. Voronsky had seen his function in bringing these writers more closely into the Communist fold, but the writers had revealed an unforeseen indifference to ideological orthodoxy. Not only had *Krasnaya nov* become the organ of the *poputchiki*, but writers from other literary groupings, once they had made their name, tended to shift their allegiance to its more glamorous pages; far from helping to guide the *poputchiki* to ideological orthodoxy, they tended to adopt their freedom of thought. In fact Voronsky himself soon abandoned his earlier simplistic approach to literary theory, and came to value more highly the aesthetic and even the subconscious aspects of art.

Naturally, this angered many of the other literary organisations. The fact that *Krasnaya nov* sold better than its rivals, its success in seducing promising writers away from them, combined with its ideological freedom, all indicated to more orthodox groups that *Krasnaya nov* and its editor were engaged on a dangerous and potentially counter-revolutionary course.

At first the Party tried to remain aloof from this controversy. It justified the existence of the *poputchiki* by an analogy with the bourgeois technical experts who were playing a vital role in the reconstruction of Russian industry. So long as the Communist writers were unable to fend for themselves, they would have to accept their inferiority; competition should speed their development and so hasten the day when there would be no more demand for the works of the *poputchiki*. In the famous resolution of 19 June 1925, '*O politike partii v oblasti khudozhestvennoy literatury*' ('On the Party's Policy in the Field of Literature'), the Party leaders effectively declared that there was as yet to be no monopoly of Soviet literature by any one group. This seemed to strengthen the hand of Voronsky and the *poputchiki*, but at the same time it denied the claim of *Krasnaya nov* to any specially privileged position within Soviet literature. As Robert Maguire has pointed out, the significance of this document lies not so much in the Party's assurances of neutrality, as in the assumption that it had a right to intervene in the dispute if it chose.[13]

Voronsky undoubtedly owed his security to friends in high places, notably Trotsky and Bukharin; but with the worsening political climate of 1925 onwards, Voronsky's position suddenly began to crumble. In 1927 he was removed as editor, and then from the journal; in the following year he was expelled from the Party and arrested as a Trotskyite. Most of his remaining years were spent in prison; he seems to have died in 1943, probably in a labour camp. The journal which he had created declined rapidly after his dismissal. Although it continued publication until 1942 it never again enjoyed the central position in Soviet literature that it had occupied in the 1920s.

The place of *Krasnaya nov,* as the forum of the *poputchiki* was taken by *Novyy mir* (*New World*) under the editorship of Vyacheslav Polonsky. Founded in 1925, it was at first overshadowed by the prestige of the senior journal, and throughout the Stalin era it remained only a pale copy, although it continued to attract the leading writers of the day. Since Stalin's death, however, *Novyy mir* was to win a new reputation under the courageous editorship of Aleksandr Tvardovsky, justifying a comparison with the great days of Voronsky's *Krasnaya Nov.*

Oktyabr

The freedom with which the fellow-travellers expressed their often heretical views was causing the orthodox increasing embarrassment. It was largely the need to redress this deficiency that motivated the *October* (*Oktyabr*) movement. This movement had originated by breaking away from the Proletkult, and it soon came to dominate all the formerly proletarian groups (except the 'Smithy') and their central organisation VAPP (All-Russian Association of Proletarian Writers, later renamed RAPP).

By taking 'October' as its banner the new movement stressed its loyalty to the Bolshevik Revolution and so to the Communist Party, which had brought it off. Most of the October writers were Party members, and they therefore claimed for themselves the Party's 'spearhead' role in the special field of literature. The group was never officially recognised as the Party's organ in cultural matters (Trotsky, Bukharin and Lunacharsky had little sympathy for its leaders or their methods) but it came to identify itself more and more with the policies and interests of the Party; its journal of the same name, *Oktyabr* (founded in 1923), has retained this character to the present day. The extreme doctrinaire wing chose a similar title for its own journal, *Na postu* (*On Guard*, later modified to *On Literary Guard*), with its characteristic overtones of militant vigilance. It was characteristic too that the October group should devote itself more to polemics and criticism than to the creation of original literature; taking a leaf from the Deborinites, some theoreticians even declared that dialectical materialism should be the method of socialist art as of socialist science (an idea that can be detected in the later definition of socialist realism).

The October group based its position on Lenin's article '*O partiynoy organizatsii i partiynoy literature*' ('On Party Organisation and Party Literature', 1905). Here Lenin had argued that, since all literature reflects the interests of some social group or party, it was important to ensure that the literature printed in the Party's journals was precisely in line with Party policy. It has often been objected (the first to do so was the editor of *Novyy mir*, Polonsky)[14] that Lenin was only talking of political literature, but Lenin's explicit references in this article to science, philosophy, aesthetics, and even pornography, show that this is not so. There is nothing inconsistent with Marxist principles in Lenin's view of literature. The real issue is not the correct interpretation of Lenin's views, but whether they possess any special infallibility in these matters. If they were correct in 1905, they were still more so in the conditions of the premature revolution, when heresy and counter-revolution still threatened.

Hence the October group valued a work of art not so much for its literary merits or for its proletarian origins, as for its ideological purity and its serviceability for the purposes of the Party. An important element in their aesthetics was therefore mass accessibility, not simply because they believed that in a socialist state all men had the right to culture, but also because they wanted the literature of the Party to reach every single citizen. They saw literature as a refined form of propaganda; they looked, therefore, for clarity of form and style, and a sharp distinction between good and bad characters. The central hero should be a model for emulation, preferably a Party member; and the ending should be optimistic, so as to boost morale in the readers. These features came to be regarded as the trademarks of 'Party-ness' in fiction.

For these purposes the oratorical flights of the Proletkult and the experimentation of many of the *poputchiki* were quite unsuitable; the October theorists preferred to advocate the example of the classical Russian writers on whose works they themselves had been brought up, though these writers were probably more accessible to the traditionally literate classes than to the masses. Tolstoy's clarity of style and Gorky's revolutionary sympathies, and above all the frequently didactic tone of both writers seemed the ideal qualities which they sought to inculcate into contemporary Soviet literature. Thus the October movement's acceptance of the classics was very much more circumscribed than that of the *poputchiki*. They valued them not in their own right, but as models for how Soviet literature should be written. In reprinting the classics, the October leaders would usually commission an introduction to explain the ideological limitations of the author, and to justify in similar terms the utility of the work in the post-revolutionary era. This practice has been generally adopted by Soviet publishing houses since the 1930s; nowadays even those works of the 1920s that are thought fit for republication are usually subjected to the same procedure.

The October group boasted a number of young poets, Bezymensky, Svetlov, Utkin, but their natural medium was prose. Here their characteristic theme was the relationship of the leaders to the led. While the Proletkult (and some of the *poputchiki*, such as Malyshkin in his story *The Fall of Dair*, *Padeniye Daira*, 1923) had idealised the masses, the October writers usually preferred to depict an individual hero, the incarnation of the strength and wisdom of the Party. In Furmanov's *Chapayev* (1923), the Communist narrator is commissioned to educate the brilliant but anarchic peasant leader Chapayev, and bring him into the Communist fold. The will of the Party has to contend not only with the Whites, but also with unregenerate human nature.

The most important novel of the October group, however, is undoubtedly Fadeyev's *The Rout* (*Razgrom*, 1927), a study of a group of Red partisans surrounded by Japanese interventionists during the Civil War. Their leader, Levinson, is the central character. He is a fascinating mixture of contradictions, not all of them intended by Fadeyev. He is shown to the reader as an unremarkable being, of lower middle-class extraction, fond of his wife and children, and constantly prey to doubts and fears; the moral would appear to be that there is no mystique of leadership. But to his subordinates Levinson presents the image of a traditional romantic hero, total assurance, immense will-power and even magnetic eyes. His men see nothing of his inner life, his emotions and uncertainties:

> Всем своим видом Левинсон как бы показывал людям, что он прекрасно понимает, отчего все происходит и куда ведет, что в этом нет ничего необычного или страшного и он, Левинсон, давно уже имеет точный, безошибочный план спасения. На самом деле он не только не имел никакого плана, но вообще чувствовал себя растерянно, как ученик, которого заставили сразу решить задачу со множеством неизвестных.*[15]

The same dual focus can be seen in the moral scheme of the book. For example it is a serious crime when Morozka steals some melons from a peasant's garden; Levinson however

> угонял коров, обирал крестьянские поля и огороды, но даже Морозка видел, что это совсем не похоже на кражу дынь.†[16]

But the difference is not explained to the reader. Presumably, the leader's special devotion to the future permits him to override the morality he imposes on others. At the end of the book Levinson fails to notice a marsh, already spotted by his scout, and leads his men straight into it with disastrous results; they are caught by the enemy and decimated. Only a handful of men survive, and Levinson breaks down in full view of them,

* By his whole appearance Levinson seemed to be showing people that he understood perfectly well why everything was happening and where it was going, and that there was nothing unusual or frightening in it, and that he, Levinson, had long had a precise and infallible plan of salvation. But in fact he not only had no such plan, but generally felt himself bewildered, like a schoolboy, who is made to solve instantaneously an equation with several unknowns.

† . . . commandeered cows, pillaged the peasants' fields and gardens, but even Morozka could see that this was not at all like stealing melons.

but finally he pulls himself together and resumes the command:

> нужно было жить и исполнять свои обязанности.*[17]

The point of the book proves to be not how the leader finally harmonises his private and public personae, as had seemed likely at this point, but how he finally overcomes his human weaknesses – and lives.

The book has long been regarded in the Soviet Union as a socialist masterpiece; the contradictions and inconsistencies of its characters and value-judgments have been explained away as the workings of the dialectic. It might be more Marxist to see in it a reflection of the new stratification of Soviet society into leaders and led, teachers and taught, and secondly, an unconscious revelation of the contradiction between the dictatorship of the Party and the democratic image that it wished to project. For the feature of the book is its uncanny prophetic quality. Written in the years of Stalin's rise to total power, *The Rout*, with its facile moral relativism and its embryonic mystique of the leader, right or wrong, might serve as an allegory of Soviet Russia in the 1930s and 1940s.

The methods and ideals of the October writers were to gain increasing influence in Soviet literary politics, and finally to form the theoretical backbone of socialist realism. But apart from Fadeyev (who never repeated the success of *The Rout*) and Sholokhov, the movement produced no other significant writers.

LEF

The LEF movement (the initials form an acronym for the LEft Front of the arts) exerted an influence in the 1920s out of all proportion to its small numbers. Although the movement was officially founded only in 1922 (the first issue of their journal *LEF* came out at the beginning of 1923), the main ideas had been formulated many years earlier.

LEF traced its origins back to the Cubo-Futurists, a small group of avant-garde poets and painters of the pre-revolutionary decade. These artists were united by a sense that technological

* It was necessary to live and fulfil one's responsibilities.

and scientific discoveries and the new modes of perception that these had brought, had rendered traditional artistic methods obsolete. This aesthetic revolution they regarded as a reflection of the imminent social and political revolution, to which they were equally devoted. They considered themselves to have been Bolsheviks in art long before 1917, and they gave themselves to the Revolution unreservedly when it came. They took the title *komfuty* (Communist futurists), and they proceeded to claim the right of 'spearheading' proletarian culture as raucously and intolerantly as any of their rivals. (Paradoxically, the only allies that they admitted were the unpolitical Formalists.) But because LEF was headed by a poet and a man of genius, Mayakovsky, it came closest of all Soviet artistic groups to establishing a valid and consistent Marxist aesthetic.

The Futurists, as their name implies, were concerned with the arts of the future. *LEF* opened its pages to the experimental photo-montages of Rodchenko; it took a keen interest in the new theatre of Meierhold, and, naturally, in the revolutionary cinema of Eisenstein. It was as ruthless as the Proletkult in its rejection of the past; indeed in the early days there was even a tacit alliance between the two groups against the October movement and the *poputchiki*, who, with their reverence for the past and willingness to work within its traditions, seemed hardly worth distinguishing one from the other. In the years when Gorky and his allies were trying to preserve the treasures of the past, the Futurist Lev Bruni advocated instead the setting up of a commission for the 'planned destruction of all monuments of art and antiquity.'[18] In the same spirit Mayakovsky once defined a member of LEF as 'anyone who treats old literature with hatred.'[19]

LEF gave the arts a definite function in the historical process:

Мы утверждаем, что литература не зеркало, отражающее историческую борьбу, а оружие этой борьбы.*[20]

Thus ran a *LEF* editorial in a clear echo of Marx's statement that the task of philosophy was not to contemplate the world but to change it. The arts should not be shut away in libraries and museums for the leisured classes, they should be out on the

* We affirm that literature is not a mirror reflecting the historic struggle, but a weapon in that struggle.

streets, a natural part of the daily life of the citizens of a socialist state. In the early years of Communist rule, Russian artists were indeed allowed to decorate the streets and buildings for the great revolutionary festivals. They threw their energies into designing posters for the Civil War, advertisements for the State shops during the NEP; their ideas even had a short-lived influence, through the Constructivists, on Soviet industrial design. Mayakovsky's propaganda poems and advertisements were a response to this utilitarian challenge, and the poet declared that he considered these works just as important as his more obviously literary ones. He wrote several poems on the short-comings of consumer goods and services, and urged other writers to do the same, instead of wasting time and energy on the useless pursuit of artistic and literary criticism.

But unlike their rivals, the Futurists realised that this new content still had to be expressed in a revolutionary form. Marx had shown that reality was not static but dynamic; it was therefore the duty of the arts to be dynamic too. LEF rejected the work of the Proletkult because it was formally so imitative; as for the *poputchiki* and the October writers, their conception of realism as a static record of actual or possible events in the past was condemned to still-birth in the new age of social and technological revolution. In their search for a dynamic art the Futurists frequently set their works in the future; some of them cultivated a 'telegram' style, omitting pronouns and prepositions; Mayakovsky instructed would-be producers of his play *Misteriya-Buff* to drop scenes that were outdated and devise new ones of greater topicality. They continued their pre-revolutionary experiments with words and syntax, unexpected rhymes and broken rhythms, with the aim of preparing the ground for the techniques of the future. If the utilitarian side of LEF required of Mayakovsky nothing but propaganda and advertising work, its theory of form could justify such poetic masterpieces as his *About This* (*Pro eto*, 1923) and *At the Top of my Voice* (*Vo ves golos*, 1929–30).

The functional and formal innovatory aspects of LEF have exerted no direct influence on Soviet aesthetic thought and practice, but two of their ideas have survived, somewhat transformed in the process. The first of these was Osip Brik's theory of the 'social commission' (*sotsialnyy zakaz*). Arguing from Marxist first principles, and Lenin's article on 'Party-literature', Brik regarded every artist as the mouthpiece of his society; the views which he expresses and the form in which he orders them reflect his social and economic allegiances. If in the past most artists had accepted this 'social commission' unconsciously, it should now be all the more effective for being fully realised and acted upon; the Soviet artist should welcome specific commissions from society. Although this theory has been officially rejected, the principle of commissioning authors and artists to write up collective farms and model factories has long been a feature of Soviet artistic life. So too has the corollary that 'non-proletarian' techniques and forms are potentially counter-revolutionary, and must be suppressed accordingly, though, of course, Brik and Soviet critics would not have agreed on the definition of 'non-proletarian'.

The second consequence was the down-grading of imaginative literature (the novel, in particular, was condemned as the ultimate in bourgeois forms) and the corresponding elevation of the documentary. In keeping with the LEF idea of art as a weapon, rather than a mirror, this meant not an objective account of the facts, but a narrative angled sharply from the class-interests of the proletariat. The semi-literate newspaper correspondents recording the modernisation of Russian industry and agriculture, and denouncing class enemies, seemed to LEF the ideal combination of art with political activity. Mayakovsky called their work 'true proletarian art' and the 'centre of gravity of literature today'.[21] He was, of course, exaggerating in the heat of polemics; the majority of these reports are badly written, and none of them reveals any of the revolutionary attitudes to words and style that he sought. However, this combination of technical progress and political propaganda was later to become an important element in the literature of the First Five-year Plan, and for some years after that. (Curiously, the genre of the slanted documentary acquired a new lease of life in the 1950s as a method of commenting *un*favourably on Soviet reality, particularly in the countryside.)

The ideas of LEF were not generally understood or appreciated at the time. Lenin disliked the Futurists, and even Lunacharsky found them rather embarrassing. Some of their early revolutionary sculptures were destroyed or removed by the unappreciative populace and there were several complaints in the press about their more bizarre productions. They were attacked by the October critics, by the *poputchiki*, and in the pages of *Na postu*. LEF, of course, revelled in controversy, and took this hostility as clear evidence of the deep-rootedness of the old arts in the mentality of the supposedly revolutionary generation. But there were also smear campaigns; the fourth number of *LEF* was accused of pornography (the pretext was an innocuous article by Shklovsky on Russian oaths). Rumours were circulated that the journal had been suppressed long before it did actually close down.

Mayakovsky, the editor, was often abroad or touring Russia, and without him the journal lost its drive. There was dissension too within the movement, and this led to inefficiency and delays. *LEF* was always in financial difficulties, and, after producing only seven numbers in nearly three years, it finally closed down in 1925. In 1927 it was revived as *Novyy LEF* (*New LEF*), and run more professionally. But this time Mayakovsky himself was under pressure; he resigned in the middle of 1928, and the last five numbers came out without him. *Novyy LEF* gave place in its turn to *REF* (*REvolutionary Front of the arts*), again under Mayakovsky's editorship, but it published nothing and collapsed as soon as Mayakovsky left it to apply for membership of RAPP at the beginning of 1930.

The views of LEF and its achievements have not yet received their due either in the Soviet Union or in the West.

Formalism

A reflection of the scientific claims of Marxism can be seen in the work of the Formalists. The foundations of this movement had, admittedly, been laid well before 1917 by Andrey Belyy and the Opoyaz group (acronym for the Society for the Study of Poetic Language), but their finest work belongs to the post-revolutionary period. As their name implies the Formalists were interested in problems of literary form, at every level, from the minutiae of stylistics to the most complex structures.

The Formalists tried to get behind the mystique of art, and to analyse it in a purely technical way. They were not interested in the biography or character of the artists; they were scornful of the programme note kind of criticism which extols the beauty or expounds the 'meaning' of a work of art. Instead, they liked to compare it to a system or mechanism, and declared that they were interested in the way it worked, not in the man who designed it. Such titles as Shklovsky's *How Don Quixote is Made* (*Kak sdelan Don Kikhot*) indicate the aims and methods of the Formalists.

But the most characteristic feature of the Formalists was their interest in the future of contemporary literature. They too believed that their function was not just to interpret it, but to assist its development. In all their studies they were conscious of the tasks awaiting the new Soviet culture. The techniques, devices and forms that they studied, they regarded as the raw materials of the trade of literature. Accordingly, many of the Formalists were friends and colleagues of the literary avant-garde, LEF and the Serapion Brothers. They were interested in the new arts, particularly in the cinema.

It might have been expected that the Formalists' strictly analytical and practical approach to works of art would have commended them to the Soviet authorities, but the growing emphasis of Marxist thinking was turning against the Formalists. They were accused of scholasticism, of one-sidedly obscuring the content of a work of art, in order to admire its form. At first the Formalists dismissed the complaints of the Marxist critics as irrelevant to their concerns. They did not deny the validity of Marxism; they simply claimed that it was inapplicable to the technical questions that interested them. Their methods were not in conflict with those of the Marxists; rather they could be used to complement one another.

However, as the Party came to feel that Marxism was the method to be applied to all fields of thought and research in the Soviet Union, the Formalists came under increasing pressure to conform. Some of them tried to compromise (notably Shklovsky, in his work on Tolstoy's *War and Peace*), by arguing that style could indicate the social origins and political presuppositions of an author much more effectively than an analysis of the content; but he succeeded only in postponing the final showdown. The movement was outlawed in 1929.

Since then the word Formalism has become one of the most serious accusations in the Soviet Union, and artists and critics alike have learnt to dread it. Yet, surprisingly, the Formalists themselves survived relatively unscathed, and reappeared after Stalin's death, faithful to their old principles, but rather more cautious in their application and formulation. Their ideas have been taken up and developed in the West, largely due to the work of the outstanding Russian Formalist critic Roman Jakobson, who emigrated from Soviet Russia in 1922. Such present day movements as Structuralism trace their origins and inspiration to Russian Formalism.

The NEP Period in Literature

As the events of the Revolution and Civil War receded into the past, a new kind of literature gradually made its appearance. Writers began to realise that the shattering experiences which had provided the bulk of their subject matter had given way to a totally changed peacetime situation, still in process of transition, but in its own way as remarkable as the events that had preceded it.

Life was settling down into a new pattern. A new class-structure was solidifying, in which the temptations of power and money seemed just as great as in the bourgeois past: the Party was evolving into a new aristocracy; while unscrupulous peasants and traders had managed to amass small fortunes. At the same time unemployment was still rampant, and the poorer classes found it hard to eke out even the most humble existence. This topsy-turvy situation was a fascinating subject for socially aware writers. Erenburg observed it with some glee in his novel *The Grabber* (*Rvach*, 1924), Leonov with rather more sensitivity in *The Thief* (*Vor*, 1927).

Ironically, it was the *poputchiki* who treated these problems with the greatest depth and objectivity. In previous years, the more committed writers had frequently reproached them for their interest in subjects remote from the present, with the implication that this betrayed a lack of commitment to the new society. Yet, as the 1920s unfolded, and the difficulties and setbacks in inaugurating the Communist millennium became more obvious, it was the Party writers who tried to deflect the limelight from the present, and to remind readers of the heroic struggles of the past. Conversely, it was the *poputchiki*, with their interest in the unusual and the unexpected, the unforeseen and the unhackneyed, who turned more and more to the contemporary scene. For a brief spell, they served as the Party's unofficial conscience.

The greater tolerance of the *poputchiki* and their concern for aesthetic values rather than political orthodoxy attracted some of the more sensitive writers from the Proletkult and the October organisations. This group took the name 'Mountain-pass' ('*Pereval*'), to suggest a half-way position between the *poputchiki* and the more doctrinaire schools (though it must be remembered that most of the *poputchiki* saw themselves in this way). The 'Mountain-pass' writers were distinguished by their humanitarianism; they preferred to deal with the problems of ordinary people rather than obviously big issues; a characteristic theme of theirs was life in the countryside, a subject that was otherwise largely ignored at this time.

They took Voronsky as their guide, and he seems to have seen in them the type of writer that he was looking for; they combined a sound Marxist outlook with a firm technical grounding and a conviction of the uniqueness of art. But the patronage of Voronsky was to become a liability from 1928 onwards, and the group were liquidated in the great purges; none of them was ever considered to belong to the mainstream of Soviet literature. Besides the older man Mikhail Prishvin, who never fitted into any category, the most remarkable writer of the group was Andrey Platonov, who was to produce his finest work during the 1930s.

An important element in the literature of the 1920s was satire. The satirists presented the other face of the 'new society' and the 'new life'. It was of course easy to mock the absurdity of the dispossessed classes, and their attempts to ingratiate themselves with the new regime; it was easy too to make fun of the confusion and hypocrisy attending the transition from bourgeois to socialist morality. Soviet satire only really began to bite, however, when the writers perceived that the abuses of Soviet society were perhaps not so very different from those of the Tsarist regime. Dozens of variations on Gogol's Chichikov and Khlestakov began to appear in books and plays from 1924 onwards. The rigidity and pomposity of the new officials and their restoration of bourgeois values were ridiculed, sometimes farcically, as in the plays of Bulgakov, or Ilf and Petrov's novel *Twelve Chairs* (*Dvenadtsat stulyev*, 1927), sometimes angrily as in Mayakovsky's later poems and plays, the productions of Meierhold, and the music of the young Shostakovich.

But the outstanding satirist of the period was undoubtedly Mikhail Zoshchenko. Zoshchenko's early stories are stylised imitations of the speech of the semi-literate proletariat, with their incongruous juxtapositions of high-flown foreign loan-words and the inarticulate vulgarisms of the vernacular. Taken individually Zoshchenko's stories present a series of ridiculous events that befall absurd people, told in ludicrous language; but their cumulative effect is one of misanthropic despair at the folly and pettiness of human nature. Zoshchenko was always a problematic writer for the Communists, because the secret of his irony lies in the tone of his writing rather than in the actual words. Thus his stories, ostensibly written for children, *Tales of Lenin* (*Rasskazy o Lenine*, 1940–1), are in fact perfectly judged parodies of the manner of Soviet hagiography. (Curiously these stories are still taken at face value by Soviet critics.)

The recurrent theme of this satire is the contrast and conflict (and sometimes too the similarity) between the old and new. Nowhere is it better exemplified than in Yury Olesha's deceptively simple fable *Envy* (*Zavist*, 1927). Olesha presents two embodiments of these abstractions: the efficient sausage-maker and loyal Party member Andrey Babichev, and the drunken layabout and artist, Nikolay Kavalerov. The new world of Babichev is inhuman and grotesque; his very profession, the transformation of flesh and blood into mass-produced, identical sausages, is a symbol at once ludicrous and horrific; his adopted son frankly aspires to become a machine. By contrast Kavalerov's surname suggests something chivalrous, almost Quixotic; he believes in such old-fashioned ideals as love and beauty, and he gets involved in a 'conspiracy of feelings' (this was actually taken as the title of the stage version of the novel) against the new society.

Olesha seems to recall Zamyatin's *We* in his rejection of the cult of efficiency and technology in the name of human emotions; but his position is much less assured. There is nothing inherently wrong about making sausages, and, if they must be made, it is clearly better that they should be made conscientiously and cheaply. At the same time Kavalerov proves unable to offer any values more admirable or relevant than those of Babichev, and at the end of the novel the 'conspiracy of feelings' has collapsed into mere indifference, 'the best of the states of the human mind'.[22] Babichev has been recognised as a soulless Establishment figure: Kavalerov as a 'superfluous' intellectual in the best nineteenth century tradition. Has anything changed?

This witty and pessimistic book has always been handled gingerly in the Soviet Union; in fact it was suppressed between 1936 and 1956. The dilemma that it treats is inherent in Marxism: can the Communist Utopia and the perfect integration of the individual into society be achieved without destroying the essence of human nature? Like *We*, *Envy* has become increasingly relevant to industrialised societies everywhere.

With the stabilisation of life and the reappearance of leisure-time in the mid-1920s, the form of the short story gradually gave place to the novel, and even to the epic novel. It was in these years that the first volumes of Sholokhov's *The Quiet Don* (*Tikhiy Don*, 1926–40) came out; Gorky had begun work on his vast, unfinished *The Life of Klim Samgin* (*Zhizn Klima Samgina*, 1925–36); Aleksey Tolstoy was re-working his earlier *The Sisters* (*Sestry*, 1920–22, composed in emigration) into the monumental trilogy, *The Road to Calvary* (*Khozhdeniye po mukam*, 1925–41); and there were several others under way. This return to large-scale forms was in itself symptomatic of the change that had come over Russian society. Writers were beginning to write for an audience that would have plenty of time for reading. It was assumed that what was of interest today would continue to be of interest to readers for the foreseeable future. The immediacy and brevity of earlier Soviet fiction, the sense that any literature was likely to be out of date almost before it was printed, the urge to break with all previous forms and established aesthetic criteria had disappeared. The rehabilitation of the long novel reflected the new sense of stability. Even when the NEP period was finally wound up, the novel, and particularly the old-fashioned three-decker, was to remain the most favoured literary form.

With the end of the NEP there were no longer any private printing firms to compete with the State publishing houses; the age of free competition in literature was at an end. And as the struggle for political power gradually resolved in favour of Stalin the scene was set for Party intervention in the arts and sciences.

At the end of 1926 an organisation for uniting the different groups of writers, the Federation of Organisations of Soviet Writers (FOSP), had been set up. The following organisations belonged: VAPP, the association of Party-orientated writers, VSP, the Writers' Union, representing the *poputchiki*, and VSKP, the peasant writers; FOSP was later joined by LEF and 'The Smithy', containing the rump of the former proletarian writers, and 'The Mountain-pass'. From the first, FOSP was dominated by VAPP with its nearly 3,000 members; the peasant writers numbered 709 and the fellow-travellers 360;[23] of the other organisations only 'The Smithy' could boast 100 members.

It was characteristic that the initial idea for this organisation should have come from the *poputchiki*, who were genuinely concerned by the ugly standards of criticism and debate that had hitherto prevailed in Soviet literary life. By the same token, it was the more ideological groups that had opposed the suggestion most passionately. The growing size of the VAPP organisation, however, and the indications that the Party was now willing to give political support to their claims encouraged them to change their attitude. The *poputchiki's* hopes that the Federation would put an end to the vicious politicking of Soviet literary life, however, proved groundless. The atmosphere grew even more intolerant; VAPP (from 1928 onwards, RAPP) used its superior numbers to rig the elections and the selection of committees. There was naturally much opposition to this high-handed behaviour, but the arrest of leading *poputchiki* such as Voronsky, and later the framing of Zamyatin and Pilnyak, showed that the Party was solidly behind RAPP. The very word *poputchik* now became heavily suspect; the *poputchik* organisation, the Union of Writers, was forced to reexamine its membership, and to take the new name of the Union of *Soviet* Writers; although it remained as before, only one among many literary organisations, it was now, like the others, subordinated in its policies and actions to the decisions of the RAPP-controlled Federation.

The Soviet literature that was to emerge from the melting-pot of the first Five-year Plan presents a curious amalgam of the main currents of the 1920s. If the dominant ideas were those of the 'October' or VAPP movement, with a few suggestions borrowed from LEF and the Proletkult, the writers who were to dominate the Soviet literary scene until 1956 were drawn overwhelmingly from the ranks of the former *poputchiki*.

6

Drama and Cinema

The revolution in the Russian theatre, like the literary revolution, can be dated back to the 1890s, with the foundation by Stanislavsky of the Moscow Arts Theatre in 1898. This was followed by an explosion of new ideas, associated with such names as Kommissarzhevskaya, Meierhold, Yevreinov and Tairov, whose methods were to play an important part in the evolution of the Soviet theatre.

The immense possibilities of the theatre as a cultural and propagandist force were recognised by the new rulers from the start. It was nationalised in August 1919. But political pressures did not at first exert any direct influence on its development. The very nature of the theatre makes overnight changes impossible; a play cannot simply be mounted at a moment's notice. Even given the existence of a suitable play, there is bound to be a timelag for the rehearsals, training of actors, designing of sets. Naturally, there were different opinions as to the forms a revolutionary theatre would take. As in the other arts, there were two main approaches to the problem. Some producers and playwrights felt that the new age required something totally fresh, both in repertory and in the relationship of stage to auditorium. Others felt that audiences who were not familiar with the theatre could not be expected to understand, let alone appreciate the new theatre, until they had been properly educated in the classical traditions.

In Tsarist Russia there had been two types of professional theatre, the Imperial theatres, and the privately-owned ones, covering a wide range from the trivial and the commercial to the experimental and avant-garde. The five Imperial theatres in Moscow and Petrograd had enjoyed official patronage and financial support; they were more lavishly furnished and endowed, and the actors were better paid; but the result was a certain conservatism, both in stage technique and in the type of spectacle put on. These theatres were the first to be nationalised; they were renamed 'Academic' and given generous support, but their essentially conservative role was thereby enhanced. They have remained the leading theatres of the Soviet Union to the present day.

The need for a national repertory theatre had been advocated, among others, by Mariya Andreyeva, the common-law wife of Gorky, herself a distinguished actress and a Bolshevik. This theatre was finally established in 1918 (it is now called the Gorky theatre); Mariya Andreyeva was appointed to the board of directors, and Blok was later made its chairman. The accent of the theatre was on heroic, melodramatic productions, in harmony with the spirit of the times. At first, there were none of the Russian classics in its repertoire. The first production was Schiller's *Don Carlos*, and it was followed by *The Robbers*, *Othello* and *King Lear*. Later some more recent plays, such as Galsworthy's *Strife*, Gorky's *Enemies* (*Vragi*, 1907) and some of the first plays by Soviet authors were added to the repertoire. These plays were shown to audiences of workmen, and Red soldiers who had never been inside a theatre before; they were introduced by a spokesman for the theatre (usually Blok himself), who took care to stress the relevance of each play to the contemporary state of Russia.

In the early days the results were impressive. The audiences reacted eagerly and attentively, and their responsiveness naturally infected the actors. However, the enthusiasm began to wear off as the conditions of life in revolutionary Petrograd became increasingly difficult. There was also a split in the theatre board. Mariya Andreyeva wanted the productions to be ideologically angled. Blok, however, saw the propagandist role of the theatre as secondary to its aesthetic effect, which he considered a far more powerful force; he found his colleague's ideas crude and over-simplified. Relations between the two deteriorated disastrously (in this quarrel Gorky seems to have inclined to the side of Blok) and ended in the resignation of Blok in 1921. But the problem of striking a balance between fidelity to the classics and the temptation to make propaganda was to plague the theatre (and the opera and ballet too) throughout the Soviet period. In the 1920s the most remarkable productions were to be found in the smaller, independent theatres, directed by a single artistic personality, or even in amateur productions.

Even before the Revolution there had been several attempts to break down the barriers between the stage and the auditorium. The egalitarianism of the early revolutionary spirit naturally gave a new impulse to this trend and the theatre soon became a genuinely popular medium; soldiers and workers evolved a spontaneous, often improvised form of theatre, sometimes for recreation, but more often for didactic or propagandist aims; the anti-religious campaign, the principles of elementary hygiene, the basics of Marxism, as well as the more immediate matter of beating the Whites, were typical topics for these playlets. This popular tradition has taken root, and most Soviet communities today can boast a theatre of some sort.

A characteristic development of this type of theatre was the TRAMs (Theatres of the Working Youth), which flourished from the mid-1920s to the mid-1930s. The workers themselves produced and acted these spectacles for their fellows in an attempt to bring the theatre into closer contact with life. They were sponsored by the Komsomol, and their aims were frankly propagandist. They staged few conventional plays, and never the classics (one of their slogans was 'liquidation of the classics as a class'). Their characteristic form was a dramatised charade of a contemporary issue, whether of domestic or international politics. Sometimes, even ordinary meetings and discussions were considered to be TRAM theatre.

The culmination of this trend was the vast theatrical spectacle with mass participation. These productions were usually staged in the open air on festive occasions, such as public holidays. Although the best-known instances took place in the capitals, many were also recorded in provincial cities. The usual theme was of the Revolution, or of its historical predecessors, the rebellion of Spartacus, or the storming of the Bastille; some of them looked forward to the triumph of the international revolution, or to the coming of the Communist Utopia. The productions were prepared by a kernel of professional actors and technicians, assisted by amateurs from local factories and army units. Audience participation was an essential ingredient, and so most of the material was improvised within a loose general framework. Performances usually ended with the singing of the *Internationale* by the massed performers and spectators. One of the most ambitious of these productions, *The Taking of the Winter Palace* (*Vzyatiye Zimnego Dvortsa,* 7 November 1920), was enacted on the actual site of the Palace Square;[1] the cast included 2,500 performers, 500 musicians, and some 35,000 spectators. The only one of these works to have survived as literature, however, is Mayakovsky's *Mystery-Bouffe* (*Misteriya-Buff*, 1918; revised 1921). As an art form the spectacle seems to have effectively died by the end of 1920; the heroic age of the Revolution was over, and the changed atmosphere of the NEP could hardly express itself in this way.[2]

The conventional theatres were for the most part in the hands of the non-Party professionals, the *poputchiki* of the theatre, and they could not be challenged, let alone replaced, so easily as in the fields of literature. It was only at the end of the 1920s that the Party could boast any qualified and reliable men of the theatre. The process, therefore, of Sovietising the theatres took the form of persuading them to stage Soviet plays, or at least, to present classical and foreign plays from a revolutionary standpoint. There were few new Soviet dramas; for the most part, theatres found it easier to adapt contemporary fiction for their purposes than to work on original plays: Seyfullina's *Virineya* (1925), Leonov's *The Badgers* (*Barsuki*, 1927), Bulgakov's *The Days of the Turbins* (*Dni Turbinykh*, 1926), from his novel *White Guard* (*Belaya gvardiya*), and Vsevolod Ivanov's *Armoured Train 14–69* (*Bronepoyezd 14–69,* 1927), among the most successful of early Soviet plays, were all taken from contemporary stories or novels.

Typical of the new role of the theatres was the situation of the Moscow Arts Theatre. After its pre-revolutionary reputation for novelty and even radicalism, it now found itself regarded with some distrust as a citadel of the old Russian intelligentsia. In 1919, when the company was on tour and cut off from Moscow by the White armies, many of its actors chose to emigrate; in 1922 Stanislavsky and his company went on an extended tour of Europe and the United States. It was only after some two years in semi-emigration that they finally decided to return to their Moscow home. Throughout the 1920s the theatre fought to defend its pre-revolutionary ideals and standards, and it continued to exert great influence both by its own example, and by means of the small studios, which, under such illustrious men as Vakhtangov and Mikhail Chekhov, had by now acquired an independent existence, and had all moved some way from the original Stanislavsky model.

Contrary to its pre-revolutionary practice the Arts Theatre in the 1920s put on few contemporary plays; instead it turned to the Russian classics from Gogol to Chekhov and Gorky. One of the few attempts to stage a revolutionary play, Trenev's *Pugachevism* (*Pugachevshchina,* 1925) was a failure, both with the public and with the Party. The Arts Theatre had made its name with the subtle polyphony and tolerant humanism of Chekhov's plays; so it was only natural that the tendentious plays of loyal Communists had little attraction for it. It was more at home with Bulgakov's *The Days of the Turbins*, a sympathetically understanding depiction of the moral and psychological collapse of the Whites in the Civil War. The production, however, was a political sensation; the dress rehearsal was nearly wrecked by the hooliganism of two Komsomol youths,[3] and the first performance was universally denounced. Lunacharsky explained rather weakly that the play had passed the censors only by an oversight, but that it would be unconstitutional to suppress it now. The first acceptable Soviet production in the Arts Theatre was the adaptation of Vsevolod Ivanov's novella *Armoured Train 14–69,* in which the theatre managed to combine its traditional humanity and objectivity with a satisfactory ideological portrayal of the Civil War.

The most revolutionary figure in the theatre was undoubtedly Vsevolod Meierhold. He was one of the few Russian intellectuals to accept the Bolshevik Revolution from the first (he joined the Party in 1920); he was promptly placed at the head of the Theatre Section of the Commissariat of Enlightenment (TEO). He held official positions in the Proletkult theatre, the theatre of the RSFSR, and the large Theatre of the Revolution, but his most important work appeared in his studios, GITIS (State Institute for Theatre Art) and TIM (Theatre of Meierhold).

In place of the traditional psychological and intellectual drama, Meierhold emphasised the physical capabilities of the human body: expressive gestures and, above all, gymnastics and acrobatics, which brought his productions closer to pantomimes and circus performances than conventional plays. This was partly a reflection of the functional ideal of art in the early revolutionary period: the actor was not an artist, but a craftsman, working with his body. But beyond this Meierhold looked forward to a Utopia when man's physical capabilities would be fully extended once again. In his *D.E.* (based on Erenburg's novel *Trest D.E.*, 1924) the West was characterised by 'decadent' jazz and modern dance, the Soviet Union by acrobatics.

In his desire to increase the involvement of the audience, Meierhold abolished the curtain in his productions soon after the Revolution, for any barrier between the stage and the audience was not only at odds with the popular origins of the drama, but was also out of place in a society committed to the abolition of all class distinctions. In the same spirit some of his early revolutionary productions made no charge for admission. To elicit maximum participation hc frequently planted stooges among the audience. Entrances would be made from the auditorium, sometimes on motor cycles or even armoured cars. In his 1921 production of Mayakovsky's *Mystery-Bouffe* Meierhold tried to give the audience the sense of participating in a mass meeting. The seats were deliberately placed askew, and the 'stage' was not distinguished at all from the auditorium. In his arrangement of Verhaeren's *Les Aubes* (Russian title *Zori*, 1920) the action was regularly interrupted at one point by the latest bulletin from the front, culminating in the news of the storming of Perekop, the last major battle of the Civil War. In his production of Martinet's *La nuit* (Russian title *Zemlya dybom*, 1922) Trotsky appeared in person to deliver an impromptu speech.

As with the Futurists, with whom he was closely connected, there was a large element of pure mischief in Meierhold's productions. Emperors appeared sitting on chamberpots; practical jokes, such as collapsing furniture, were common occurrences. He responded to Lunacharsky's appeal 'Back to Ostrovsky' with his notorious production of *Forest* (*Les*, 1923), in which the text was so transformed by means of film captions, funny business, and the stage context, as to be unrecognisable. Ostrovsky's characters were updated into Komsomols and

NEP profiteers. Meierhold explained that 'Back to Ostrovsky' was better reformulated as 'Forwards, even with Ostrovsky. . . .'[4]

Like the Futurists, Meierhold believed that content in itself was no guarantee of modernity, unless it was also reflected in the form. He was as opposed to realistic productions of contemporary plays as of the classics; his own sets were usually non-representational. In the most drastic of all his productions, Crommelynck's *Le Cocu Magnifique* (Russian title *Velikodushnyy rogonosets,* 1921), he dispensed with all scenery and stage props, except for a wooden platform, beyond which could be seen the brick walls of the theatre; the actors were dressed in overalls and their faces were not made up. He treated the text and spirit of a play, and indeed all traditional interpretations with unprecedented freedom; he rearranged, rewrote, cut scenes and added totally new ones, in order to create the effects he wanted.

But Meierhold could not create his spectacles without plays. There were few contemporary plays that interested him, but those that he did choose, Mayakovsky's *Mystery-Bouffe, The Bedbug* (*Klop,* 1929) and *The Bathhouse* (*Banya,* 1930) and Erdman's *The Warrant* (*Mandat,* 1925) were among the best of the decade. For the most part he had to make do with Russian classics, adapted and updated. In his hands Gogol's *The Inspector General* (*Revizor,* 1926) and *Woe to wit* (*Gore umu,* 1928), his arrangement of Griboyedov's *Woe from wit* (*Gore ot uma*), were transformed into satires on the ossification of the revolutionary spirit and the Communist Party. These implications were spelt out in the subsequent productions of Mayakovsky's *The Bedbug* and *The Bathhouse* which are both set in the Soviet present and future. Though considerably modified by the censors the two plays were bitterly criticised; *The Bathhouse,* in fact, was taken off after only a few performances, and the rebuff probably played some part in Mayakovsky's suicide. These indiscretions were not forgotten by Meierhold's many enemies either.

Meierhold's productions were probably the most remarkable artistic phenomenon of the entire post-revolutionary period. One of his admirers, the brilliant director Vakhtangov, said as early as 1922 that each one of them contained suggestions for a whole new style in the theatre. Meierhold was at the height of his powers. The more intellectual Bolshevik leaders admired and supported his work, while the popularity of his shows with servicemen won the admiration of prominent military figures. In the 1920s these connections gave Meierhold immense powers. Unlimited funds were available for his productions; actors and actresses, budding directors and technicians eagerly accepted invitations to work with him, and he was able to build a company entirely according to his own ideas. However, the decline in the fortunes of his patrons, the deepening distrust of any experimentation, and also the peculiarities of his own temperament, had by the end of the decade brought about a lessening of official support, the calibre of his company and the quality of his productions.

All his productions were controversial. Krupskaya distrusted everything connected with Meierhold. Lunacharsky liked the more propagandist and superficially traditional productions; but on other occasions he is known to have walked out in disgust. Meierhold went too fast for his sympathisers too. Those who approved his productions of Soviet plays were indignant at his resurrection of the classics; Mayakovsky, who admired his production of *The Inspector General,* called his *Forest* repulsive. Unfortunately, only photographs and Meierhold's copious notes survive from these performances. In the 1960s these have inspired a revival of the Meierhold tradition, but the essentials of his theatrical style, his inventiveness, his range, his sheer genius as a practical man of the theatre can never be resurrected.

Like their counterparts in Soviet literature, the great theatre directors of the 1920s were in some respects even more doctrinaire, intolerant and tendentious than their Party-line successors in the 1930s and 1940s; nor were these vices always redeemed by the artistic success of their productions. But the wide variety of styles, the sheer range of attempts to realise the full potentialities of the theatre, and the unlimited scope for innovation and experiment, presented the theatre-going public with an inexhaustible choice of plays, interpretations and techniques. For all their flaws, the 1920s in the Soviet theatre were one of the most brilliant periods in stage history.

Cinema

The possibilities of the cinema were recognised from the first by the Bolsheviks. Lenin said: 'The cinema is for us the most important of all the arts.'[5]

The most obvious advantage of the cinema as a medium for communication lies in the mechanical processes which it exploits. A film can be reproduced cheaply, and innumerable, identical copies made; it can then be shown with a minimum of trained personnel or technical equipment. In this respect it is far superior to the stage play, which is not easy to transport or to establish in backward areas.

But the very ease of reproducing and circulating film-material has its disadvantages. The spectator of a film remains passive; he is not watching real people, but their pictures. In a Meierhold play the spectator might rise from his seat and join the actors on the stage; indeed there might well be an actor sitting next to him. But in the cinema, however excited and moved the spectator may be, however keen his desire to participate, the limitations of the medium prevent him from doing anything about it. And with this lack of contact between screen and spectator the spectators too tend to be isolated from one another. The darkness of the cinema and the passivity of the experience make the medium an escapist rather than a participatory one. It is perhaps for these reasons that the Soviet cinema even in its golden age, 1925–7, never became the 'most important of the arts' in the official or in the popular mind.

At first, however, the possibilities of the cinema seemed immense. Because of its technological basis, it seemed ideally suited to the new age; it was free too from the oppressive weight of tradition which hung over the other arts. Small wonder then that the cinema attracted some of the most creative minds in the Soviet Union. Mayakovsky made his first films in 1918, and he continued to write film scenarios for the rest of his life, among them one of his most important works, *How Do You Do?* (*Kak pozhivayete?* 1926). The Formalist Shklovsky was the leading film critic of the day; and in the 1930s he too applied his talents to the composition of scenarios. Unfortunately, the young Soviet cinema was exposed to the competition of romances and melodramas surviving from the pre-revolutionary period or newly imported from the West. The general Russian public far preferred these alien productions to the work of their own countrymen and contemporaries. It was effectively the West that discovered the great Soviet directors.

The Russian film industry had been well-established even before the First World War. In 1917 however, the majority of owners emigrated, taking their equipment with them; many of the leading actors and technicians followed suit. The Soviet cinema had to recreate itself from scratch. The basic materials, camera, film and lights, all had to be purchased from the West. The loss of the directors and actors, however, proved something of a blessing, as it enabled a new approach to the problems of film to spring up with little opposition. The first Soviet directors were extremely young. Kuleshov directed his first film at the age of seventeen; Dziga Vertov was put in charge of all film coverage of the Civil War when he was barely twenty.

The first important Soviet films were Vertov's newsreels of the Civil War. It was his experience at the front that helped Vertov to formulate his ideas, which were to have a lasting effect on the development of the Soviet cinema. He held that the essence of the film is documentary, that it can only record what has actually happened; accordingly, he called his method *Kinoglaz* (Cine-eye). At the same time he realised that the chaos of raw experience is in itself meaningless; the director's task is not just to record events, but, by cutting and re-arrangement, to bring out their pattern and rhythm, and so to suggest their meaning. After the Civil War he continued this approach with newsreels of scenes of Soviet life, in a series called *Kino-pravda* (Cine-truth), which he envisaged, as the name suggests, as a cinematic equivalent to the newspaper *Pravda*. The brilliance of Vertov's photography, the effectiveness of his editing of material, and his attempt to create a cinematic rhythm, however schematic, were all to exert considerable influence on later Soviet directors.

If the documentary was intended primarily for propaganda purposes, the feature film was conceived in terms of its educational or cultural potential. The first Soviet films in this category were usually based on a well-known play or story: Tolstoy's *Father Sergius* (*Otets Sergiy,* 1918), *The Power of Darkness* (*Vlast tmy,* 1918), *Living Corpse* (*Zhivoy trup,* 1918), and *Polikushka* (1919), Garshin's *Signal* (1918), Gorky's *Mother* (*Mat,* 1920), Merezhkovsky's *Peter and Alexis* (*Petr i Aleksey,* 1919), Andreyev's

Story of Seven who were Hanged (*Rasskaz o semi poveshennykh,* 1920). These were usually performed by professional theatre actors, and filmed with little attempt to break away from the conventions of the stage. The idea was simply to familiarise audiences with their cultural heritage. There were a few attempts to exploit the possibilities of the new medium, such as Mayakovsky's *Not Born for Money* (*Ne dlya deneg rodivshiysya,* 1918) and *Fettered by Film* (*Zakovannaya filmoy,* 1918), but these, though the scenarios are of interest, did not succeed as films, and are now lost.

The great breakthrough in Soviet cinematography came with the application by Lev Kuleshov of Vertov's methods to the feature film. Like Vertov, he had worked with newsreels during the Civil War, but he had carried the experiments with montage rather further. He had explored the way in which the brain attempts to organise and interpret the raw material presented to it by the eye, and the possibilities of constructing a purely visual logic. His discoveries enabled him to refine on Vertov's straightforward documentary realism, by stimulating the spectator's imagination and expectations. He applied his new techniques in a variety of genres, from the satirical *The Extraordinary Adventures of Mr West in the Land of the Bolsheviks* (*Neobychaynyye priklyucheniya mistera Vesta v strane Bolshevikov,* 1924) to the intense and tragic *According to the Law* (*Po zakonu,* 1926, based on a story by Jack London, *The Unexpected*). Kuleshov also worked with old newsreels, and his combining of old materials in new patterns was to pave the way for Esfir Shub's creative use of the documentary in such films as *The Fall of the Romanov Dynasty* (*Padeniye dinastii Romanovykh,* 1927), *The Great Road* (*Velikiy put,* 1927) and *Lev Tolstoy and the Russia of Nicholas II* (*Rossiya Nikolaya II i Lev Tolstoy,* 1928).

All these ideas were synthesised and developed in the work of Sergey Eisenstein. Eisenstein came to the cinema comparatively late. During the Civil War he had worked as a poster artist, and this led to his being hired as a scene-painter in Meierhold's Proletkult Theatre. In 1923 he put on his first independent production, Ostrovsky's *Simplicity enough for Every Wise Man* (*Na vsyakogo mudretsa dovolno prostoty*). This production surpassed even those of Meierhold in its inventiveness; the original play disappeared in a fantastic whirl of circus and music hall turns, topical satire and film strips. For his next production, Tretyakov's *Gasmasks* (*Protivogazy*), Eisenstein moved out of his theatre into the Moscow Gas Factory. The parts were taken by the workers themselves, and the dangers of gas were really confronted by the actors on the stage. Eisenstein had pushed the theatre as far as it would go in the direction of documentary; the film was the logical next step.

Eisenstein's training in the Proletkult theatre was of immense importance for his later development. Meierhold's stress on the visual rather than the verbal element in the theatrical experience was valuable to any potential film director, but particularly in the days before the invention of sound films. From Meierhold too came Eisenstein's fondness for grotesque caricatures and stylised movements. Above all, it was the devices of the music hall and the circus, and the structural principles behind them, that influenced Eisenstein in his own theories about the cinema. He even took over the term '*attraktsion*' (advertising-jargon for a 'turn') from this source. He built up his films on the pattern of contrasting episodes, each striking in itself, but revealing its full meaning only in its context. His films exploit the possibilities of every sort of contrast and contradiction. He applied this device not just to adjacent episodes or shots, but as the basic principle of structure. He argued that this collision of opposites reflected the Marxist dialectic in action. This somewhat dubious idea has given Eisenstein's films the reputation of being intellectual, and in the Soviet Union this was soon to lead to accusations of Formalism.

In fact, Eisenstein's films, though they may be composed on intellectual principles, depend as much as the Futurists' poetry and Meierhold's productions on startling shock effects. Eisenstein rejected Vertov's Cine-eye as too neutral; he preferred the term *Kino-kulak* (Cine-fist). His first film *Strike* (*Stachka,* 1924) may have begun as a documentary film (one of a series on the 'dictatorship of the proletariat'), but it soon turned into a passionate and imaginative denunciation of capitalist Russia. Eisenstein used the discoveries of Kuleshov to create new visual metaphors. Simple juxtaposition forces the spectator to equate police spies with owls and foxes, the massacre of the strikers with the slaughter of an ox. In *The Battleship*

Potemkin (*Bronenosets Potemkin,* 1925), the images are worked more subtly into the texture of the film, as for example the breaking wave at the beginning, the mechanical march of the soldiers down the Potemkin steps, the tarpaulin covering the condemned men. Eisenstein continued to explore the possibilities of extending the language of the cinema, but in his next film, *October* (*Oktyabr,* 1928), the use of associative imagery becomes overindulgent: a popular Russian obscenity (usually translated from the Russian subtitles as 'Think of your mothers!') is followed by a series of shots of mother-figures throughout human history.

There are no professional actors in Eisenstein's films of the 1920s. He chose his cast out of thousands of workers, peasants and unemployed, not for their acting skill, but for the expressive power of their faces and their ability to suggest the character that he wished to convey; thus to portray Lenin in *October* he chose a metal-worker, Nikandrov; even for the crowd scenes he selected each participant individually. The special techniques of the cinema, and its ability to pick out individuals momentarily from the mass are of course particularly well-suited to crowd scenes; even so Eisenstein's skill in conveying the mood of a crowd remains unsurpassed. But his main purpose in dispensing with professional actors in favour of ordinary men and women was to reinforce the theme of the films, the Revolution by and for the masses.

In the Soviet Union, however, Eisenstein's early films seldom achieved any great success. The general public preferred foreign imports, and even the Party critics distrusted the unconventional means by which he achieved his effects. *October*, which appeared at the end of 1927, fell foul of the Party, because it depicted Trotsky's role in the Civil War, and he was forced to remake the film. His film on the modernisation of agriculture, *The General Line* (*Generalnaya liniya,* 1928), was held up by the censors because the Party line on collectivisation had changed: as a result Eisenstein was forced to change even the title to *Old and New* (*Staroye i novoye*), to avoid any suggestion of official approval; for all that the film was suppressed shortly afterwards. Even *The Battleship Potemkin* was at first appreciated only abroad, and it had to wait for Stalin's death (and Eisenstein's) before it won general acceptance inside the Soviet Union.

Very much more accessible to Soviet taste has been the work of Vsevolod Pudovkin. Like Kuleshov and Eisenstein, Pudovkin believed in the supremacy of the director. His work was closer to the theatre, however, than theirs. He made use of professional actors, and his films usually tell a fairly clear story. Where the other Soviet directors cut and rearranged their material after it had been filmed, to obtain their effects, Pudovkin relied more on the preparatory composition of the scene before any filming began. He found his inspiration in literature rather than in the medium of the film itself. His famous films *Mother* (*Mat,* 1926), *The End of St Petersburg* (*Konets Sankt-Peterburga,* 1927) and *The Descendant of Genghis Khan* (*Potomok Chingis-khana,* 1928, shown abroad as *Storm over Asia*) were all based on works of fiction, the first two on novels by Gorky and Andrey Belyy respectively, the third on a story by Novokshonov. But Pudovkin's films are more than mere screen versions of a book. He was interested in the fate of individuals and the portrayal of psychological development; his films are intended to involve the spectator by taking him inside the character portrayed, rather than by shocking him into political generalisations. Pudovkin's fondness for glossy photography and a strong storyline were to exert a lasting influence on the later development of the Soviet film. His frequent lapses into sentimentality and crude propaganda have, regrettably, also been imitated by his followers.

If it is the great heroic and satiric films of the 1920s that have attracted international attention, there were also some striking films on problems of everyday life. Outstanding among these was Abram Room's *Third Meshchansky St* (*Tretya Meshchanskaya,* 1927, shown abroad as *Bed and Sofa*), a sensitive study of the interaction of the housing shortage and marital problems. Ermler's *Parisian Cobbler* (*Parizhskiy sapozknik,* 1928) was even more outspoken in drawing a contrast between the cynical attitudes to sex of the Komsomol and the wisdom of ordinary Russians. Both these films aroused intense interest inside Russia, but their fatalistic and anti-Party tenor soon led to their withdrawal.

The art of cinematography had risen to its peak by 1928. After the destruction of the Russian cinema during the Civil War, only eleven full length films had been produced in 1921;

by 1924 this figure had risen to 157. If at the beginning of the decade Russian films were heavily outnumbered by foreign imports, by 1926 they had drawn level,[6] and by the end of the decade they had virtually squeezed out all foreign productions. The Soviet film industry was self-supporting at last.

This trend was of course assisted by Government pressure, and the growing isolationist sentiment of the Party. As in other branches of culture, the Party had begun to take a closer interest in the affairs of the cinema. The position of RAPP in the literary world was paralleled by the official support now given to Vertov and his followers. The other directors of the 1920s were to be temporarily obscured; many of the leading Soviet actors emigrated in protest. Eisenstein too went abroad in August 1929; but he was to prove no more fortunate in the West than in his own country.

7

The Peasantry

History

Marx's thought was primarily concerned with the proletariat; he regarded the peasant as essentially conservative and individualistic, and so unripe for revolution or for socialist life. Unlike the proletarian, who was so alienated from the goods that he helped to produce that he had 'nothing to lose but his chains', the peasant was still deeply attached to his land and his few possessions. Where the advanced proletarians aspired to revolution, the successful peasantry aspired only to becoming members of the bourgeoisie.

Marx therefore saw the future of the peasantry largely in terms of industrial development: only under the leadership of the urban proletariat could the peasantry hope to pass into the classless Utopia. He looked for the abolition of all private holdings, and the adoption of co-operative and centralised forms of organisation. Trends in Western Europe seemed to be moving in this direction, but they held little comfort for Marx's disciples in Russia, where the peasantry constituted some 85 per cent of the population, and the countryside was still hopelessly backward. Nonetheless such was the reverence of the Bolsheviks for the views of Marx and Engels that they accepted this recipe as a model for the development of Russian agriculture.

This placed them in a dilemma. They shared Marx's disdain for the peasantry, but they realised too that, if they were to seize and retain power, it was essential to win at least the passive support of the peasantry. Throughout the summer of 1917 they vied with the Social-Revolutionaries for the loyalties of the peasantry; they outbid their slogans and even adopted their policies. They encouraged the forcible expropriation of the landlords and the anarchism of the rioting rural mobs; the general breakdown of order was an essential pre-condition for their coup. But once they had come to power, the Bolsheviks looked on these activities very differently. They soon broke with the Social-Revolutionaries, and their measures against the peasants were frequently harsh. In no field of Soviet life was the paradox of the premature Marxist revolution to have such tragic consequences as in the history of the dealings of the Communist Party with the Russian peasantry.

The Bolsheviks believed at first that the mere power of good example and the evidence of good intentions would be sufficient to bring the peasants over to collective forms of organisation. The peasants were theoretically equal partners in the state with the proletariat; their sickle was intertwined with the workers' hammer on the Soviet flag; and Kalinin, a former peasant from the Tver (now Kalinin) district, was elevated to the head of state. (Actually his work had been predominantly in the cities.)[1] From 1918 special State Farms were instituted which were to serve as models for the development of Soviet agriculture. The members worked as state employees, with fixed wages in place of the peasant's notoriously unpredictable earnings. They received the benefits of large-scale organisation and of such mechanical aids as were available. However, this example did not impress the peasants unduly; they preferred to persevere with their own, often uneconomic, small-holdings, where they felt themselves to be unchallenged masters. The fact that the redistribution of the land had resulted in only a fractional increase in the size of their holdings was even a cause of dissatisfaction.

As a result friction with the central government was inevitable. It was not long delayed. With the collapse of the currency and of industry, there was no return in goods or in cash that the peasants were willing to accept in exchange for their produce. They therefore preferred not to deliver it to the cities, but to store it at home in expectation of better times. By May 1918, food supplies in the cities were running low and the Government was forced to take emergency measures. Bands of armed townsmen were sent into the countryside to requisition produce for the cities; in the villages themselves the Government tried to force the issue by appealing to class resentment; it formed committees of the poorest peasants (*kombedy*), and encouraged them to extract the grain from the richer peasants themselves; in return the *kombedy* received most of the few goods that were available to the peasants, but they made themselves extremely unpopular in the process. This attempt at fomenting a social revolution in the villages was soon abandoned. The scheme had proved self-defeating, for, with the lack of incentives, the peasants had refused to produce; and agricultural production had dropped to only half of its pre-war figure.

The Communists thus came up against the passive resistance of the peasantry, their traditional skill in frustrating the orders of the central government, and the fact that agricultural production cannot be planned or produced to order like industrial goods. The Communists' ideological distrust of the peasantry was confirmed by their experiences in the first years of the revolution.

The compulsory requisitioning of grain did something to ensure regular supplies to the cities, but the black market remained a more plentiful, though also more expensive, source throughout the years of War Communism. However, the experience of grain-requisitioning alienated the peasants from the Bolsheviks; their traditional resentment of the city authorities now reasserted itself, and with the end of the Civil War this broke out into open hostility. A series of anti-Communist risings spread rapidly through the Russian countryside, culminating in the Tambov revolt of February – April 1921. Coinciding with the Kronstadt mutiny, this evidence of popular dissatisfaction forced the Government to back down for the time being from the authoritarianism of War Communism.

The introduction of the NEP was intended primarily to assuage peasant dissatisfaction. The attempt to re-organise the peasantry on industrial lines had failed. In any case, the mechanical equipment required to exploit the advantages of large-scale farming did not yet exist, and so there was little advantage in insisting on Marxist methods of agriculture. Meanwhile, the hostility between the city and the countryside which had been fostered during the period of War Communism was now a liability; instead a new campaign was launched emphasising the need for solidarity (*Smychka*) between the peasantry and the proletariat, and pointing out their mutual interdependence.

These slogans were backed by substantial concessions. The hated system of grain-requisitioning was replaced by a tax on kind; all restrictions were removed on the peasant's right to do as he chose with the remainder of his produce. But the introduction of the NEP in March 1921 came too late to affect the spring sowing that year; the summer was marked by a severe drought, the harvest failed, and a disastrous famine ensued, which hit the most fertile areas the most cruelly. At first the Bolsheviks tried to conceal the existence of this famine, but a committee of intellectuals, headed by Gorky, persuaded the Government to appeal to the West for assistance. (Once the crisis was over, many of the intellectuals who had signed Gorky's appeals were arrested as foreign agents; they were released, however, after international protests and expelled from Russia.)[2] It has been argued that this famine, from which three to five million are estimated to have died, played a greater part in breaking peasant resistance than did the Red Army.[3]

There were further concessions to the peasantry in 1922. To encourage them to produce more they were even allowed, within certain limits, to lease land and hire labour, a complete reversal of earlier socialist ideals. They were allowed to produce what they chose and how they chose. As a result many of the few collective farms broke up into individual small-holdings once again; in the mid-1920s the State and collective farms provided only 2 per cent of the total grain production, and claimed just over 1 per cent of the total land under cultivation.[4] In effect, the peasants had reverted to their pre-revolutionary way of life.

It was easier, however, to make concessions to the peasants than it was to satisfy them. There was a marked rise in grain production, but this led to a fall in prices. On the other hand, the industrial and consumer goods which had been promised to the peasantry were still pitifully scarce. Unchecked inflation on top of the shortage of goods meant that the value of money seriously depreciated before it could be turned into goods (the graph showing the falling agricultural prices and rising industrial prices led to Trotsky's expression 'the scissors crisis').

The peasantry naturally responded by consuming more of their produce themselves.

In 1924 there was another drought; the wealthier peasants were able to ride it out, but the poorer ones were in many cases forced to hire out their labour, to borrow money, or even to sell their land (though these last two were illegal). This intensification of class differences within the village led to fears of the re-appearance of the *kulak*, the energetic but grasping rich peasant, who made his living by usury as well as by farming. The old type of *kulak* had been virtually exterminated since the Revolution by the joint operation of Government decree and lynch-law, but the traditional hatred and fear were easily re-awakened as some peasants acquired greater wealth and influence. From 1924 onwards the word *kulak* with its powerful emotional connotations began to be applied indiscriminately to any rich peasant, regardless of how he had acquired his wealth or of how he used it.

The emergence of a new rich peasant class led to heated discussions within the Communist Party. Trotsky and Zinovyev feared their potential power; they foresaw a day when the rich peasants would be able to blackmail the Central Government into further retreats from socialist ideals. Stalin and Bukharin, however, claimed, with considerable justification, that the need to build up a stable and efficient peasantry was inherent in Lenin's NEP, and that it would provide a steady internal stimulus for industrial development. The Bolsheviks would remain militarily and economically in command, and a few rich small-holders would present no serious challenges to their authority. Bukharin even coined the slogan 'Enrich yourselves' on the principle that the whole of society stood to gain from the peasants' prosperity.

These policies seemed to pay off between 1925 and 1927. The harvests were good and the exchange situation improved; manufactured goods were more plentiful, and the currency was practically stabilised. Even so the Party's position was still weak in the countryside. It was represented largely by urban-bred members who had little understanding of peasant needs and aspirations. The rural communities withdrew into their traditional patterns of life, largely indifferent to outside concerns. The old village commune remained a more effective force for social organisation than either the Party or the local soviets. (When in 1926 and 1927 the Party tried to overcome peasant apathy by allowing free elections to the village soviets, the Communists were roundly defeated by the non-Party candidates; the experiment has not been repeated.)[5] As in the old days the richer and more successful peasant, the *kulak*, was the dominating figure in the typical village. Since he was not allowed the vote, he was hardly sympathetic to the Communists, and his influence was not favourable to them.

But although the rich peasant was unlikely to be a supporter of the Communists, he was in no position to hold the State to ransom, as Trotsky and Zinovyev had suggested. It was estimated that only some 4 per cent of the peasantry could be classified as *kulaks* (the definition was concerned only with the land and livestock a man owned, not with the way in which he exploited his property), and they accounted for 13 per cent of all produce. The bulk of agricultural supplies (85 per cent) came from the middle peasants (*serednyaki*), some 75 per cent of the total peasantry. The remainder, who owned no land or insufficient to support themselves, were classified as poor peasants (*bednyaki*).[6] At first the Party moved cautiously; it tightened the controls over the *kulaks*, raised their taxes, and restricted the leasing of land. Measures were taken to increase the powers of the village soviets at the expense of the traditional peasant institutions; but even at this stage it still seems to have hoped to achieve collectivisation by persuasion and co-operation rather than by brute force.

The uneasy truce between the Party and the peasantry began to crack towards the end of 1927, when grain supplies to the cities diminished sharply, necessitating the re-introduction of food rationing. In fact the total grain harvested was not inadequate by the standards of previous years, but there were now more peasants to feed, and the concessions of the NEP had encouraged all peasants, rich, poor and middle, to aspire to a higher standard to living; they preferred to keep more grain for themselves and their livestock, rather than sell it cheap on the market. There was thus much less surplus left over for the needs of the cities, though it is likely that the Party exaggerated the shortfall in order to justify the new measures it was envisaging. Compulsory requisitionings followed, and the peasantry in turn sowed less again. The situation in 1928 was considerably worse than it had been in 1927. The Government took alarm; its fears of a rich peasantry acquiring political power hostile to the Bolsheviks reawakened. It claimed that the *kulaks* were threatening national security, and that emergency measures were required. There was, of course, evidence to support this view; but it is also undeniable that the Party line was hardening in all other spheres of Soviet life at just this time. The campaign against the peasantry was not an isolated instance; it was part and parcel of the emerging pattern of Stalinism.

In retrospect, the years 1925–7 came to seem the golden age of Soviet agriculture. The pre-war levels of production and living standards which they had attained and surpassed were not to be approached again until after Stalin's death.

The Peasantry in Literature

The theme of the peasantry had been central to Russian literature of the nineteenth century. Both Slavophiles and Westernisers, in their different ways, were obsessed with the paradox of a superficially Western civilisation based precariously on an alien mass of primitive peasants. On the one hand they tended to assuage their sense of guilt by idealising the peasantry for their long-suffering and crediting them with an immense cultural potential; on the other, they were instinctively afraid of the peasants' overwhelming numbers, their appalling record of bestiality, and their nihilistic contempt for all cultural values.

The Bolsheviks inherited these contradictory attitudes, further complicated by their own preconceptions of the nature of culture. They were incapable of interpreting any artistic self-expression other than in terms of class interests; they therefore reacted distrustfully to any spontaneous manifestations of peasant culture. It could come only from the better-educated (and therefore better-off) section of the peasantry, and so it was automatically suspect as *kulak* propaganda. Some Communists felt that if the entire countryside was eventually to be urbanised and industrialised according the the Marxist blueprint, then any interim peasant culture was inevitably bound to be reactionary.

On the other hand the nineteenth-century habit of identifying the Russian 'people' with the peasantry was too strong to be broken overnight, and many Soviet writers, particularly the *poputchiki*, were drawn to them rather than to the proletariat. In the literature of the Civil War, notably in the stories of Pilnyak, Vsevolod Ivanov and Artem Veselyy, it is the peasantry and not the proletariat which is identified with the spirit of revolution, destructive and anarchic, an elemental force, before which urban civilisation is helpless. The peasantry are shown as indifferent to all ideologies, and interested only in land. They live their lives by the seasons, so that even their anti-Bolshevik campaigns are called off once the sowing season approaches.

This non-ideological approach offended Party critics, who naturally felt that the Revolution was the work of the Communists, not of hordes of illiterate peasants. They looked for rather more positive signs of the Revolution's impact on the village, such as the benefits of education and technology that it had brought. Much literature on the peasantry is coloured by these well-intentioned, optimistic assumptions. Lidiya Seyfullina's story *Virineya* (1924) tells of a peasant girl who is saved from a life of drink and promiscuity by her love for a young Communist, until she is finally ready to give her life for the cause. In Leonov's *The Badgers* (*Barsuki,* 1924), the peasants for all their hostility to the city come to realise that it is essentially well-intentioned, 'like an elder brother'[7] as one of the peasants puts it. The leader of the peasant rebellion finally surrenders, because he recognises that the Communists, led, symbolically enough, by his elder brother, 'are building nature's own process and you're obstructing us'.[8]

The greatest literature on peasant themes came from the peasants themselves, the lyric poetry of Oreshin and Pimen Karpov, the novels and poems of Klychkov (pen-name of Leshenkov); but these names have been overshadowed by the two major figures, the poets Nikolay Klyuyev and Sergey Esenin. From 1912 (the date of Klyuyev's first book) until 1929, peasant literature was to form one of the main streams of Russian literature. But it is a paradox inherent in the whole idea of peasant literature that just as the writers establish themselves in the literary world, so their links with the peasantry tend to weaken. By the nature of the case, the greater peasant poets could hardly speak for the illiterate and inarticulate mass of the Russian peasantry. Yesenin's poetry has always appealed much more to the urban youth, and so, no doubt, would Klyuyev's, were it ever to be published again in Russia. The very nature of literary production and the technical processes it involves, leaves a peasant poet no option but to come to terms with the city. If Koltsov could not escape this dilemma in the nineteenth century, his successors in the twentieth had even less chance of doing so.

The peasant poets were naturally more sympathetic to the Social-Revolutionaries than to the Bolsheviks, but they seem to have taken little part in political activities. Under the guidance of Ivanov-Razumnik they formed a movement, called *Scythianism* (*'Skifstvo'*); besides the peasant poets, such figures as Blok, Belyy and Remizov were closely associated with it. The 'Scyths' revived the old Slavophile faith in the Russian peasantry, as a bastion of spiritual values in an age of materialism. They regarded the 'dictatorship of the proletariat' as a merely temporary aberration, and they envisaged the eventual rejection of all European standards and values, and the affirmation of uniquely Russian features, which had been suppressed ever since the time of Peter the Great. They called for a spiritual revolution to complete the political and social revolutions already begun. In opposition to the materialism of Marx they stressed religious and even mystical values; Christian and especially sectarian imagery is strong in all their work. Usually the 'Scyths' were concerned with purely Russian questions, but Blok's poem *The Scyths* (*Skify*, 1918), which is addressed to the nations of the West, reveals a chauvinistic and aggressive side to the movement. The ideas that they preached were surprisingly influential, chiefly because of the traditional predisposition of the Russian intelligentsia towards the peasantry; but they are now associated less with the original 'Scyths' than with such writers as Pilnyak.

The ideas of the movement are very similar to those advocated by Klyuyev for many years, and he was undoubtedly very influential within it. Klyuyev was an Old Believer; in his youth he had even been a missionary for one of the flagellant sects. His poetry was from the first influenced by the Symbolists, and in their manner, he treated the everyday details of peasant life and the manifestations of nature as symbols of a higher mystical reality; they were signs that peasant Russia had a Messianic role to play. Klyuyev therefore denounced the Westernised Russia of the industrialists and the intelligentsia; only a return to the old pre-Petrine faith could redeem her, and lead in its turn to the salvation of the world. Like the Symbolists, he believed in an imminent cataclysm, which would sweep away the corruption of the old world and create a new and better one in its place. For these reasons he welcomed both the Revolutions of 1917, as successive stages in the re-establishment of a peasant heaven on earth.

Early on, however, Klyuyev began to lose faith in the Bolsheviks, partly because of their anti-peasant tendencies, but also because of his growing conviction that the Russian peasantry were not capable of seizing their opportunity. For some time, however, he continued to put his faith in Lenin, in whom he claimed to detect the fanatical spirit of the old Russian Churchmen;[9] in one poem, indeed, *The Aery Ship* (*Vozdushnyy korabl*), he even claimed that Lenin himself had been betrayed by the Revolution.[10] The weird titles of his books express the duality of his vision in these years: *The Bronze Whale* (*Mednyy kit*, 1919) combines the idea of metal with the whale of the prophet Jonah, a symbol of a mystical rebirth after the triumph of the proletariat: *Lions' Bread* (*Lvinyy khleb*, 1922) expresses the corruption of the peasants' grain by the lions of revolution.

In his later poems Klyuyev expressed his disillusionment openly. He now saw no prospect of the spiritual revolution in his lifetime, and he comforted himself with pathetic visions of the transfigured world to come or furious denunciations of the false prophets of his age. He began to feel that the present was dedicated to the destruction of all peasant and spiritual values.

From 1922 onwards he was persecuted ruthlessly. His books were withdrawn from circulation and destroyed; editors were reprimanded and even sacked for publishing his poems. But it was in just these years that Klyuyev wrote his finest poetry, notably in a series of long poems, *Mother-Sabbath* (*Mat-Subbota*, 1922), *Lament for Yesenin* (*Plach o Yesenine*, 1926), *The Village*

(*Derevnya,* 1927), and *Martyrdom by Fire* (*Pogorelshchina,* 1928). Although denounced by the Soviet authorities, on the rare occasions when they are mentioned, these works are not so much attacks on the Soviet system as on the twentieth century, and its cult of material progress. Klyuyev was finally arrested in 1933, and exiled for '*kulak* agitation'; he died in 1937, and he has still not been officially rehabilitated.

Although denounced as a spokesman for the *kulaks* it is unlikely that Klyuyev spoke for any class other than that of poetry-lovers. He was a peasant poet only in the sense that he used peasant imagery as the basis of his philosophy. His combination of extreme erudition with the idealisation of primitive peasant life is one of many paradoxes in his life and work. Many critics regarded his beliefs as mere affectation; but actually, Klyuyev was not capable of dissembling his beliefs even to curry favour. For example, one of his last poems to be published in the Soviet Union, *Youth* (*Yunost,* 1927), tries to extol the red neckties of the Komsomol youth, but the idiosyncratic imagery with which Klyuyev develops this crude theme is far more intelligible in the light of his own earlier work than in terms of Communist ideology.

The case of Sergey Yesenin is rather different. Yesenin had been decently brought up, and adequately educated, but he quite lacked Klyuyev's intellectual and religious depth. His early poetry is largely idyllic, concerned with the beautiful sights and sounds of the Russian countryside. Peasants and the peasant way of life are described only incidentally; they are part of the scenery, not the basis of his poetry. Yesenin himself passed a fairly leisurely childhood, so the harsher side of the peasant's life does not penetrate into these poems. When he came to Petrograd in 1915, Yesenin was quite happy to play the role of the naive country boy, and to allow his listeners to believe that his was the voice of the Russian peasantry. Such was his social success that he was able to dedicate one book of poems to the Empress Aleksandra. However, since the book only came out after the Tsar's abdication, he quickly withdrew this incriminating inscription.

In the years immediately following the Revolution Yesenin changed his style drastically. He tried the terse and dramatic rhythms of the Futurists, the outrageous similes of the Imaginists, and the eschatological trappings of Klyuyev. Out of this unlikely amalgam he still contrived to make something recognisably his own, but it is unlikely that he ever took this eclecticism very seriously; he had dropped both the style and the mystical gestures by the end of 1919.

Unlike Klyuyev, who followed his own path with few concessions to popular taste, Yesenin was always sensitive to literary fashion. Again unlike Klyuyev, who divided his time between the Russian countryside and the cities, Yesenin effectively settled in the city from the time he first visited Moscow in 1913. He enjoyed the Bohemian life of the artistic world, he revelled in the absurdity of a Russian peasant, dressed in top hat and patent-leather boots, reading his poetry in sophisticated nightclubs. Throughout this period of his life he suffered from a certain dizziness at the prospect of the distance he had travelled, and an insatiable appetite for ever more recognition. This period culminated in his disastrous marriage to Isadora Duncan, and the eighteen-month fiasco of his travels to Western Europe and America.

It is largely on his poems of 1920–4 that Yesenin's reputation as an original peasant poet rests, yet this poetry hardly speaks for the peasantry in any meaningful sense. Rather the conventions of peasant poetry are used to depict the dilemmas of Yesenin himself. He writes about the rape of the countryside by the city, the ugliness and brutality of pylons and locomotives, not in order to condemn the twentieth century, but as an externalisation of his own personal tragedy.

Yesenin's heroes during these years are Pugachev and the Ukrainian anarchist Makhno. Both men are seen as solitary individuals, battling against the tyranny of the State, and betrayed by their friends. The dramatic poem *Pugachev* ends with the hero's despairing monologue, whose final maudlin appeals are not so different from the drunken confessions of Yesenin's own poems in *Moscow of the Taverns* (*Moskva kabatskaya*, 1923). The famous image of the foal trying to race the locomotive in *Mass for the Dead* (*Sorokoust*, 1920), generally taken as a symbol of the bewildered Russian village, at first suggested to Yesenin the figure of Makhno;[11] in his play *Land of Scoundrels* (*Strana negodyayev*, 1923) the hero's name Nomakh is a transparent anagram of Makhno. Yesenin's Pugachev and Makhno do not propose any sort of peasant ideology; they are peasants only by reason of their association with historical peasants of the same name; both are more or less wishful transmutations of Yesenin himself.

Even the famous poem *I am the last poet of the countryside* ('*Ya posledniy poet derevni*', 1920) is concerned with the imminent end of Yesenin, rather than with the fate of the Russian peasantry or the Russian peasant poets. When eventually Yesenin did return to his native village, such poems as *Soviet Russia* (*Rus sovetskaya,* 1924) show that Yesenin realised that he had no following there. His search for an identity and for some roots became a nightmare; he made some sporadic attempts to become a conventional Soviet poet, as in his *Ballada o 36* (1924), a story of the escape of Bolshevik political prisoners from exile, and *Poema o 26*, an account of the execution by the British of twenty-six commissars in Azerbaidjan; but these works were written in a forced style, quite unlike anything else that he wrote before or after. The poems of his last year, 1925, are entirely self-regarding and have no peasant orientation.

In spite of his drunken and, often enough, crudely anti-Soviet outbursts of hooliganism, Yesenin was always treated by the Soviet authorities with surprising tolerance. He was backed by Voronsky, the editor of *Krasnaya Nov*, but it is unlikely that he could have enjoyed this protection much longer. The charge that Yesenin was reactionary (which was true enough), perhaps even a *kulak* poet, was being heard more and more loudly towards the end of his life. With the disgrace of Voronsky and the onset of collectivisation, not even Yesenin's immense popularity could have saved him. In the event his suicide in 1925 inspired a whole epidemic of imitations, which infected the youth of all the big cities. The Government was quite bewildered by this development; it coined a word '*yeseninshchina*' for the phenomenon, and endless meetings throughout the country discussed means of countering the threat; (Mayakovsky composed his *Sergeyu Yeseninu* in 1926 as part of the campaign). From 1927 onwards the publication of Yesenin's works, except for the most innocuous, was discouraged; but since he was only a bad example, and not a class-enemy, his works were never actually suppressed, and they continued to circulate freely, until Stalin's successors decided to reclaim Yesenin as a Soviet peasant poet after all.

By the end of the decade the original peasant poets were either dead like Yesenin, on the run like Klyuyev, or protesting hopelessly like Oreshin. A new type of peasant writer, like Mikhail Isakovsky, was being groomed for the role in the 1930s – a sort of literary equivalent to Mikhail Kalinin.

8

Vladimir Mayakovsky

Vladimir Mayakovsky stands at the opposite end of the poetic spectrum from Aleksandr Blok. The son of an impoverished nobleman, reduced to working as a forester, he spent his childhood in the Caucasus far from the fashionable capitals. His education was superficial, and even though he travelled widely in later life, he never acquired more than a smattering of foreign languages. Where Blok for most of his life was content to remain within the conventions of nineteenth-century poetics, an established literary language, standard metres and the cult of a mellifluous smoothness, Mayakovsky was from the start a modernist (even a 'futurist') poet; he revelled in colloquial diction and slang, 'barbaric' sound effects, and broken jazzy rhythms. Where Blok was an almost involuntary mouthpiece for his age, Mayakovsky was more of a coach vigorously urging mankind and time itself onwards into a better world:

Он [поэт] должен подгонять время.*[1]

The toughness and aggressiveness of Mayakovsky sometimes blind readers to the intense lyrical power of many of his works. His love-poems, such as *The Spine-flute* (*Fleyta-pozvonochnik*, 1915), and *Letter to Tatyana Yakovleva* (*Pismo Tatyane Yakovlevoy*, 1928), rank among the greatest in the Russian language; the depths of humanitarian compassion sounded in such poems as *But All the Same* (*A vse-taki*, 1914), *War and the World* (*Voyna i mir*, 1915–16), *About This* (*Pro eto*, 1923) and *At the Top of my Voice* (*Vo ves golos*, 1929–30) relate him to the social reformers of nineteenth century Russian literature. It is these twin elements of intense lyricism and technical iconoclasm that form the basis of Mayakovsky's poetry.

* The poet must drive time onwards.

Mayakovsky's poetry was revolutionary – in every sense; he was a born rebel. The earliest surviving document we have in his hand is a letter of 1905, when he was eleven, containing a sympathetic reference to the revolutionary events of that year. In 1908 he joined the Bolshevik Party, and he was arrested later the same year for helping some women political prisoners to escape from prison. In July 1909 he was arrested again, and this time he was kept in solitary confinement for several months. At this point, however, he dropped his interest in direct political action; he left the Party (he never rejoined it) and turned to art.

Mayakovsky's earliest ambitions were in painting; characteristically he turned at once to the modernist movement, particularly Cubism. It was only during his spell of solitary confinement that he first tried his hand at writing poetry; but these works have not survived (much to Mayakovsky's relief); the extant poetry begins in 1912. For the next few years Mayakovsky moved mainly in the circle of poets and painters who, like him, had broken with the established traditions of art, and were experimenting with cubism, abstractionism and other new techniques. As their name suggests, the Russian Cubo-Futurist poets hoped to discover new techniques from the experience of modern painting, and, if possible, to apply them to the problems of creating a new literature, appropriate to the contemporary urban and industrial scene, with its noise, power and speed.

Where, however, many of the Futurists were excited primarily by the technical and formal possibilities of their experiments, Mayakovsky's poetry was from the first rich in content and above all in emotional involvement. He depicts the urban scene too, but not in its technological glory – rather in its dehumanising features, its disease, poverty and corruption. Mayakovsky is never content merely to observe or to record; he must participate. His compassion for the world's suffering leads him into hatred for the powers that are responsible, both divine and human. He storms Heaven to deliver his protest, or looks for an imminent revolution to correct these injustices. Sometimes he combines the two motifs as in *A Cloud in Trousers* (*Oblako v shtanakh*, 1914–15) where the revolution appears in the guise of Christ:

> Где глаз людей обрывается куцый,
> главой голодных орд,
> В терновом венце революций
> грядет шестнадцатый год.*[2]

But these Christian references have more in common with Blok's *The Twelve* (which it anticipates by three years) than with any established creed. Like Blok, Mayakovsky looked for a spiritual as well as a political revolution.

Mayakovsky called his poem a denunciation of the old world, which could be summed up in four slogans: 'Down with your love! Down with your art! Down with your society! Down with your religion!'[3] These four nouns range from the most intimate of human concerns to the most public, and they may be said to contain the heart of Mayakovsky's poetry both before and after the Revolution. This extraordinary diapason enables him to step instantaneously from private to public matters and helps to justify his assumption that his own personal experiences are of crucial importance for the whole of humanity. Indeed Mayakovsky frankly offers himself as a prototype for the new man of post-revolutionary society. In his poem *Man* (*Chelovek*, 1916–17), the title refers both to man in general and to Mayakovsky himself, а небывалое чудо двадцатого века.†[4] He was always conscious of his own immense physical and spiritual potentialities. One of his most extraordinary poems, *To his Beloved Self the Poet Dedicates these Lines* (*Sebe, lyubimomu, posvyashchayet eti stroki avtor*, 1916), is constructed on a characteristically outrageous and yet tragic hyperbole: 'If only I was as tiny as the Great Ocean. . . . If only I was as beggared as a millionaire . . . as tongue-tied as Dante or Petrarch . . .' with the clear implication that life would be so much simpler if he was; the poem ends with a despairing description of himself 'so huge and so useless.'[5]

This need for some superhuman mission in life leads Mayakovsky on to his theme of himself as the Redeemer and

* Where the dock-tailed eye of man fails,/at the head of starving hordes,/In a thorny crown of revolutions,/comes the year 1916.

† an unprecedented marvel of the twentieth century.

Saviour of the contemporary world, as in the poems *But All the Same*, *War and the World* and the monodrama *Vladimir Mayakovsky. Tragediya* (1913). Here he identifies himself with the outcasts of the world, the unhappy, the prostitutes, the maimed and the deformed, accepts the burden of their suffering and guilt, in order that the world and human nature may at last realise their full potentialities. Where God has failed, the poet Mayakovsky may succeed.

By 1917 Mayakovsky seemed to have reached an impasse. His passionate desire to change the world and his confidence in his own ability to do so had been repeatedly frustrated by the dead weight of the established order of things, personal, social and cosmic. The March Revolution, therefore, affected him as a personal liberation, and he greeted it rapturously in the poem *Poetochronicle* (*Poetokhronika*, April 1917) with the famous lines:

Граждане!
Сегодня рушится тысячелетнее "Прежде".
Сегодня пересматривается миров основа.
Сегодня
до последней пуговицы в одежде
жизнь переделаем снова.*[6]

However the stagnation under the Provisional Government, the lack of any dramatic change in Government policies, let alone in human nature, soon disillusioned Mayakovsky, just as they had Blok. The November Revolution seemed a miraculous renewal of hope: in his autobiography he described his reactions to it:

Принимать или не принимать? Такого вопроса для меня (и для других москвичей-футуристов) не было. Моя революция.†[7]

Mayakovsky's deep emotional commitment to the Revolution was not entirely a matter of political, or even artistic, conviction; it was also a psychological necessity. Here, for the first time, he was confronted by a challenge that he regarded as worthy of his genius; it was both an admirable cause in itself and on a

* Citizens!/Today the thousand year-old 'Yesterday' is collapsing. Today the foundations of the world are being re-examined. Today/we shall remake life all over again/Down to the last button on your clothes.

† To accept it or not? This question never existed for me (or the other Moscow Futurists). *My* revolution.

suitably gigantic scale. The poet was not restricted merely to writing about it; he could actually do something at long last. Having once decided to devote himself to this cause Mayakovsky regarded no chore as too menial in its service. For three years (1919–22) he worked full-time in the Russian Telegraph Agency (ROSTA) in the propaganda department. He designed posters and composed captions to them (to date his authorship has been established in the case of nearly 700, but the real total is probably twice as big). The majority of these posters are of course on Civil War themes; to raise morale in the Red Army, and to encourage civilians to send food and clothing to the front. In the period immediately following, he urged people to guard against epidemics by boiling their drinking water, tried to explain to the peasantry that it was their revolution too and that they should cheerfully share out their grain with the cities, while he urged the workers to put in even more effort to get the economy back on its feet. These slogans and jingles are of course not great poetry – they are ephemeral doggerel. But, as Mayakovsky saw it, this was part of his mission; it was the sort of job that could be done better by a qualified poet than by a literary novice. His genius no doubt found a certain satisfaction in translating official policies into accessible language and in inventing memorable rhymes and images for getting them across.

At the same time, however, he remained vitally concerned by the fate of the arts. Changing society was quite meaningless for him unless the arts were revolutionised as well; the whole of human activity hangs together; a revolution is either total, or it has failed. Culture, as he frequently told his readers, was not just a matter of museums, exhibiting universally accepted, but dead masterpieces; it was a case of a new living art, manifested in the way people live here and now. The old arts were hopelessly compromised by the old world that had produced them, and unless they were overthrown the Revolution would fail. In his notorious poem *Too soon to Rejoice* (*Radovatsya rano*, 1918) Mayakovsky expressed these ideas with his usual forthrightness:

Белогвардейца
найдете — и к стенке.
А Рафаэля забыли?
Забыли Растрелли вы?

А почему
не атакован Пушкин?
А прочие
генералы классики? . . .
Скорее!
Дым развейте над Зимним —
фабрики макаронной.*[8]

Soviet commentators have often tried to explain away these outrageous views, but Mayakovsky usually meant what he said, and he wasn't afraid of saying it. Beauty was not just for contemplation; it had to earn its keep like any Soviet citizen, if it was to survive. The fact that Mayakovsky knew long passages of Pushkin and Blok by heart does not demonstrate how devoted to the classics Mayakovsky really was (as some critics have maintained); but, on the contrary, how difficult he found it to break free of their charms, and how strongly he needed to make the break.

On the other hand, the coming of the proletarian revolution forced Mayakovsky to reconsider his role as a poet. This had been plain enough before 1917, when the poet had felt himself naturally to be a rebel, outcast and redeemer, but in the proletarian era this role was hardly appropriate any more. In the poem *The Poet-Workman* (*Poet-rabochiy*, 1918) he tried to demonstrate that a poet too is just as useful as any proletarian:

Конечно,
почтенная вещь — рыбачить.
Вытащить сеть.
В сетях осетры б!
Но труд поэтов — почтенный паче
Людей живых ловить, а не рыб.
Огромный труд — гореть над горном,
Железа кипящего класть в закал.
Но кто же
в безделье бросит укор нам?
Мозги шлифуем рашпилем языка.
Кто выше — поэт
или техник . .?
Оба.

* If you catch a White officer/to the wall with him. But have you forgotten Raphael? Have you forgotten Rastrelli? . . . And why/ is Pushkin not attacked? And what about the other White generals among the classics? . . . Quick! Over the Winter Palace – raise the smoke/of a macaroni factory.

Сердца — такие ж моторы.
Душа — такой же хитрый двигатель.
Мы равные
Товарищи в рабочей массе.
Пролетарии тела и духа.*[9]

If in these views Mayakovsky sometimes comes close to the Proletkult, he had in fact little use for their poetry, which he considered to be stylistically imitative and formally weak. More importantly, where the Proletkult remained satisfied with this formulation of the responsibilities of a proletarian poet, Mayakovsky could not accept such a facile parallel for long.

The two major works which Mayakovsky wrote in these years are *Mystery-Bouffe* (*Misteriya-Buff*, 1917–18) and *150,000,000* (1920). They are aimed at mass audiences, and so by comparison with his pre-revolutionary poetry they are simpler, sometimes even crude. *Mystery-Bouffe* is a light-hearted allegory of Russian history since the beginning of 1917 (it was in fact begun in the spring of that year). The Revolution is depicted in terms of a Second Flood. The pairs of 'clean' and 'unclean' that enter the ark are re-interpreted to correspond to the class-distinctions in pre-revolutionary society. The unclean do all the work, think of all the bright ideas, and finally build the ark; the 'clean' give the orders, take all the credit, eat all the food, and discuss questions of kingships and presidencies among themselves. Finally the workers in exasperation hurl them overboard; but now left to themselves, with a storm rising, with no food and no knowledge of navigation, the workers suddenly panic. The blacksmith and a farm labourer (symbols of the proletariat and the peasantry) try to restore order; but the situation is only finally saved by the appearance of a man walking over the waves; not actually Christ, or even any of the Bolsheviks, but 'the most common-or-garden man', the 'undeflectible spirit of eternal rebellion',[10] a part which was taken, predictably enough, by Mayakovsky himself at the first performance.[11] He

* Of course,/a fisherman's job is decent enough. Pull out your net/and hope for a sturgeon! But how much better – the work of poets,/fishers of men, not just of fish. It's a strong man's job – to sweat at the furnace,/and temper the hissing irons . . . But who/will accuse us of idleness? We polish brains with the rasp of our tongues. Who is nobler – the poet/or the engineer?. . . . Both. Hearts are engines too. The soul – just an ingenious motor. We are equals. Comrades in the working mass. Proletarians of flesh and spirit.

enters their hearts and souls, and leads them via Hell, which carries no terrors for the workers who have seen far worse in this world, via Heaven, whose miserable diet and archaic standards only earn their scorn, into the Promised Land, which proves to be this world transfigured. Their tools leap into their hands, the soil brings forth the crops unasked. The play ends with a vision of the proletarian Utopia, and an appeal to the rest of the world to join the Russian workers there.

The poem *150,000,000* occupies a lesser place in Mayakovsky's work. It looks forward to the final showdown between Communist Russia and capitalist America, in the form of a gigantic boxing match between a bloated Woodrow Wilson and Ivan, a composite of the 150,000,000-strong population of Russia. Ivan is, predictably, the winner, and this inaugurates Communism all over the world. In an attempt to break with Mayakovsky's earlier individualism the poem was originally published anonymously, or as the first line puts it: 'The name of the author of this poem is 150,000,000.'[12] However, the true authorship was an open secret from the first, and Mayakovsky made no attempt to deny it in the second or later editions.

In spite of difficulties and misunderstandings the years 1917–21 were a period of honeymoon for Mayakovsky and the Bolshevik Party. He accepted its decrees unquestioningly, and saw his poetic activity almost as an arm of Government. The material difficulties of these years, the shortages, the atmosphere of crisis – military, economic and political – he accepted as a romantic challenge. But the change of tempo and policy brought by the NEP found Mayakovsky uncomprehending and resentful. The Revolution's whole purpose had been to throw out the old world, lock, stock and barrel; and here it was re-introducing the past through the front door. If in his propaganda poems he was at first able to make out a case for the NEP:

Всероссийская конференция РКП отвечает на эти сомнения:
недоверию места нет,
новая экономическая политика установлена
на́ долгий ряд лет.*[13]

* The All-Russian Conference of the RKP answers these doubts; this is no time for distrust./ The New Economic Policy has been set up to run for many years.

his own reservations could not be satisfied so easily. At times he even began to fear that the proletarian revolution had been succeeded after all by a dictatorship of the bourgeoisie:

Да и то
в Октябре
пролетарская голь,
до хруста зажав в кулаке их, —
объявила:
“Не буду в лакеях!”
Сегодня,
изголодавшись сами,
им открывая двери “Гротеска”,
знаем —
всех нас
горчицами,
соусами
смажут сначала:
“НЭП” — дескать.
Вам не нравится с вымазанной рожей?
И мне тоже.
Не нравится-то, не нравится,
а черт их знает,
как с ними справиться.*[14]

The only solution Mayakovsky sees is to learn from the bourgeoisie, so that the Communists will be able to do without them when the real revolution eventually comes.

IV Internatsional (1922; the title indicates Mayakovsky's impatience with the Third International, established by Lenin, and his desire to design a rather more grandiose one) opens with a picture of the bad old bourgeois world that has been blown up by Marx and the Revolution, in order to prepare the world for Communism. Mayakovsky decides for a change to describe what Communism will *not* be like, and this brings him back inescapably to the present, the restoration of the bourgeoisie,

* And then too/in October/the ragged proletarians/crushed them, [the bourgeoisie] in their fist/and declared: 'I will not be a slave!' To-day,/starving ourselves,/opening the doors of nightclubs to them,/we know – all of us/will be smeared/with their mustards/and sauces:/'The NEP' – they call it. You don't like having your face smeared? Neither do I. But for all that/Hell only knows what we do about it.

the turning-back of the calendar:

К гориллам идете!
К духовной дырке!
К животному возвращаетесь вспять!*[15]

This Revolution has failed, but Mayakovsky still has faith in its ideals, and he looks forward to a new revolution to complete the work of February and October, 1917:

Взрывами мысли гóловы содрогая,
артиллерией сердец ухая,
встает из времен
революция другая —
третья революция
духа.†[16]

This prophecy of revolution is remarkably similar in its phraseology to the equivalent passage in *A Cloud in Trousers* and the implication is plain – that Communist Russia is in a pre-revolutionary stage, not a post-revolutionary one. But the full implications of these lines are only apparent when it is remembered that the call for a 'third revolution' was one of the slogans of the ill-fated Kronstadt rising just a year earlier. The poem ends in the spirit of Mayakovsky's early works, with the poet-hero undertaking a single-handed mission to redeem all humanity and an invitation to all to come and learn from him.

No doubt, Mayakovsky himself was horrified at the anti-Soviet direction his poem had taken. He started work on a new poem, *The Fifth International* (*Pyatyy Internatsional*, 1922), a vast project in eight parts, to be as optimistic as the *IV Internatsional* had been pessimistic. But this poem, with its ambitious hopes of depicting the arts in Utopia, petered out in some high-spirited pranks which lead nowhere; only two out of the projected eight cantos were written.

The most ambitious of Mayakovsky's post-revolutionary poems is *About This* (*Pro eto*, 1923). Here the poet confronts the *revanche* of the bourgeoisie head-on. In many ways the poem is a

* You are headed for the apes,/for a spiritual dump,/you are returning to the beasts again.

† Juddering heads with explosions of thought,/Thumping with the artillery of hearts,/There rises out of the ages/a new revolution – a third revolution – of the spirit.

Soviet version of *A Cloud in Trousers*, but the urgency is now far greater because the Revolution has come and gone, leaving hardly a trace. The poem itself stresses its *pre*-revolutionary connections by references to *Man*, completed in just such a mood in the middle of 1917. Mayakovsky is still tormented by love, he is still horrified by the existence of the bourgeoisie both as a class and as a state of mind:

> Тот быт, который ни в чем почти не изменился, тот быт который является сейчас злейшим нашим врагом, делая из нас мещан.*[17]

The poem is built round two situations: the poet's love for a woman (Lilya Brik, the wife of his closest friend) and the theme of universal love. Both lead to suicide. His love for Lilya is tragic, because of her indifference (at least as portrayed in this poem), while his longing to serve and redeem humanity is equally frustrated by the world's apathy. The poet who is ready to die for humanity discovers that humanity is not interested; and though redemption by one man may have been good enough for Christianity and the young Mayakovsky, it is not good enough for Communism:

> Что толку —
> тебе
> одному
> удалось бы?
> Жду,
> чтоб землей обезлюбленной
> вместе,
> Чтоб всей
> мировой
> человечьей гущей.
> Семь лет стою,
> буду и двести
> Стоять пригвожденный,
> этого ждущий.†[18]

* That way of life which has hardly changed in a single respect, that way of life which is now our bitterest enemy, making bourgeois of us all.

† What is the point – just you alone, could you succeed?/I am waiting till the whole love-starved world together,/Till the whole wide world in a human mass – /I have waited seven years, I can wait for two hundred/Crucified here, awaiting the day.

Finally, Mayakovsky comforts himself with the thought that one day the world will become one vast family, and the problems of the individual and society will have been solved. But this distant prospect seems to be attained by science rather than by revolution.

Mayakovsky now began to discover evidence of the bourgeois restoration all round him. He was naturally concerned primarily with the literary world; he attacked the pompous language of contemporary poets, journalists and politicians.[19] The whole of literary and literate Russia comes under his lash in the poem *Four Stories of Trash* (*Chetyrekhetazhnaya khaltura*, 1926). From the editorial policies of the State Publishing House (GIZ), the technical incompetence of most Soviet writers, the ignorance and chauvinism of Soviet criticism, down to the illiteracy of the contemporary reader, Mayakovsky found the 'tree of literature bare'.[20] But this mentality was not just confined to the literary world. In 1928 he began work on a series of poems satirising the Soviet variants on Tsarist or universal types: SovPompadour, SovPlyushkin, SovCoward, SovHack (*Sovkhaltursheik*); the prefix 'Sov-' has since been dropped from Soviet editions of these poems, but the word '*sovmeshchanin*' (SovBourgeois) has succeeded in entering the language.

Ironically, it was during the NEP period that the logic of events forced Mayakovsky himself to become a champion of bourgeois values. In 1923 he was invited to compose some advertisements for the State shops to counter the attractions of the private traders. No doubt, Mayakovsky accepted the challenge as an extension of his earlier propaganda work in ROSTA during the Civil War years. However, it is not easy to combine commercial advertising with socialist moralising, and Mayakovsky's grandiose claims on behalf of the cigarettes, biscuits, teas and beers of the State shops, even texts for the wrappings of sweets, seem peculiarly inappropriate among his collected works. Above all, his poems in support of the State lottery, with their blatant appeals to human acquisitiveness – one of these poems is entitled *The Poet's Dream* (*Mechta poeta*, 1926) – run clean counter to the values that he was asserting elsewhere at the same time. In 1928, after the end of the NEP period, Mayakovsky was to accuse those who had actually won money on these lotteries of wilfully sabotaging the economy.[21]

Mayakovsky's defiantly revolutionary attitudes and his innovatory literature were not to the taste of everybody. But the main opposition came from the Party bureaucracy. *Mystery-Bouffe*, which had been written for the first anniversary of the Revolution in Petrograd, was taken off after only three performances; plans for putting it on in Moscow were completely thwarted. When, in 1921, Mayakovsky revised and expanded the work for a new production, repeated attempts were made to stop it reaching the stage. It was, however, put on for the May day celebrations after considerable obstruction. These attempts culminated in more delays by the State Publishing House (GIZ) in publishing the work, and its subsequent unwillingness to pay Mayakovsky any money at all. (Mayakovsky took the case to court and won.) As for *150,000,000* Lenin himself complained to Lunacharsky:

> Как не стыдно голосовать за издание *150,000,000* Маяковского в 5,000 экз.
> Вздор, глупо, махровая глупость и претенциозность.
> По-моему, печатать такие вещи лишь 1 из 10 и не более 1,500 экз., для библиотек и для чудаков.
> А Луначарского сечь за футуризм.*[22]

Giz once again resisted publication of the work under various pretexts. In 1925 it unilaterally tore up its contract with him for a 'Collected Works' in four volumes, on the grounds that his work didn't sell.[23] Similar delays and obstructions were repeated up to the last year of his life.

The charge that his works were not accessible to the general public infuriated Mayakovsky more than any other; it challenged his whole claim to be a revolutionary poet. He retorted that the failure to understand was part of a deliberate ruse by the bourgeoisie to prevent his poetry from reaching the workers; the fact that Soviet literary critics also failed to appreciate his aims and achievements simply proved to Mayakovsky how bourgeois they were. He pointed to the success of his readings in factories and barracks as evidence of his accessibility

* You ought to be ashamed of voting for the publication of Mayakovsky's *150,000,000* in an edition of 5,000 copies. It's nonsense, stupid, utterly stupid and pretentious. In my opinion only one in ten of such things should be published, and then in an edition of 1,500 at the most, for libraries and cranks. And Lunacharsky should be whipped for his futurism.

and popularity among those who were willing to make the effort; but, in fact, there were occasions when Mayakovsky came under attack at his public readings.[24] Even his poem *Vladimir Ilich Lenin* (1924), now regarded as a masterpiece in the Soviet Union, was not well-received at first. The *poputchiki* considered it to be hackwork, while the Party critics seized on misprints and misinterpretations to insinuate that the poet was fundamentally anti-Soviet.

The major works *Vladimir Ilich Lenin* and *Good!* (*Khorosho!*, 1927) on which Mayakovsky's reputation in the Soviet Union largely depends today, have been underestimated in the West. They are public and oratorical statements, but by no means so impersonal or merely propagandistic as is sometimes made out. They are both concerned, on a deeper level than the titles suggest, with an attempt to find a place for the poet in the revolution. The funeral of Lenin performs the miracle in the earlier poem: Mayakovsky is swept off his feet by the surge of popular emotion:

Я счастлив.
Звенящего марша вода
относит
тело мое невесомое. . . .
Я счастлив,
что я
этой силы частица,
что общие
даже слезы из глаз.*[25]

and the poem ends with a re-discovery of the status of the poet in the world revolution alongside the workers and Party leaders:

. . . мы,
людей представители,
чтоб бурей восстаний,
дел и поэм
размножить то,
что сегодня видели.†[26]

* I am happy. The waves of a ringing march/sweep away my weightless body . . . I am happy to be a particle of this power/and that even the tears in my eyes are common to all.

† . . . that we, the representatives of man, in a tempest of risings, of deeds and of poems,/should multiply what we have seen here today.

Good!, a poem to which Mayakovsky attached the greatest importance (he compared it to *A Cloud in Trousers*), was composed for the tenth anniversary of the Revolution. Here he continues the theme of the individual and the masses less obtrusively, through his use of the pronouns. At first 'I' and 'we' are differentiated; then, in the sixth canto, the coming of socialism is signalled by the switch into 'we' and 'ours'. In the last canto, a picture of the Communist Utopia, the 'we' changes back again into an all-embracing 'I' – the individual no longer just merges with the collective (as at the end of *Vladimir Ilich Lenin*); each individual is the embodiment of the society as a whole:

Улица —
моя.
Дома —
мои. . . .
. . . в моем
автомобиле
мои
депутаты.*[27]

As a practising Futurist, Mayakovsky was always fascinated by the possibilities of science and technology. If at first he tended to stress the fairy tale aspects, as in *Mystery-Bouffe* and *150,000,000*, or looked to it to provide a solution to the problem of death, as in *About This*, his travels abroad opened his eyes to its real possibilities. The first of his trips outside the Soviet Union took place in 1923; he was to travel abroad at least once a year thereafter up to 1929. He developed a surprising affection for France, which he visited almost every year; but it was the technological marvels of the United States that really impressed him. If in some of his comments he displays a chauvinistic determination not to be over-awed, in the famous *Brooklyn Bridge* (*Bruklinsky most*, 1925) he was reduced for once to sheer amazed contemplation:

* The street is mine. The houses mine. . . . my deputies/ride in my automobile.

Смотрю,
как в поезд глядит эскимос,
впиваюсь,
как в ухо впивается клещ.
Бруклинский мост —
да . . .
Это вещь!*[28]

On his return home he began to campaign vigorously for the 'Americanisation' of Soviet Russia.

Mayakovsky was therefore delighted by the announcement of the first Five-year Plan. It marked an end to the NEP, and it held out the promise of his cherished Americanisation, thus hastening the coming of true Communism. He travelled around Soviet Russia, looking at the building sites, and felt that he could see the new Russia already rising out of the mud and filth; he wrote a large number of poems on the subject. The excitement of the Plan even reminded him of the heady days of 1918, but the comparison strikes an ominous note; Mayakovsky was no longer judging the present in terms of the future but of the past.

This note of nostalgia grows stronger in Mayakovsky's last years. He begins to lament the lost placards of the Civil War years, and to wish that they had been preserved for posterity in museums. The famous poem *Conversation with Comrade Lenin* (*Razgovor s tovarishchem Leninym*, 1929), written on the fifth anniversary of Lenin's death, provides a striking illustration of this change. Mayakovsky swears that Lenin's name and spirit are still vital forces in Soviet Russia, but the final lines can only repeat the first ones:

Двое в комнате.
Я
и Ленин —
фотографией
на белой стене.†[29]

After all the grandiose claims made earlier in the poem, this

* I gaze, as an Eskimo stares at a train,/I drink it in, like a nit in an ear. Brooklyn Bridge – Yes – that's something.

† Two in the room. Me and Lenin/in the photograph on the white wall.

refrain strikes a doubly pathetic note. The poem returns to its starting point, like a prayer or an incantation; the fact that the final line is syntactically unnecessary creates a drooping, almost a melancholy intonation. Lenin is supposedly alive in spirit and deed, but all we have here is a photograph, and on a *white* background at that.

The two satirical plays that Mayakovsky wrote at the end of his life, *The Bedbug* (*Klop*, 1928–9) and *The Bathhouse* (*Banya*, 1929–30), reflect his growing disillusionment and bitterness. If the second of these plays satirises the Soviet Establishment and its bureaucracy, the first casts doubt on the very goals and ideals of Communism. In the first half of *The Bedbug* Mayakovsky depicts a typical NEP profiteer, Prisypkin (in the original version he was a Party member; under pressure from the censors, Mayakovsky compromised on 'ex-Party member'). By a freak of nature this Prisypkin is deep-frozen and resuscitated some fifty years later when Communism has come. He is now exhibited as a specimen of the horrors of the bad old days, when suddenly, by a brilliant change of focus, the reader's sympathies are switched to Prisypkin away from the sterile robots of what should be Utopia. This world with all its imperfections is for the first time in Mayakovsky's work shown to be more attractive than the goal which he had been advocating for so long. Mayakovsky no longer identifies himself with victorious Communism, but with the fallible and the fallen in a world of growing inhumanity. It is not so much that he sensed his own approaching exclusion from the ranks of good Communists, as that he had begun to doubt whether he wanted to stay with them any longer.

He still did what he could to show his loyalty. In August 1928 he abandoned his LEF group; in January 1930 he applied for membership of RAPP, which had always criticised him for his individualism and his unwillingness to join the Party. After a month's delay and several humiliating interviews, he was finally accepted. In March he was granted the apparent distinction of an exhibition of his life's work, 'Twenty Years of Mayakovsky'. But the exhibition was ostentatiously ignored by most of the literary world; even the chairman for the opening ceremony failed to appear.[30] Overcome by acute depression, Mayakovsky committed suicide a few days later. He left behind him a handful of unfinished poems, among them *At the Top of my Voice*, his apologia addressed, like so many of his poems, to the future:

Потомки,
словарей проверьте поплавки:
Из Леты
выплывут
остатки слов таких,
как 'проституция',
'туберкулез',
'блокада'.
Для вас,
которые
здоровы и ловки,
Поэт
вылизывал
чахоткины плевки
Шершавым языком плаката.[31]

The poet's mission to redeem a world of evil and suffering, the humiliating self-sacrifices ('treading on the throat of his own song')[32] which this entails, and the appeal to a better world to judge and vindicate him, are typical themes of Mayakovsky's early poetry; but now a revolution has come and gone, and nothing has changed. For Mayakovsky this was the final tragedy.

Mayakovsky's last years were rich in ironies. In the poem *Gloom about Humourists* (*Mrachnoye o yumoristakh*, 1929) he had enquired why there was no good Soviet satire, and pooh-poohed the *poputchik* complaints of censorship; but when his own works began to be cut and altered he was, naturally enough, extremely indignant.[33] In the poem *Zeus the Refuter* (*Zevs oproverzhitel*, 1929) Mayakovsky had attacked the Soviet citizen who has been denounced in the press and writes to clear up misrepresentations in self-defence; within a few months Mayakovsky was receiving the same treatment.

Just four years earlier Mayakovsky had reproached the dead

* Posterity, check the floats of your dictionaries,/And out of Lethe will bob up the fragments of such words/as 'prostitution', 'tuberculosis', and 'blockade'. For you who are so fit and smart,/the poet licked away the expectorations of consumptives/with the rough tongue of his posters.

Yesenin for taking the easy way out. His own suicide was therefore greeted angrily by the Soviet press, and was used as additional evidence against him; work on a collected edition of his works was temporarily suspended. Later on, however, a chance remark of Stalin's to the effect that he was 'the best and most talented poet of our Soviet epoch'[34] led to a complete rehabilitation. A statue depicting him as an arrogant man of bronze was erected in the centre of Moscow. His approved works were dutifully taught in all schools of the Soviet Union.

The Soviet canonisation of selected poems from Mayakovsky's Soviet period completely distorts the true image of the man and poet. Mayakovsky frequently emphasised that his work was all of a piece; he spoke of *A Cloud in Trousers* in the same breath as *Good!*; the principles of Futurism were for him not an outgrown aberration, but a vital ingredient in his later poetic theory and practice; even while he was waiting for his acceptance by RAPP, he still wanted to know what was going on in REF. Selected poems can make Mayakovsky sound like a prison camp guard, but even these acquire rather more meaning and poignancy in the light of Mayakovsky's own experience at the hands of RAPP and the Party; the revolutionary and tragic aspects of Mayakovsky are discernible even in the long poems that are held up as masterpieces for emulation by all right-thinking Soviet poets.

Formally, Mayakovsky's poetry has exerted a wide but ultimately superficial influence on Soviet literature. Many poets have tried to adopt his aggressive postures without realising, still less experiencing, the complex emotions that lay behind them. His characteristic device of arranging poetry step-wise across the page to assist declamation has been facilely imitated by poets who have failed to attract any audiences to declaim to. Others have simply borrowed expressions and lines wholesale from his work, and like Bezymensky (whom Trotsky held up as a model to Mayakovsky) then boldly accused him of plagiarism. Yet the myth of Mayakovsky has continued to exercise a potent influence at another level. The idea of the poet as revolutionary and spokesman for humanity, redeemer and Saviour, and the stubborn assertion of values that are otherwise honoured only in the letter, emerged again in the 1950s to inspire a new generation of Russian writers.

If persecution and suicide were the fate of Soviet Russia's greatest poet, a man unreservedly devoted to the Bolshevik revolution and a fearless champion of its principles, the omens were not encouraging for minor talents in the years ahead. The first decade of Soviet literature ends, as it had begun, with the death of the greatest Russian poet of the day.

Part II

1929-46

1

Social and Political History

The Five-year Plans

If the NEP may be seen as the consequence of the premature revolution of November 1917, the new phase that Russia entered, with the inauguration of the first Five-year Plan in 1928, was an attempt to bring about the socialist revolution. Private enterprise and private property (though not, of course, personal property) were finally abolished. The few remaining entrepreneurs of the NEP period were squeezed out: their supplies were cut off; they were subjected to crippling taxes, and, in the last resort, to arrest and exile in the labour camps. In 1930 Stalin declared that the country was now entering the stage of socialism and in 1936 he was to announce that it had been attained.

Stalin called 1929 the 'year of the great break', and so it proved to be in almost every sphere of Soviet life. The social upheaval caused by the implementation of the new policies, the widespread resistance to them and the countermeasures of massive repression that this provoked, were to effect another revolution, even more far-reaching than that of November 1917. It was this revolution that has largely formed the Soviet Union as it is today.

But the revolution of 1929–30 was not the result of unmanageable tensions within society; it was the consequence of political and administrative decisions imposed from above. Industrialisation was introduced to facilitate the transition to socialism, instead of socialism evolving from industrialisation. The First Five-year Plans in industry and agriculture were a first step towards the complete proletarianisation of the population, already supposedly experiencing a 'dictatorship of the proletariat'. The Communists claimed that, having mastered the theory of historical development, they were now proceeding to the higher stage of putting it into practice. By the same argument 'consciousness' was also expected now to determine 'social existence'.

The abrupt switch to intensive industrialisation and mass-collectivisation were the more unexpected in that Stalin had earlier opposed these policies, while they were associated with Trotsky and Zinovyev. They were, however, consistent with his own doctrine of 'socialism in one country'; for if Russia could not hope for any immediate revolutions in Western Europe to assist her development, she would have to build up her own industrial and military might in self-defence against their hostility.

Thus the socialism built in the Soviet Union during the 1930s was still 'socialism in one country', still trammelled with the consequences of the premature revolution. The leading role of the Communist Party showed no sign of merging into a proletarian, still less a classless, society; indeed the dictatorship of Stalin became even stronger. Preoccupied with its internal affairs, the Soviet Union largely abandoned its internationalist and revolutionary ambitions to concentrate on its own security. The earlier ideal of national self-reliance degenerated into chauvinism. Even the non-Russian nationalities of the Soviet Union were affected; the word 'Soviet' lost its original meaning, and became merely a synonym for 'Russian', as in the new phrase of the 1930s, 'Soviet patriotism'.

The new line was sincerely welcomed by many Russians. After the frustrations of the NEP period they felt that they were returning at long last to the revolutionary spirit of the early days. Such expressions as 'mass-attacks' and 'storming a fortress' evoked the heroism of the Civil War period. In dramatic contrast to the rapid growth of Russian industry and technology was the disaster of the Great Depression in the West; many European and American technicians and engineers, who had lost their employment, now came to Russia. Marx's prophecies of the collapse of capitalism and Russia's age-old dreams of outstripping the West seemed on the point of realisation. Thus in the First Five-year Plan Communist ideology and Russian patriotism came together.

Once again history seemed to be on the side of the Communists, and many Russians threw themselves into work with fanatical devotion, believing that their exertions would bring about the millennium in their own time. Men and women showed themselves willing to work fantastic hours in appalling conditions. The newspapers were full of incredible feats of record-breaking in production and construction, of norms being overfulfilled by astronomical percentages. Young Communists went out to build the city of Komsomolsk in the Far East and endured extraordinary hardships and privations in creating a large city out of nothing. Great new enterprises, like the city of Magnitogorsk, an industrial giant, were created in the space of a few years. The urge to achieve the impossible found its embodiment in the slogan 'Complete the Five-year Plan in four years'.

In this pursuit of records and overfulfilling norms, the original idea of the plan was somewhat obscured. In a truly planned economy, overfulfilment is, strictly speaking, as unhelpful as underfulfilment;[1] if resources are limited the excess taken by one industry in the name of overfulfilment can only come at the expense of another. Plans were often established not on a rational assessment of the forces involved and the materials required but on an emotional commitment to produce more than anyone had thought possible, or as a demonstration of political orthodoxy; in such circumstances to argue the case for a lower but more practicable target was to risk the charge of insufficient loyalty or even sabotage. Grandiloquent slogans had taken the place of rational planning. The Government too contributed to this imbalance. By its pursuit of ostentatious prestige projects, such as grandiose hydro-electric stations and the Moscow underground railway, for which there was little economic justification, it too contributed to the overheated atmosphere of the times.

In many respects this chaotic substitute for planning led to absurd situations: machinery accumulated and deteriorated in one place where there was nowhere to house it, while in another new factories were standing idle for lack of the same machinery. New and sophisticated products were often damaged by unskilled workmen, ignorant of their correct treatment and maintenance, while elsewhere qualified technicians had to make do with outdated apparatus. Much of the damage and wastage of valuable resources in these years was the result of the unplanned nature of the Plan. Calculations based on these enthusiastic estimates only multiplied the errors.

More serious were the administrative consequences. The failure of the Government to distribute resources rationally, or to supervise the workings of the Plan critically, served to divert the energies of management away from the spirit of the Plan to an irresponsible, and even cynical observance of its letter. It was in these years that dishonesty, falsification and corruption became endemic among Soviet officials. The cult of statistics and percentages led to the sacrifice of quality to quantity. Related industries would co-operate with one another in exchanging their products, so that they could be counted twice in calculating output. The unpredictable demands of the Plan encouraged the hoarding of scarce resources, and so a new unofficial profession grew up, that of the *tolkach* (or pusher) who specialised in easing their circulation.

These abuses had the effect of unnecessarily delaying Russia's development into a fully industrialised state. Consumer goods of a notoriously shoddy standard were shamelessly imposed upon a population that had nowhere else to turn. The emphasis on quantity and the habit of hoarding men and resources effectively discouraged innovations; the next target-date was too close to admit of any rethinking of production methods. There were other long-term effects. This prolonged period of intense work took a heavy toll of the health, both physical and psychological, of the workers involved. Elementary precautions were spurned as soft and unproletarian. As a result, industrial accidents increased sharply; in the new cities, because of inadequate hygienic measures, there were several major epidemics.

Thus the Plan failed to meet most of its targets by the end of 1932. In spite of all the feats of endurance and hard work and the genuine enthusiasm of many workers, the rate of growth in these years, though remarkable, was not significantly higher than it had been during the NEP period. The exact figures are still uncertain, because of the unreliability, either involuntary or deliberate, of Soviet statistics. The plans, which had been opportunistically raised during the first years of the Plan, were drastically lowered in the final year, in an attempt to approximate to the real situation; but even so, it fell short.

Although the regime continued to pay lip-service to the proletariat in these years, the conditions of the working-class deteriorated, and their remaining privileges were curtailed. In the years 1930–32, they lost the right to choose where to work; employers were forbidden to hire those who had left their previous employment without authorisation. The re-introduction of the Tsarist system of the internal passport (which had been denounced by Lenin before the Revolution) provided an effective check on their movements. In practice, management was often so short of labour that factory officials connived at violations of the code in order to attract workers.

At the same time, the liabilities of the workers increased formidably. They were made personally responsible for any damage or injuries at work. Prison sentences could be imposed for minor violations of labour discipline, while theft of State or industrial property could be punished with death. A day's unauthorised absence from work could incur instant dismissal. Since housing and food-rations depended on the job, and there was no longer any unemployment relief (on the grounds that there was no longer any unemployment) the worker was defenceless. With the disappearance of private traders, the State became the only employer, and the right to strike was withdrawn, since it could now only be used against the State. The Trades Unions were no longer empowered even to negotiate wage settlements on behalf of their members. Tomsky, the head of their organisation, tried to intervene on their behalf, and was promptly sacked; he committed suicide in 1936 to avoid arrest.

For the majority of Russians life in these years continued to be difficult. True, Russian workers had acquired the benefits of paid holidays and guaranteed sick pay, but work hours were long and demanding, and leisure time was further curtailed by the necessity of attending interminable political meetings. Housing was extremely scarce and of poor quality. The new cities were surrounded by shanty towns of mud huts and sometimes mere holes in the ground. Throughout the first half of the 1930s certain basic foodstuffs were rationed. The elimination of the private craftsman meant that such services as shoe repairs, interior household jobs and private dressmaking ceased to exist.

With the disappearance of the itinerant NEP traders small but essential household items, needles and thread, shoelaces and buttons became scarce. These shortages naturally hit the poorest people hardest, as they could least afford to replace the clothes and goods that could not be repaired.

The goal of maximising production was assisted by the encouragement of 'socialist competition', so called because it was the workers who were meant to compete rather than the bosses as in capitalist states. (This kind of competition extended to other walks of life too. The writers' newspaper, *Literaturnaya gazeta*, of these years is full of public challenges, issued by individual writers to their rivals to contribute as much money, if not more, than themselves to the State Loan.) The new pattern was cemented by the introduction of high differentials in wages. Most workers were put on to a piecework basis (though this had been denounced by Lenin as a typical technique of capitalist exploitation); it was later to culminate in the Stakhanovite system, whereby certain workers were helped to set astonishing records of productivity, and the work norms for other workers correspondingly increased. Not surprisingly, this created widespread ill feeling; many Stakhanovites were attacked and in some cases killed, by their disgruntled fellows. Not only wages but food rations too, as in the Civil War, were distributed on these principles. Strictly speaking, of course, the practice could be justified by the definition of socialism as 'from each according to his ability, to each according to his work'.

Theoretically, with the approach to socialism, the class-basis of Soviet society might have been expected to weaken, but to forestall any suggestion that the leading role of the Party and the State might decrease correspondingly, Stalin declared that the class-struggle would intensify, not diminish, as society drew closer to socialism. (This argument was later to serve as a justification for the great purges of the 1930s.) The actual experience of Soviet life certainly suggested an increasing stratification within society. The differentiation of wages and salaries now went to extremes; the maximum salary that a Communist had been allowed to receive in the 1920s was effectively abolished in 1929,[2] and the top officials received high salaries and generous perks. The disproportion was further increased by a heavy turnover tax on all goods and foodstuffs, and a mild income tax, both of which discriminated against the lower-paid. The institution of prizes and awards for those who were already highly paid tended still further towards the stratification of society. The Soviet information media too preferred to exalt a few favoured individuals, whether in sport or in industry, in the arts or in contemporary aviation, at the expense of the collectives behind them.

These class distinctions reflected of course the stabilisation of Soviet society. This in turn led to the rehabilitation of the family as a social unit, and the introduction of much stricter laws governing marriage and divorce. With the concept of a legally registered marriage, and the regulation of the rights of the children, the distinction between legitimate and illegitimate births re-appeared. The schools too re-introduced the concept of discipline, the authority of the teacher was restored, and the pattern of studies became more conventional. This was in part a reaction against the excesses of the 1920s, but it was also symptomatic of the need to stabilise, and retrench, that is typical of all societies after a series of convulsions. In the Soviet Union this reaction was correspondingly extreme.

This sense of stability was reflected in the structure of the new Constitution, which was worked out in 1935–6. On the face of it the Soviet (or Stalin) Constitution is the most liberal document of its kind ever promulgated. But the democratic freedoms that it guaranteed only enjoyed protection if they were exercised 'in conformity with the interests of the working-class and in order to strengthen the socialist system'.[3] Since it was the Party, and not the judiciary, which was the arbiter of these matters, the Soviet citizen still had no means of redress against the State. The Party remained above the law as before. In certain respects the laws now became extremely harsh. For example, children were made legally responsible for their actions at the age of twelve, and so were liable to capital punishment at that age. In 1934, families of political prisoners were made liable, regardless of their actual complicity, for the 'crimes' of their close relatives. (During and after the war, this clause was often to be used against the wives and children of prisoners-of-war.) Even if they were not always arrested, relatives could lose their jobs, and were subject to various kinds of official harassment.

At the end of 1932 the First Five-year Plan was officially

declared to have been 'completed'; the Seventeenth Party Congress of 1934 took the title of 'Congress of Victors'. An important stage in the building of socialism had been reached: 99 per cent of all industry was now owned by the State, and 90 per cent of the peasantry had joined collective farms. It was intended that the Second Five-year Plan should root out the last vestiges of private enterprise, the peasants' individual garden plots, and the black market. The Second Five-year Plan (1933–7) was thus a less dramatic undertaking, but it probably achieved rather more; it was intended to consolidate the foundations already laid. The Third Five-year Plan (begun in 1938) was interrupted by the German invasion of 1941.

The First Five-year Plan was a turning-point in the history of the Soviet Union; it created the pattern for Soviet society down to the present day. It has also sunk deep roots into Soviet mythology. The legend of the Plan has quite eclipsed the fatalism of Marx's 'social being determines consciousness'. On the contrary, modern Russians are brought up with a prodigious faith in the ability of human will-power and endurance to achieve miracles. For the Russian as for the ambitious Westerner, consciousness is all. Yet this consciousness must be directed by the Party; spontaneity is still suspect, as in the first years of the premature revolution. Indeed, the precursors of Stakhanov were often prevented from pursuing their time-saving methods because the initiative had not come from the management. Even under socialism in one country the workers cannot be trusted to work harder without constant exhortation from above. Slogans, a technique often used in the 1920s, now became the only way in which the Party communicated with the people. Thus politics, a force which Marx had relegated to the superstructure, became the prime mover of Soviet life.

This primacy of politics was achieved only by a vast extension of controls, and, in particular, of the power of the Secret Police, which was now to become the most important arm of Government. From the first it had acquired its own troops, and it had always been used ruthlessly against counter-revolutionaries, dissidents and *kulaks*. The opposition to collectivisation and the widespread resentment of the workers at the brutalities of forced industrialisation were crushed in the same way. In the popular mind, the Party had become indistinguishable from the Security Police.

The Purges 1933–9

Although the Congress of Victors was a somewhat grandiloquent title, there were real achievements which the delegates could see for themselves. First and foremost, the foundations of industrialisation had been laid, and the resistance of the peasantry had been broken, without splitting the country or weakening the Party. Since these policies were those of Stalin himself, it was only natural that he should receive the chief credit.

The success of Stalin lay in his organisational abilities rather than in any personal brilliance. He had none of the graces of social charm or imagination; he spoke Russian badly with a thick Caucasian accent. It has been suggested that the early death (probably by suicide) in 1932 of his wife Nadezhda Alliluyeva had a decisive effect in transforming him into a morose and suspicious despot, but there is little evidence to suggest that he had ever been very different. If anything it was the immense possibilities of unrestrained power that led to his later megalomania, the incessant fears of a palace coup, the recurring thirst for blood, and at the same time the insatiable craving for praise and popularity.

The direct consequence of his style of dictatorship was the creation of a group of court favourites, whose word on any subject had the force of law; this led inevitably to the cultivation of influential connections, and so to every kind of political corruption. The system had created an elite with an overwhelming interest in preserving the *status quo* and immense powers to prevent any changes which threatened its own position. One of the uglier consequences of this feudal system was the creation of hundreds and thousands of little Stalins, modelled on the life style and mannerisms of the leader. For these reasons Stalinism outlived Stalin.

The creation of the popular image of Stalin was thus a miracle of public relations. From 1929 onwards he was presented as a being of superhuman wisdom and humanity; he was depicted with a benign smile on his lips, surrounded by children and flowers. Actually, he saw few people outside his immediate entourage; the Kremlin churches and gardens which had once been open to Muscovites and visitors were now closed and guarded. Yet Stalin still succeeded in persuading the vast majority that he was a devoted 'father of his peoples'; they were prepared to believe that the iniquities of the system were to be blamed on his underlings, that he himself was ignorant and therefore innocent of them. By the time that war broke out, soldiers were ready to die with Stalin's name on their lips.

However, in the atmosphere of comparative relaxation that accompanied the end of the First Five-year Plan, the Communist leaders who knew Stalin's ruthless and overbearing character began to question his suitability for the quieter times thought to be ahead; more moderate and reasonable leadership seemed to be called for. In the summer of 1932, a group of senior Communists produced the 'Ryutin platform'. Although this document has never been published, it seems clear that its authors were calling for a return to more democratic methods, a reduction in the pace of industrialisation, greater liberties for the peasantry, and also greater freedom inside the Party. The document was aimed directly at Stalin 'the evil genius of the Russian Revolution'.[4]

On the other hand the Communist Party was not prepared to contemplate any weakening of its own position above the law. The mentality that had frustrated reform in Lenin's time was to return under Stalin with redoubled potency. The Communists still felt themselves to be an unpopular minority, and many of them feared that relaxation might lead to a total loss of control, even to the overthrow of the Bolshevik Party. From this angle the very successes of the last few years and the pressures for moderation seemed to be a potential threat to the Party. Even Trotsky in exile warned against the risks of removing Stalin; the consolidation of Communist rule was far more important than the possible degeneration and corruption of Communism. All the forces within Russian Communism now conspired to block any possibility of peaceful change. In this atmosphere it was naturally the extremists who triumphed, as before.

The purges of 1933–6 were undertaken on a large scale, but they were not essentially different from previous ones, in that they were primarily concerned with the membership of the Russian Communist Party. At the beginning of this period there were three and a half million Party members; in the first two years, almost a third of these were to be expelled. By the autumn of 1934, however, the rate had fallen off; the temptations to relax had extended to political life too. In this situation the murder of Kirov, the Party boss of Leningrad, on 1 December 1934, served as the signal for a new crisis and a new series of emergency measures. By a somewhat suspicious coincidence, Stalin had only the same day introduced new legislation against 'terrorists', depriving them of the right of defence and of appeal.

The 'Ryutin platform' and the Kirov assassination were the main foundations of the reign of terror that was to ensue. Although Kirov had shown himself enough of a hardliner in the 1920s, there is some evidence that he had urged moderation upon the more blood-thirsty leaders over the Ryutin case. He had acquired a certain popularity in Leningrad, to the extent that he could afford a much smaller bodyguard than his colleagues; at the Seventeenth Party Congress his reception rivalled that given to Stalin. If the opposition were looking for a leader, Kirov might have seemed the ideal candidate, and, though there is no indication that he aspired to this role, it is plain that to a suspicious despot he might have seemed as serious a threat as the straight-forward opposition of Ryutin and his sympathisers.

That Stalin connived in the murder of Kirov is now generally accepted. In any case he was to exploit the crime unscrupulously for his own ends; over the next four years it was blown up into a vast 'conspiracy' of criminal negligence, espionage and sabotage. First, Kirov's comparative 'moderation' had been shown to have been unfounded; by implication all moderate Communists were guilty of insufficient vigilance. In particular, the crime served as a pretext for purging the Leningrad NKVD for its inefficiency; Stalin then proceeded to purge his own bodyguard. From the NKVD the charges spread to the Party. Kirov's assassin had been a Zinovyevite in the 1920s, and so Zinovyev and his former associates were forced to admit that their oppositionist views had been an indirect factor in the crime; later still they were to be accused of complicity. Finally in the years 1937–8, the campaign was to culminate in the arrest, exile and death of millions of innocent Russians. At the back of the whole fantastic 'conspiracy' supposedly lurked the master-mind of Lev Trotsky.

The purges within the Communist Party that had taken place in earlier years were only a dress rehearsal for the full-scale terror to be unleashed from August 1936 to March 1939. One contributory factor in the timing may have been the death of Maksim Gorky in the summer of 1936, the last single individual with the international prestige to speak up effectively. (It is probable that he too was murdered.) Previous waves of terror in history, even in the Soviet Union, had been directed by one section of the population against another for religious or political motives; but no one was safe during the years of the great purges. Two chiefs of the secret police were removed; interrogators and informers were frequently sent to join the prisoners that they had helped to condemn. Diplomats were recalled from abroad, only to disappear without trace. Peasants, workers, servicemen were no more fortunate than intellectuals, artists, and officers.

Historians have tended to concentrate on the slaughter among Party members, which is easier to document; it was also, naturally enough, the subject of most concern to the Party, when it came to re-examine the Stalin period in 1956. The greater part of the delegates to the Seventeenth Party Congress of 1934 were to disappear during the next five years; only fifty-nine out of nearly 2,000 delegates were to attend the next Congress in 1939; 1,108 are known to have been arrested, and there were probably many more. For many years even the documents of the ill-starred Congress of Victors, which contained so many unmentionable names, were to be suppressed. But the purges were not confined to the Communist Party alone. Certainly in proportion to its representation among the population it suffered heavily, but for every Party member there were approximately seven non-Party members arrested.

The charges were usually fantastic: espionage on behalf of England, France or Japan; attempts to sabotage the country's security, either by preposterous 'conspiracies' or by retailing political jokes; plots to assassinate Lenin and/or Stalin, or murder vast numbers of Soviet workers. The evidence was often demonstrably false; in other cases it was based on such evidence as the non-Russian surnames of the accused, or a chance conversation with another 'enemy of the people'. Confessions (the preferred type of evidence) were extracted by torture, both physical and psychological, and they were framed in such a way as to incriminate others. In fact many of those implicated in this way were to remain unscathed, but the charges were fabricated just in case they might be needed later.

The ordeal of the purges did not end with the brutality of the arrest and preliminary investigation, or even the mockery of a trial. Those who escaped summary execution, and did not take their own lives or die under torture, were dispatched as convicts to the most inhospitable regions of the country, the Arctic Circle, the wastes of Siberia or the deserts of Central Asia, where they were defenceless against the rigours of the climate, the inhuman exploitation of the camp officials, and the mockery of the common criminals who openly lorded it over them.

Stalin was well aware of the role that exile had played in the growth of the Russian revolutionary movement under the Tsars, and he was determined that Siberia should not father a new opposition. If, in the 1920s, Soviet political prisoners had still enjoyed the comparative liberties of their predecessors, the right of receiving food parcels and books, of corresponding with friends and relatives, of pursuing their own intellectual interests, under Stalin there were no such concessions; even the right of correspondence was severely restricted. The prisoners were given gigantic sentences, usually of eight or ten years (twenty-five year sentences were introduced in 1938); the labour was physically exhausting, and the meagre food rations depended on success in fulfilling the norm. Underfed, inadequately clothed, deliberately reduced to a lower level than the common criminal, the political prisoners had no illusions that this labour was 'corrective'. The majority died within a few years.

Many justifications have been given for the purges. At first many people credited the accusations and confessions as essentially if not wholly correct – the charges were so fantastic, that it seemed inconceivable that they could have been completely baseless, but Khrushchev's revelations at the Twentieth Party Congress in 1956 have shown that they were. Others, like Isaac Deutscher, have seen in the purges a logical extension of the desire of any ruler to strengthen his position; but although

Stalin may have strengthened his own personal power, he weakened the country considerably; the purges in the Army had the effect of killing off almost the entire upper officer corps, and this was to prove almost disastrous for Stalin himself in the first months of the German invasion. Others again have seen an economic rationale behind the purges; the provision of massive slave labour to create the capital required to support the industrialisation campaign. But here too the wastage hardly balanced the gains. As Marx had pointed out, slave labour is not economic. Forests were felled for export so as to gain foreign currency, but the felling was unplanned, and not matched by the planting of new trees; this led to a deterioration of the soil and the creation of marshland; unforeseen climatic and ecological changes followed.[5] Vast railway lines were laid, but they were never connected to the existing network, or even among themselves, and so were never used.[6]

But worst of all was the senseless wastage of human life and initiative. Some twenty million men, mostly in their thirties and forties, lost their lives in Stalin's concentration camps.[7] Hundreds of thousands of able-bodied men were employed in the unproductive labour of guarding these innocent prisoners. Even those who survived physically unscathed, whether captives or captors, suffered deep psychological traumas. Thus the shadow of the purges has fallen on Stalin's heirs too. They served under Stalin and co-operated in the execution of the purge. Their guilt by association and their fear of the truth still haunts their actions and attitudes.

With the consolidation of Stalinism the lie came to dominate Soviet life. The falsifications, official and unofficial, of facts and figures, established during industrialisation and collectivisation, the distorted picture of life outside the Soviet Union, and the fantastic accusations of the purge trials, now spread to well-known and easily verifiable facts and events. In 1935 the works of Trotsky, Kamenev, and Zinovyev were removed from public libraries; contemporary history was being re-written in full view of those who had actually watched or participated in it. Even the existence of the labour camps, familiar to every Soviet citizen, was unmentionable. This trend reached its apogee in the *Short Course of the History of the All-Union Communist Party, Bolsheviks* (*Kratkiy kurs istorii vsesoyuznoy kommunisticheskoy partii bolsheviki*), (1938), with its grotesque falsifications of Stalin's role during the Revolution and Civil War, and its hysterical abuse of names that had since fallen into disfavour.

With the introduction of mass terror the lie became a way of life. People learnt to dissemble their feelings, to deny their natural impulses, to reject what they instinctively believed to be true; even to remain silent required immense courage. Words had lost their meaning. The consequences for social life, for the arts and sciences were catastrophic.

The factual and historical confusion was paralleled by the moral and legal uncertainty. All were technically guilty of something, even if only of having been incriminated in someone else's forced confession; most were morally guilty of having kept silence when they should have spoken out, or of having lied when they could have said nothing; not that this equivocation was any guarantee of survival. In these circumstances matters of life and death became totally unpredictable. The laws were often so vaguely formulated that a citizen had no way of knowing whether he had committed an offence or not; the extension of legal guilt to other members of the family only intensified the general insecurity. The inevitable result was a terrible corrosion of the moral fibre of society by fear, guilt, opportunism and plain cynicism. It was the liars, the informers, the traitors that had the best chance of survival.

By the autumn of 1938 the country had been reduced to an epidemic of neurosis. Production was declining, and that at least was unacceptable. Yezhov, the Chief of the Secret Police, disappeared (some hold that he went mad, others that he was shot). He was succeeded by the last of Stalin's appointments to this post, Beriya, himself to be shot soon after his master's death. In March 1939 Stalin declared that, though there had been excesses, the purges had by and large been successful, and the 'great terror' gradually abated; Trotsky, the last of the victims of the great purges, was murdered in Mexico on 20 August 1940.

What had the purges achieved? Their most important service was the creation of a new class of administrators and technicians. They were young – many of them had only recently graduated. They had no memories of the pre-Stalin era; Lenin and the Civil War were simply legends to them. They owed everything to Stalin, indeed they knew nothing but Stalin. The Party had finally shed its grassroots, revolutionary image; it had become a professional elite.

But effective power had now passed out of the hands of the Party, and into the grip of the Secret Police. With its own private army, its unlimited powers of arrest and sentence without trial, the NKVD was strong enough to purge even the Red Army unchallenged. Even before the great purges began, the man-power held down in the labour camps made it the largest single employer in the country, with an enormous economic, industrial and military complex of interests, which the Party has not succeeded in bringing under control even today. The great purges completed the formation of Stalinist Russia.

Meanwhile, another ordeal was awaiting the Russian people. On 22 June 1941, Hitler invaded the Soviet Union.

The Outside World and the War

'Socialism in one country' was primarily a slogan intended for internal consumption. Its implications of Russia's isolation in a hostile non-socialist world were no less far-reaching, however, for foreign policy. Stalin realised that this isolation could serve both as a patriotic rallying-cry and as a means of consolidating his own personal power. It is therefore no accident that his rise to power coincided with the deepening isolation of Russia from the outside world. Unlike the other Bolsheviks Stalin had passed his periods of exile in Siberia, not in the West; he had travelled to Western Europe before 1917 only occasionally, and strictly on Party business; his longest stay outside the frontiers of Imperial Russia, before or after 1917, lasted only six weeks. He was uninterested in the European socialist movements, and he distrusted the Westernised intellectuals of Lenin's entourage. He preferred to replace them by men who, like himself, knew little of the outside world, and so would be less easily distracted from the goal of socialism in one country.

The same assumptions can be seen in his attitude to the Comintern. Under Lenin it had been dedicated to the cause of world revolution; Stalin, however, had little faith in the ability of foreign Communists to bring off successful revolutions in their own countries, and he regarded the Comintern, therefore, primarily as a battleground in his own power struggle.

Both Zinovyev and Bukharin were to be outmanoeuvred there, the first moves in their eventual defeat. Later in the 1930s foreign dissidents and moderates were to be purged as ruthlessly as their Soviet comrades.

With the apparent failure of the policy of co-operation with foreign socialist parties, at least in England and China, Comintern tactics swung back to a harder line. After using the moderates in his struggle against Trotsky, Stalin now needed the Left wing to support him in discrediting Bukharin, and he adjusted his foreign policy to suit. In December 1927, two years before the Great Depression, he declared that the stability of capitalism was faltering; events were moving Russia's way, and in that case Communists should be wary of any unnecessary compromise with the socialist parties of the West. But this policy too was to lead to disaster, not only for the Soviet Union, but this time for the whole world.

The largest Communist Party outside the Soviet Union was in Germany, and though by itself it was not strong enough to challenge the Nazis, an alliance with the German Social-Democratic Party, might well have been decisive; but Stalin, struggling with the moderates at home, refused to contemplate the possibility of a Social-Democratic Government in Germany. The German Communists were instructed, therefore, to give no support to the socialists, even to the extent of backing Nazi-led strikes and election campaigns. Stalin later explained that he had thought dissatisfaction with Hitler would accelerate the revolution in Germany. In fact, once they had come to power, the Nazis imprisoned or executed the greater part of the German Communist Party.

Shaken by the collapse of this policy, which had simply created a new and powerful enemy in Central Europe, Stalin was still cautious enough to continue observing his side of the Rapallo bargain, and in 1933 he even renewed the treaty with Hitler (it was to last until the end of 1935). He did not even protest at the execution of German Communists. At the same time he began to look for opportunities of securing defensive alliances against Nazi Germany. Soviet Russia applied and was admitted to the League of Nations; she signed treaties with France and Czechoslovakia. The Western Communist parties were now instructed to form a united front with other socialist or even with consenting bourgeois parties in defence of 'democracy' against Fascism.

The crucial test came with the outbreak of the Spanish Civil War. This placed the Russian Communists in a dilemma. Their new policy inclined them to support the Republicans, but they were afraid that a Communist success might create a backlash effect in the countries where Communism was just beginning to acquire sympathy and respect. In the event Stalin delayed any action until after Germany and Italy had intervened in support of Franco. Indeed, the Russians' extreme caution disappointed many of their friends; they refrained from any ambitious revolutionary claims, while their efforts inside the republican camp were primarily disruptive, aimed at creating a unified, Soviet-style Communist Party out of the motley Left wing groups. The pursuit of Stalin's feuds against the Trotskyites, and indeed the entire non-Stalinist Left in Spain, was simply an extension of purge techniques against heretics abroad. Such activities did little to assist the Spanish Republican cause, or even that of Communism. Once the outcome was clear the Russians broke off their assistance; many Spanish Communists fled to Russia, where most of them soon disappeared into the labour camps.

Meanwhile Stalin had still found no reliable alliance against the Nazi threat. He had anyway little confidence that such treaties could bring any real security. With his Marxist inclination to see little essential difference between bourgeois regimes, whether democratic or Fascist, he assumed that the Western powers would, in the last resort, side with one another against Communist Russia. Meanwhile, the resurgence of a belligerent Japan to the East confronted Russia with the possibility of a war on two fronts. Stalin saw the main hope therefore in a conflict between the European powers, from which he could stand aloof. If Russia was faced by a threat from the West, then any alliance, however fragile, was desirable for the temporary security it might bring.

Thus throughout 1938–9 Stalin began to put out feelers to the European powers. The Germans were interested, because of their own fears of fighting on two fronts. England and France, however, never seriously contemplated the possibility of a Nazi-Communist alliance, and took their time accordingly. They had no more reason to put any faith in the Russians' adhering to a treaty than the Communists had in the bourgeois powers. They were not entirely innocent either, of the hope that Hitler might continue to expand eastwards; the nations that had failed to defend Republican Spain and democratic Czechoslovakia were hardly likely to intervene on behalf of Communist Russia. But the procrastinations of the Western powers only increased Stalin's suspicions of them, and he gratefully accepted the first firm offer he received. On 23 August 1939 Molotov and Ribbentrop signed their notorious non-aggression pact, with its secret clauses dividing Eastern Europe into spheres of influence between them.

On 1 September the Nazis invaded Poland, and two days later England and France declared war. Once the Polish armies had been defeated in the West, Stalin invaded from the East. He next persuaded the Baltic states to grant him strategic bases for stationing Red troops; Finland, however, refused, and the Red Army invaded at the end of November. But the Russian soldiers, unused to the conditions of a northern winter war, and demoralised by the havoc of the purges and the inexperience of their new commanders, were at first humiliated by the determined and resourceful Finns. Eventually, however, their superior numbers and artillery forced the Finns to accept peace on Russian terms; they lost territory, but they kept their independence. Three months later the Russians staged coups of 'liberation' in the Baltic states and incorporated them into the Soviet Union. All potential dissidents, and in some cases even foreign tourists in the occupied territories were rounded up and dispatched to the labour camps. The Polish officer corps was massacred at Katyn outside Smolensk.

The collapse of resistance to Hitler on the European mainland alarmed Stalin, who saw that the Nazis, with their Western flank secured, would be free to turn on Russia. The Germans soon began to take a more hostile line; they openly disregarded the frontiers of their spheres of influence in the Balkans, defaulted on their deliveries of machinery under the terms of the pact; German planes began increasingly to intrude on Russian airspace, troops massed on the frontiers. Stalin, however, was still playing for time. He continued to observe his side of the bargain scrupulously; he even handed over to Hitler German

Communists and Jews who had taken refuge in Russia. He ignored intelligence reports of the impending attack, and only a week before the invasion, he publicly stated that he was fully satisfied with the way the Germans were honouring their part of the deal.

The invasion of 22 June 1941 destroyed many illusions. The alliance with Nazi Germany had never been popular inside Russia. Germany was the traditional enemy in Central Europe, and memories of the 1914–18 war and the peace of Brest-Litovsk had not yet faded; the intensive propaganda campaign against the Nazis from the middle of the 1930s had been much more successful with the population than its abrupt reversal in 1939. The Communist parties in the West too had found it difficult to adjust to the new policy in 1939, but they had dutifully followed the Moscow line, trying to foment mutinies among the troops and strikes among the industrial workers of the Allies. It was partly this instinctive resistance to the Molotov-Ribbentrop pact that enabled the Communists to execute their astonishing *volte-face* so smoothly on the day after the German invasion of the socialist homeland.

The first five months of the German campaign brought a series of overwhelming disasters. The ravages of the purges had in themselves been 'greater than any defeat in history':[8] the costly Finnish war had further lowered the morale of the army. On top of this the Soviet leaders had failed to take advantage of the breathing space they had gained by the alliance with Hitler. There were no adequate mobilisation plans for a military emergency; there were not even any military fortifications along the frontier; in occupying Poland, the Russians had demolished their old defence system, but had not yet erected another.

These failures of the High Command continued even after the invasion. It was six hours before the Russians received the order to return the Germans' fire. By that time some 90 per cent of the aircraft at the front had been destroyed on the ground. On the day of the invasion the artillery units were engaged in training exercises in the rear. In spite of the officers' protests they were at once ordered to proceed to the front, in broad daylight, where they provided a sitting target for enemy bombers. Further tactical blunders resulted in the loss of 90 per cent of the front-line tanks.

Thus, although on the day of the invasion the Russians actually outnumbered the Germans, and even their equipment was not far inferior, the blunders of their leaders placed them in a hopeless situation. As a result of the orders not to retreat under any circumstances, over three million Russians were taken prisoner in the first five months of the campaign. Those officers who succeeded in withdrawing their men on their own initiative were arrested, and usually shot, by the reinforcements coming to meet them. These reinforcements were shortly to be confronted with the same dilemma, once they had reached the front. Stalin was so used to an entourage of flatterers that some of his senior officers were executed merely for bringing him the unpalatable truth.[9] By November Leningrad had been surrounded, and the Germans were within twenty miles of Moscow; the Ukraine on which Russia depended for the bulk of her grain supplies was in enemy hands; in the South the Germans had almost reached the Caucasus.

The bewilderment of the fighting men was matched by the consternation of the Government. Molotov was left to break the news to the Russian people; Stalin himself spoke only on 3 July, but even then he could not bring himself to admit the full extent of the catastrophe. As the Germans advanced, government ministries and foreign embassies were evacuated to Kuybyshev (formerly Saratov) on the Volga. This created a panic in Moscow; there was looting of foodstores, and several members of the Party were lynched. In the areas threatened by the German advance the NKVD murdered political prisoners wholesale, for fear they might desert to the Germans.

Morale was restored only by the news that Stalin had remained in Moscow. On 7 November, the anniversary of the Revolution, he appeared as usual on the Lenin mausoleum to review the traditional parade, and to make a determined speech. This act of identifying himself with his people (he addressed them as 'brothers and sisters') did much to restore his credit. The atrocious crimes of the pre-war years, the military blunders of the preceding months were forgotten. Popular adoration of Stalin revived miraculously.

Stalin fostered this cult by appealing to patriotism rather than to Marxism. The cry was for Russia and for Stalin, not for the Soviet Union and the Communist Party. In particular he stressed the parallels with Napoleon's invasion of Russia in 1812, and its miserable end; hundreds of thousands of copies of *War and Peace* were printed and avidly read; it was at this time that Prokofyev began to think of turning the book into an opera. Later, Stalin was even to claim that he had based his campaign on Kutuzov's in 1812–3, with the difference that he had contrived not to surrender Moscow to the enemy.

This patriotic appeal had many consequences. In his earlier thinking Stalin seems to have believed that a world war between the major capitalist countries could be fanned into an international proletarian revolution, much as Lenin had hoped to do in 1917. But when the war came it proved to be no time to encourage Russian soldiers at the front to fraternize with Germans; it was a struggle for national survival not for world revolution. The *Internationale*, which had been the national anthem of the Soviet Union since the Civil War, was replaced by the frankly nationalistic '*An inviolable union of free republics*' ('*Soyuz nerushimyy respublik svobodnykh*'). In 1943 the Comintern was disbanded. If the First World War is known in the Soviet Union as the Imperialist War, the Second is entitled the Great Patriotic War.

In October 1942 the revolutionary origins of the Red Army disappeared in a mass of new reforms aimed at increasing its fighting efficiency. The political commissars, through whom the Party had kept a close watch on military affairs, were removed, and decisions were now taken in accordance with tactical and strategic considerations. This gave the military commanders the unity of authority which was essential if orders were to be carried out promptly and effectively. Such symbols of the Tsarist regime as epaulettes and saluting were brought back to boost army morale. Stalin even gave some encouragement to the Church, whose hold was still strong outside the cities. The rigours of collectivisation were reduced. It was not so much the ideological principle that mattered as the need to unite the whole people into a maximum effort to win the war.

In retrospect, the first winter seems to have been the decisive moment of the Russian campaign. If the Germans had not left their invasion until so late in the summer, Moscow could scarcely have withstood their onslaught; but in October the severities of the Russian winter set in a few weeks earlier than usual, and this time it was the Germans who were unprepared. They had neither the clothing nor the technical equipment for such conditions. It was now that Stalin delivered a counter-attack that forced the Germans back. Strategically, the gains were not particularly significant, but in terms of morale the results were incalculable. The Russians discovered that the Germans were not invincible, while the German armies were actually forced to retreat for the first time in the war. In the euphoria of the moment Stalin actually began to dream of victory in 1942.

But, although the Russians had done something to right the balance, their situation was still desperate. German forces occupied a large part of European Russia, with its agricultural and industrial resources. In the first few months the greater part of these industries were dismantled and transported to the Urals; but there was naturally a serious timelag before it could be fully mobilised again. At the same time, the tyrannical behaviour of the Communists had created a great deal of disaffection, especially among the non-Russian nationalities of the Soviet Union, and German propaganda was quick to exploit this possibility. In the Ukraine the invaders were often welcomed with open arms, but the Nazis' contempt for the Slav peoples soon lost them all their potential support. They dispatched the men to German labour camps, requisitioned the grain, and showed an indiscriminate brutality to the women and children that drove them back into the arms of Moscow. Even so some Slavs, notably General Vlasov, were willing to collaborate (Vlasov had been one general always trusted by Stalin, and so had survived the army purge).

The second summer of the war saw the Germans advance still deeper into Russia until they reached the Volga to the South-East of Moscow. Here the campaign centred on the city of Stalingrad, which, by reason of its name, had become a symbol on which both sides staked everything, though its strategic importance was comparatively unimportant. The Russians even brought in divisions from the Far East, which were essential in case of a Japanese attack. But the gamble was justified. At the beginning of 1943 the siege of Stalingrad was lifted; the German besiegers were themselves surrounded; the Commander-in-chief, twenty-three generals and their troops surrendered.

This colossal victory proved to be the turning-point of the war. By the summer of 1943 the Red Army had regained most of the territory that had been lost in the previous two years and the outcome could no longer remain in doubt. The Russians had serious problems still, the continuing siege of Leningrad and the acute shortages of food and clothing for the civilian population, but these were likely to improve with time. Stalin's bargaining position was now much stronger, and in November 1943, at the Teheran Conference with Churchill and Roosevelt, he began to prepare for the eventual peace settlement.

Although the Western powers had supplied the Soviet Union with food, clothing and transport, Stalin still felt suspicious of their intentions. Their failure to launch a Second Front in Europe until 1944 alarmed him with the thought that perhaps they were waiting to let Russia and Germany exhaust themselves; perhaps they were even contemplating an alliance against Russia. Since he had done just this himself in 1939, it was natural for him to suspect others capable of doing the same.

The first hint of trouble, however, came over the Polish question. The Soviet Union could hardly be expected to relinquish the Polish territory she had received from Hitler, and which was still hers when she was invaded; on the other hand, from the Western point of view, the rape of Poland was the immediate cause of the war, and to tolerate the continuance of this injustice made the whole war pointless. The Polish Government in exile in London bitterly opposed any sell-out, but it was helpless in the face of the facts of power. The Great Powers proposed to divide up Europe into spheres of influence; the Russians gave certain guarantees of the democracy of Poland, but as the Red Army approached the Vistula, they betrayed their intentions for the peace unmistakably. The Poles inside Warsaw rose against the Germans, partly in the hope of throwing the Germans off balance, but also in an attempt to forestall liberation by the Russians. The Germans put down the rising brutally; the city of Warsaw was razed almost to the ground. Meanwhile the Russians failed to come to the help of the Poles; they were themselves pegged down by a German counter attack; but they refused even to let the Western allies fly in supplies and reinforcements.

In February 1945, the three Allied leaders met at Yalta to

prepare for the peace; the division of Europe, and in particular of Germany, was settled, and so the seeds sown for further dissensions. The Great Powers were agreed on the need to smash Germany's military and industrial potential, but they pursued their policies in different ways. While the Western powers preferred to disarm Germany with a view to letting her develop as a peaceful capitalist state, in the East the demands were for heavy reparations – though, in fact, it had been the Russians who had been most critical of this form of vengeance after the 1914–8 war. In the Eastern sector, German industry was dismantled and removed to the Soviet Union.

At the end of the war the Russians were in an immensely strong position internationally. The victorious saga of the Red Army, the popular image of a wise and grizzled Stalin, had completely effaced the fears and prejudices of earlier years. In Western Europe, the Communist Parties profited by a wave of popular sympathy, quite oblivious of their discreditable and disloyal activities in 1939-41. In Eastern Europe too, which had been liberated by the Red Army, there was a natural inclination towards Russia. As after the First World War, so now it was the Western governments who had most to fear.

At the same time the Soviet Union had good cause for concern. The Western possession of the atomic bomb once again underlined the relative weakness of Soviet Russia, and the fate of Japan showed that the Americans would not hesitate to use it. In the face of such a threat, even the Red Army seemed less invincible. At home the weakness and the sheer exhaustion of the Russian people posed another serious problem. The official figure of the dead was put at seven million; Western estimates are nearer double that figure.[10] On top of this there were the cripples, the orphans and the homeless. Cities had been devastated, industry had been largely destroyed, and agriculture, in Western Russia at least, would have to start all over again; the same cheerless prospect as in 1921 seemed to face the Russian people.

In the 1930s Stalin's authority had been achieved largely by the efficiency with which he had isolated his country from the outside world. Western political developments were grossly over-simplified or simply ignored; cultural novelties, both artistic and scientific, had been virtually unknown. Even foreigners were hardly ever seen by the average Russian. They were confined to the cities, and they lived in blocks set apart for them.

During the war however, these barriers crumbled. There was more information available. The very success of the alliance in defeating Nazism seemed to give the lie to previous claims that the West was plotting the downfall of Soviet Russia. Soviet citizens once again came into contact with foreigners. Officers who had established friendly relations with their Western counterparts could not fail to see that some cherished Soviet beliefs about the West were not true; in the final campaigns of the war in Europe the ordinary soldiers on both sides met one another. Even prisoners-of-war, for all the brutality of their treatment by the Germans, had caught glimpses of a far higher standard of living than the vaunted achievements of the Soviet Union. Not that these impressions were entirely favourable. The Russians could not easily forget the barbarities of the Germans, and anyway, they have never been over-impressed by the achievements of Western civilisation.

Stalin, however, was well aware that the previous 'patriotic war' (against Napoleon), and the triumphal march of Alexander I's troops into Western Europe had led to the awakening of political thought in Russia, and to the Decembrists' rising of 1825. At the end of the war there were about five million Russians in Western Europe, prisoners of war and forced labourers, deserters and refugees. Under the terms of the Allied agreements, they were all subject to repatriation, regardless of their wishes. Just as in the pre-war years all Russians who had had any dealings with the West were once again automatically suspect; arrest and exile or execution were all that awaited them in Stalin's Russia, and many committed suicide rather than return.

Well before the end of the war, Stalin was preparing the ground for a new isolationism. In 1944 he warned that, although the war with Fascism might be ending, the struggle with capitalism was only just beginning. In February 1946 he re-affirmed that war was inevitable while capitalism still existed. Although this was widely interpreted as a foreign policy statement (in the following month it was answered by Churchill's 'Iron Curtain' speech at Fulton), it was probably intended primarily for a Russian audience; nothing could be more terrible to the average

Russian than the prospect of another world war. The creation of external enemies to justify repression at home had been a natural tactic for the Communists ever since the Allied Intervention during the Civil War.

In the months after the war Stalin set about restoring the primacy of politics over all other considerations once again. The popular hero of the war, Marshal Zhukov, was eased out of the limelight, and all the credit for the victory given to Stalin. The peasants who had grown comparatively fat during the war years when they were encouraged to produce food, and no questions were asked about collectivisation, had to be brought to heel once again. The Church, which had gained a new hold on the hearts of countless Russians, had to be reminded of its position in a Communist State. Entire nationalities were deported to the most distant corners of the Soviet Union as punishment for the sympathy, if not the collaboration, of a few individuals with the invaders. On the cultural front, a new campaign, denouncing 'servility to the West' even in matters of historical fact, was vigorously and unscrupulously pursued. With the break-up of the wartime alliance Russia's East European allies were taken over by Communist puppets and forced to act as her satellites.

By 1947 all the wartime hopes of liberalisation and peaceful co-existence had once more been crushed.

2

Maksim Gorky

It may seem odd to include Maksim Gorky (pseudonym of Aleksey Maksimovich Peshkov) in an account of Soviet culture in the 1930s. He wrote practically no fiction in this decade and he was an ageing man in his middle sixties. None the less his prestige and power were such that he was able to exert considerable influence in Soviet cultural life of the 1930s. This chapter will attempt to estimate that influence and the use made of that power.

Gorky's early life was one of great hardship; much of it was due to the social conditions of the time, even more to the accidents of his biography. His earliest memory was of the death of his father; he had been infected with cholera by his son. Gorky's mother could never forgive the boy for his part in this tragedy, and she did little about bringing him up (she died when he was ten). The boy was brought up by his maternal grandparents. The new household was an unhappy one; quarrels and fights and beatings were common occurrences. The boy could dimly remember that his own parents had lived more peacefully and happily, and this sense of a golden age tragically lost was to accompany him throughout his life.

At the age of ten he was sent out to earn his living. Now the backbreaking conditions of work, the cynical and cruel behaviour of his masters and comrades almost drove him to despair; he found his solace in books. He read voraciously anything that came to hand, snatching hours which he needed for sleep. His first books were mostly trash, but helped by some discriminating adults, and above all by his own natural good sense, Gorky gradually learnt to distinguish worthwhile literature from rubbish. He was particularly impressed by the portrait of the Russian intelligentsia that emerged from these books. He decided that he would enter university and, with this ambition, he made his way to the university town of Kazan.

Gorky never managed to get into the University (the title of the third volume of his autobiography, *My Universities,* is ironic). He did, however, meet several students who took an interest in him; but for all their admiration for his efforts at self-education, they could not help patronising his lack of any formal education. At first Gorky was impressed by their high-flown language, but when he talked to the ordinary workmen of Kazan, he was shocked to discover that these same students who talked so eloquently about beauty and truth flouted them in practice by their cynical and immoral behaviour. This double view of the intellectual world, its past nobility and its present degeneration, was to cause Gorky much soul-searching in the years to come.

At the age of twenty, Gorky joined a group of Populists, and left Kazan to work in the village of Krasnovidovo. Unfortunately this venture lasted only a few weeks. The peasants were deeply suspicious of their visitors and were easily incited to violence against them; they set fire to the house in which Gorky and his friends were sleeping, and he was lucky to escape alive. These experiences gave him a dislike and distrust of the Russian peasantry that was to last the rest of his life. When he next began to take an interest in social changes, it was the Marxists, not the Populists, who attracted him. The next four years (1888–92) he spent in travelling all over Western Russia, partly looking for work, but partly too looking for the answers to his questions about life, about Russia, about society, and about man; he called on Tolstoy, and even tried to found a Tolstoyan colony.

Thus it was that when, in 1892, his first story *Makar Chudra* was published in a provincial newspaper over the pseudonym M. Gorky (M. the Bitter), he had acquired an extraordinarily rich and contradictory knowledge of different kinds of life and people. On the one hand there was the nobility of man's ideals, the heights of selflessness which they often inspired, and on the other the cynicism and brutality of man's (often the same man's) actions. Which was man's true nature? and how could one encourage the better side to triumph? This question remained at the centre of all his work.

His own experiences seemed to provide an answer. He had

had to face all kinds of hardships in his life; yet remarkable changes in his fortunes had been brought about by the people who had helped or encouraged him, and by the books he had read. Life then was not hopeless; neighbourly co-operation, cultural activities, and above all sheer will-power could help a man to build a new life for himself. The fantastic success of his stories, which brought him national fame in 1898, and an international reputation a year or two later, only confirmed him in these beliefs. Indeed, his own life and writings could in themselves provide a source of inspiration, visible evidence that a man could rise from the lower depths.

Gorky's early stories try to illustrate these ideas. Many of them, *Makar Chudra* (1892), *Old Izergil* (*Starukha Izergil,* 1894) are wildly romantic, with their high-flown language, and their semi-legendary heroes. These stories may seem mere escapism, but the important thing is that the escapism is upward. Men are reminded of their fabulous super-human heritage, and encouraged to emulate their forebears.

But Gorky soon came to see that these stories by themselves could hardly achieve very much, for they would be read not by the illiterate masses who had most need of them, but by a leisured, cultured class in search of literary novelty. Accordingly, he also composed a series of factual accounts of what he himself had seen during his wanderings. The backwardness, the bestiality, the cynical exploitation of the Russian people were sickeningly well-known to the masses of the population who lived through them; they were hardly even guessed at by the bourgeoisie and intelligentsia, who made up the bulk of the reading population. Stories such as *At the Saltmarsh* (*Na soli,* 1893) and *Running the Gauntlet* (*Vyvod,* 1895) were not intended to be read as fiction, but as fact: the latter story ends with the words:

> Это я видел 15 июля 1891 года, в деревне Кандыбовке, Херсонской губернии, Николаевского уезда . . .*[1]

If it is not fact, then the story loses its whole *raison d'être.* The reader is meant to be shocked into action.

In the best stories of this early period, *Chelkash* (1895), and

* I saw this on 15 July 1891, in the village of Kandybovka, in the province of Kherson, in the district of Nikolayev . . .

Twenty-six Men and a Girl (*Dvadtsat shest i odna,* 1898), Gorky succeeds in combining these two contradictory strains. The defiance of the smuggler Chelkash and the pathetic ideals of the twenty-six bakery workers grow naturally out of their surroundings, and provide, if not an escape, then at least a refuge, in which men can retain some shreds of humanity. As a symbol of this life-line, Gorky frequently quotes or describes folk songs, for in them the everyday words are transfigured by the other-worldly, and yet universal beauty of the melody.

But the existence of these two streams in itself raised a problem. If a good book has such a good effect on the reader, does a sordid or depressing book necessarily drag him down? Gorky is continually asking: should a writer try to inspire his readers at the cost of having to fudge the truth? or should he tell the truth at the risk of discouraging his readers and destroying their will to resist? When a hostile critic pointed out that Gorky could hardly complain about the pogroms, since he had contributed to them by putting anti-Semitic sentiments into the mouth of one of his characters, the disreputable cobbler Orlov, Gorky was horrified, and he at once removed the offending passage.[2] He did not think of questioning the validity of this accusation; literature and life could not be separated.

The most notable treatment of this dilemma in Gorky's early work is his play *The Lower Depths* (*Na dne,* 1902). Here Gorky tries to unmask the specious charms of the 'ennobling falsehood', embodied in the plausible comforter, Luka. Luka's advice is shown to lead to disillusionment and suicide. Gorky's position is stated by Satin:

> Ложь — религия рабов и хозяев . . . правда Бог свободного человека.*[3]

Thus the problem is shifted on to a social plane: when society is a better place, then the dilemma will cease to exist.

But Gorky's attempts to discredit Luka cut both ways. For example, Luka assures the dying Anna that she can die happily because there will be no punishment or torments after death. Paradoxically, Anna's response is a willingness to put up with the pain of her illness a bit longer. By this very human, but

* The lie is the religion of the slave and the boss; the truth is the god of the free man.

illogical reaction, Gorky meant to refute Luka, but the paradox is only superficial. Luka's words do not turn Anna against death; on the contrary they succeed admirably in putting her into a state in which she can die happily. Looked at from another angle, Luka is only re-stating Gorky's own materialistic attitude to the after-life; from Gorky's point of view, he is actually telling the truth, and the effect of his words, the reconciliation of Anna to life, is surely a praiseworthy action in any scheme of values. Either way the 'lies and truth' debate in this scene (and the same could be shown in the other scenes too) can be argued in Luka's favour. It is true that in the final act, Satin makes an attempt to define 'truth':

Человек — вот правда! .. Чело-век! Это — великолепно! это звучит гордо!*[4]

But this truth means little more than that man's potentialities are unlimited. Admirable as a statement of faith, Satin's drunken optimism differs from Luka's consoling philosophy only in that it is expressed more vigorously.

The Lower Depths reveals the full extent of Gorky's confusion in the philosophical issues he had raised, and he never again attempted to treat the subject from this angle. Instead he concentrated on the social aspects of the dilemma. For the next ten years his works *Mother* (*Mat,* 1907), *Confession* (*Ispoved,* 1908), *The Town of Okurov* (*Gorodok Okurov,* 1909), *The Life of Matvey Kozhemyakin* (*Zhizn Matveya Kozhemyakina,* 1911), deal with the grisly realities of Tsarist Russia, and contrast it with the ideal of a romantic, revolutionary, sometimes even religious, hero. But these works are generally regarded as inferior to the works he wrote before and after.

This involvement in social and political issues led Gorky to the revolutionary movements, particularly the Bolsheviks (from 1902 onwards), but he never joined any of them. He was finally forced to leave Russia for his activities during the 1905 Revolution, and this only reinforced his revolutionary sympathies. Once abroad he had plenty of opportunities for meeting the leaders; he met Lenin in 1907. But Gorky's humanity and sincerity often made him an infuriating ally, and his relationship with Lenin was marked by periodic storms. These differences

* Man – that is truth! Man – that's splendid! That sounds proud!

of opinion did not prevent him, however, from contributing to Bolshevik funds or from opening the pages of *Chronicle* (*Letopis*), the journal which he started in 1914, soon after his return to Russia, to their writings.

Like most other Russian intellectuals, Gorky welcomed the March Revolution. He opened a newspaper, *Novaya zhizn* (*New Life*); the first issue appeared in the middle of April) and the title was indicative of his attitude to events. He conceived the hope that the intelligentsia might complete its historic mission by taking over the government of Russia. But the revolution began to develop its own momentum. Violence began to increase: there were peasant risings, and a serious risk of democracy collapsing into anarchy. Gorky who had once opposed the war, now began to feel that its continuation was the only way of stabilising a deteriorating situation. While denouncing the ambitions of the military and the Right wing extremists, he saw also the danger to the Provisional Government from the Bolsheviks, and warned against them. When the Bolsheviks' attempted coup of July failed, and the leaders had to flee, he denounced them angrily for this 'setback to the workers' cause'. In November he allowed Zinovyev and Kamenev to betray Lenin's plans for an imminent coup, to the understandable fury of the other Bolsheviks. Stalin's denunciation of him was particularly vicious.

When the Bolsheviks did seize power, Gorky continued to oppose them in the pages of *Novaya zhizn*. He denounced their policy of fomenting class hatred, which, he said, appealed to the same snobbish attitudes that Communism should eradicate. The mass executions and the unscrupulous exploitation of the lives of innocent hostages appalled him. Instead of correcting the abuses of Tsarism, the Communists seemed bent on multiplying them.

Novaya zhizn stood alone in its opposition to the Bolsheviks, as the other publications were gradually silenced. But Gorky's enlightened attitudes, his clear recognition of the threat of extremism from both the Left and the Right wing, weakened the impact of his writings, and prevented *Novaya zhizn* from offering any practical alternative to the Bolsheviks. Various countermeasures were taken against the paper; strikes were organised, threatening letters were written to the editors, some issues were suppressed, and it was finally closed down in July 1918.

Now that all outlets for opposition were closed to him, Gorky decided to co-operate with the new regime. This turn-about was characteristic of him; his ability to change his mind was both his strength and his weakness. Through his articles in *Novaya zhizn* he had hoped to avert anarchy; but now anarchy had come. The country was torn by civil strife; public order and administration had broken down; the atrocities committed by the peasants against their landlords, and even against one another, horrified Gorky, who remembered his own experiences at their hands. His hopes that Western pressures would help to restore moderation had been shattered by the Allied response of military intervention. In this situation the Bolsheviks alone seemed to have the will and the strength to re-impose order. In the name of Russian culture, Gorky was prepared to co-operate with the men he had just been denouncing. His activities for the next three years have already been mentioned.

He does not seem to have felt particularly bitter about his departure from Russia. One of the first works he wrote in exile was the film scenario, *Stepan Razin* (1921–2). Significantly Gorky introduces a poet-minstrel into the rebel camp. Like Gorky, he cannot stomach the deceptions and cruelties of the revolutionaries, but when he is finally turned away by Razin-Lenin, he comes to see that the artist has no right to criticise in times of revolution; he composes a new song:

> Кто людям послужил, тот и Богу послужил,
> А грехи его тяжелые — не нам судить.*[5]

This abdication of responsibility was to be prophetic of Gorky's activities under Stalin.

Gorky continued his cultural activities as best he could in emigration. At first he settled in Germany, like most other Russian *émigrés* at this time. He founded a new periodical, *Beseda* (*Colloquy*), in the hope of inaugurating a dialogue between the two halves of the Russian intelligentsia; but the Communists refused to admit *Beseda* across the frontier. From Germany he

* He who has served men has served God, and as for his grievous sins, they are not for us to judge.

moved to Italy and finally settled in Sorrento. For several years his home there was to become a Mecca for Russian writers. He subscribed to all the Soviet literary periodicals he could, and encouraged budding writers to send him their manuscripts for comment and advice. He read all these works carefully and sympathetically; he answered every letter, and frequently initiated correspondences himself. Among Russian writers, even ones as sophisticated as Pasternak, Gorky's comments were eagerly sought and highly valued. When conditions became easier, many Soviet writers travelled out to Sorrento to spend a summer holiday with him.

Gorky's own writings in these years are various and fascinating. From an artistic point of view they are the richest that he ever produced. The memoirs of Lev Tolstoy and Leonid Andreyev, written in Petrograd at the height of the Civil War, are justly acclaimed. Less well-known are some masterly short stories, and the novel *The Artamonov Business* (*Delo Artamonovykh*, 1924–5), the most compact and unified of his novels. He also began work on a vast fictionalised history of the Russian intelligentsia from the 1870s down to 1917, *The Life of Klim Samgin* (*Zhizn Klima Samgina*, 1925–36), but this is less successful, and was never completed. Most of these works are set entirely in the pre-1917 era; *The Artamonov Business* ends abruptly with the shock of the Revolution. Only in *The Story of a Hero* (*Rasskaz o geroye*, 1923) does Gorky peer briefly into subsequent events.

This concern with the past did not prevent him from following closely all developments within the Soviet Union. He was very disturbed to hear of the application of censorship not just to new literature, but even to such classics as Plato, Kant and Tolstoy (for a time, indeed, he was even tempted to renounce his Russian citizenship as a protest). He was particularly upset by the attacks on *Krasnaya Nov* in 1924 and 1925, when Voronsky was temporarily removed. Gorky supported him by withdrawing all his works from *Krasnaya Nov* until Voronsky was fully re-instated. In this case Gorky's tactic was effective, but other undertakings were not so successful. The journal *Russkiy sovremennik* which he had founded in an attempt to bridge the gap between the generations in contemporary Soviet literature was abruptly closed down after only four issues. One of his closest associates on *World Literature*, A. N. Tikhonov, was sacked in spite of Gorky's protests, and even imprisoned briefly afterwards.

Gorky's influence in these matters was founded on his international reputation. It is the more impressive in that inside the Soviet Union he was still frequently criticised as an *émigré* (the true explanation that he had emigrated for reasons of health, and at Lenin's insistence, was not put out until rather later). Gorky's origins in the petty bourgeoisie were often used to suggest his unsuitability for proletarian readers, and his failure to produce any literature on developments since 1917 was taken as evidence of his alienation from the Revolution. The State Publishing House, which held sole rights in his works inside the Soviet Union, made little attempt to publish them (though there was a clear demand for them), and obstinately ignored Gorky's suggestions that it should grant these rights to other publishers if it was not interested.

The turning-point came with Gorky's memoir of Lenin. This literary tribute, the most impressive from any Russian prose-writer (in it Gorky said that Lenin's death had caused him even more grief than Tolstoy's), was taken up by the Soviet press, and Gorky began to receive more favourable notice; his critics began to play down his bourgeois origins and to emphasise his services to the proletariat instead (Lenin had termed Gorky an 'outstanding representative of proletarian art'[6]). Even so opinions were divided. In January 1924, there was a sensational case of embezzlement in the GUM department store, and the newspaper *Izvestiya* went out of its way to implicate Gorky in the case. (The editor, Steklov, had been sacked by Gorky from *Novaya zhizn* in 1917.) In protest Gorky refused to allow any Soviet periodical, even *Krasnaya Nov* of which he was nominally joint editor, to publish any of his works, even the memoir on Lenin. *Izvestiya* finally withdrew its insinuations in April, and he at once restored publication rights. Even as late as 1927 the critic Veshnev could sum up Gorky's most recent works:

Я хотел доказать, что редчайшие виды уродств, многообразный садизм, патологический эротизм, непостижимые извращенности человеческой природы находят в Горьком, как находили в Достоевском, Розанове и Сологубе, тщательного собирателя, и любовного изобразителя. Кажется, что теперь слово 'человек' вряд ли звучит для Горького 'гордо'.*[7]

In spite of these attacks, Gorky's ties with his country were growing steadily stronger. He was beginning to feel his isolation among the *émigrés*, and he was worried by political trends in Europe, particularly by the rise of Fascism. He was often homesick. In November 1925, *Pravda* invited him to contribute a brief article for the anniversary of the Revolution. Although he did not oblige on this occasion he was coming to identify himself more and more closely with the Soviet Union. In a letter of June 1927, he speaks for the first time of 'our Union',[8] and by the end of the year he had begun to contribute articles to the Soviet press. Even the renewed campaign against Voronsky did not affect his decision now. True, he suspended publication of *The Life of Klim Samgin* in *Krasnaya Nov* in protest, but by October he had succumbed to the appeals of the new editorial board. When Voronsky was finally dismissed in January 1928, he does not seem to have reacted in any way.

The fact that the most universally respected living Russian writer still preferred to remain an *émigré* was a standing reproach to the Communists; a successful visit would be an immense fillip to their prestige. Accordingly, efforts were made to attract him back to the Soviet Union for the tenth anniversary celebrations in November 1927; but he declared that his health was still unsatisfactory, and that he wanted to finish *The Life of Klim Samgin* first. Instead, he contributed an article *Ten Years* (*Desyat let*), in which he spoke of the gigantic strides taken by the Soviet Union in the creation of a new culture. The shortcomings of Soviet life, he said, were insignificant by comparison with the achievements, and could easily be accounted for as survivals from the past. Yet Gorky was still living outside the country; he had no way of judging except from the literature he read and the reports he received. The fact was that he had already decided to return; he wanted to believe in the new Soviet Russia; any facts which spoilt this image, he now began instinctively to minimise. He finally abandoned his hopes of serving as a bridge between the *émigrés* and Soviet intellectuals

* I have tried to show that the most recondite monstrosities, sadism in all its varieties, pathological eroticism, incomprehensible perversities of human nature, find a painstaking collector and loving painter in Gorky, just as they used to in Dostoyevsky, Rozanov and Sologub. The word 'man' hardly seems to sound 'proud' to Gorky nowadays.

with the publication of a scurrilous article *On White Émigré Literature* (*O beloemigrantskoy literature*, 1928). He even admitted his 'errors' of 1917–18, explaining that he had been afraid that the Bolsheviks would be swept away by the anarchic mass of the peasantry. This was not quite what he had said in his articles in *Novaya zhizn*, but the explanation was accepted.

He was unable to return to Russia for the celebrations of his sixtieth birthday, but he was officially greeted that day (29 March) in the press by the Soviet Government as the 'greatest writer and fighter for the cause of the working-class'.[9] He finally came back on 30 May, and the Government leaders, accompanied by a vast crowd of ordinary people, came to the railway-station to meet him. (It is outside this station that his statue stands today in Moscow.) On the following day he made a speech summing up his first impression of the new Russia:

> Что это громадное дело, я вижу на каждой улице, в том человеке, который ходит по Москве другой походкой чем десять лет назад. Я вижу все. Человек мне жалуется, жалуется на то, что начальство затирает глаза, показывает блестящие вещи, что меня обманывают. Жалобы эти я и раньше слыхал. . . . Мне как-то кажется, в чем я почти уверен, что обмануть меня довольно трудно всякими блестящими вещами, если они придуманы, выдуманы, но когда на самом деле блестящие вещи, я это вижу. Если есть темные пятна, я вижу, что это темные пятна.*[10]

He visited the mausoleum of Lenin, and said of the dead leader: 'I loved him as I loved nobody else.'[11]

The chief cause of concern to Gorky was the literary situation. He already knew about the ideological squabbles and unscrupulous manoeuvrings of the various literary groups, but the actual evidence which met him in the Soviet Union saddened him. His attitude to Soviet writers became very much more

* That this is a colossal undertaking I can see on every street, in the man who walks through Moscow with a gait quite different from that of ten years ago. I see everything. One man complains to me that I am being deceived, that the authorities are throwing dust in my eyes by showing me only the brilliant successes. I have heard these complaints before ... but I am pretty sure that I cannot be deceived so easily by brilliant successes if they are spurious or imaginary; but when they really are brilliant successes I can see it. If there are dark patches I can see that they are dark patches.

critical. He was particularly resentful of writers who pointed to the many survivals of Russia's bourgeois past in her revolutionary present. Characteristically, he felt that the publication of such truths risked disheartening those who were genuinely searching for a new world, while providing encouragement to Russia's enemies in the West. He came to the conclusion that if only people knew how much was being done all over Russia, they would gain a much fairer perspective. He therefore founded a new journal, *Nashi dostizheniya* (*Our Achievements*; the first number came out early in 1929), which would record the industrial and cultural re-birth of Russia for the whole world.

In his own articles *Around the Union of Soviets* (*Po soyuzu sovetov*, 1928–9) for the journal Gorky noted some of his impressions from his grand tour of the country. He visited factories where he had once worked as a common labourer, and recorded his amazement at the improvement of working conditions, the development of technology, and the rational and humane use of labour since his time. He even visited the notorious labour camp Solovki, and contrasted the cultural backwardness of the monks, who had once lived there, with the enlightened Soviet programme for rehabilitating criminals; apparently without any irony he admired the fine old Russian folk songs which he heard in the camp, though he could not help noticing that the words were not the traditional ones, but a 'distorted' modern variant. However, he deduced from the men's love of the music that their rehabilitation was progressing satisfactorily.[12]

When Gorky left for Italy in October, he promised to return again in the following spring. The visit had been a great success, and he was to wax enthusiastic about the 'new man' that he had seen. But the spectacle of the squabbling writers had shocked him; the letters of advice, warning and complaint that he had received on his arrival seemed to him to be the work of a carping intelligentsia, more concerned with petty facts than with the grandeur of the whole design. To their complaints that they had been reduced to a 'mechanical existence' he retorted with the article *To the Mechanical Citizens of the USSR* (*Mekhanicheskim grazhdanam SSSR*, 1929), in which he showed himself now completely unsympathetic to their plight; to the *lishentsy* who were deprived of their democratic rights he gave the advice that they should not blame the working people of the Soviet Union for their position, but rather the enemies of the working people[13] (by which presumably he meant themselves). His contempt for the intelligentsia now spread backwards in retrospect to the pre-revolutionary era, and he accused them of 'having sat in prisons before 1917 only because they were hoping to ride on the backs of the working class afterwards'.[14]

His determination to glorify every aspect of contemporary Russia led him into absurd contradictions; he would point to the epidemic of suicides in the West as a sign of its degeneracy and impending collapse, while the similar wave of suicides in the Soviet Union he interpreted as the self-destruction of the bourgeois survivals, and therefore a healthy phenomenon. Of the suicide of Mayakovsky he observed:

> Маяковский сам объяснил, почему он решил умереть. Он объяснил это достаточно определенно. От любви умирают издавна и весьма часто. Вероятно, это делают для того, чтобы причинить неприятность возлюбленной.*[15]

Gorky visited the Soviet Union each year thereafter (except for 1930) for the months of May–October, until 1933 when he finally settled there. He still had hopes of hastening the coming of socialism by his journalistic ventures. As a twin to *Nashi dostizheniya* he founded *Za rubezhom* (*Abroad*; the first issue appeared in June 1930) to publicise the horrors of life in the West and the growth of the revolutionary movement there. He opened a new journal *Literaturnaya ucheba* (*Literary Training*; the first number came out in April 1930) for the benefit of young and inexperienced writers. This had once been the aim of *Krasnaya Nov*, but Gorky did not now think of inviting Voronsky, his former friend and co-editor, to join him in this new venture.

Most of the energies of Gorky's last years were to be devoted to these and other journalistic ventures; but none of them was to satisfy him or create any significant impact on the cultural scene. He was a domineering editor, and the growing irritability of his last years only worsened this fault. The difficulties of trying to edit a Soviet journal from Sorrento were immense,

* Mayakovsky himself explained why he chose to die, and he explained it pretty clearly. People have been dying of love for countless centuries. Probably they do it so as to embarrass their loved ones.

and Gorky's insistence on getting his own way often meant wholesale rejection of articles that his colleagues had accepted, while the time-lag often left the editors in Moscow with no time to replace or rewrite the articles that he had thrown out. On one occasion he rejected almost a whole issue of the journal *Kolkhoznik*.[16] He soon gave up hopes of persuading the established writers to work for his publications, and his disillusionment with them led him to down-grade all imaginative literature, and to advocate instead the documentary sketch. Here he felt that a young writer's weaknesses would be minimised; he would be confronted with facts, and all he had to do was to give them a literary form.

This utilitarian approach to literature now facilitated Gorky's reconciliation with RAPP, which he had previously opposed, and he co-operated with its leader Averbakh in thinking up new schemes.[17] One of the few Soviet books that he praised in the 1930s was *Donbass the Heroic* (*Donbass geroicheskiy*, 1931) and he refused to correct even the grammatical mistakes in the text:

> Книга рабкора Еремеева воспринимается мной не как литература, а как нечто большее — более важное, более активное. Это сырье, из которого со временем будут выработаны прекрасные драмы и романы, это подлинный документ истории, которую создает именно масса.*[18]

Yeremeyev was offered a place at a writers' training college on the strength of this book, but he refused it because he had a more important job to do in the mines. This was the ideal that Gorky now held out to the writers of Russia.

By contrast with the enthusiastic, selfless labour of the workers, Gorky often felt that writers had an unfairly easy life. They were sometimes better paid than doctors, engineers and teachers, and yet, by the irregular and subjective nature of their art, and the haziness of their contribution to the national effort they seemed to be mere parasites:

> чувство социальной ответственности развито у литераторов значительно слабее, чем у других мастеров культуры.†[19]

* For me this book of Yeremeyev is not literature, but something greater, more important and more dynamic . . . This is the raw material out of which beautiful plays and novels will one day be fashioned; this is a true historical document, created by the masses alone.

† The sense of social responsibility is developed very much more feebly in our writers than in our other masters of culture.

and he constantly warns that:

> наш читатель скоро будет культурно и идеологически грамотнее писателя.[20]

Gorky had once seen literature in the vanguard of progress; now it seemed to be lagging far behind.

It is generally believed that Gorky intervened on behalf of several Soviet writers during the 1930s, but the only case so far documented is that of Zamyatin. There is no evidence even of this in Gorky's works, as published, and if we did not know of it from Zamyatin it would be difficult to credit, in view of such comments on *We* as a 'desperately bad book'.[21] Therefore the possibility that Gorky intervened privately on behalf of writers whom he criticised publicly is not to be excluded. Even so his contacts with writers, especially with those who needed help, diminished markedly during the 1930s. Particularly revealing are his correspondences with Voronsky and Zazubrin; up to 1927 he had supported them morally and practically, but after their dismissal and arrest, when they and their families needed all the help they could get, he does not appear to have made any attempt to contact them or to intervene on their behalf. Of the established writers, he seems to have corresponded regularly in his last years only with Fedin; he remained on friendly terms with Prishvin and Vsevolod Ivanov, but some writers such as Babel and Leonov, whom he had encouraged and supported earlier, he now left to their fate. In these years, he must have been aware of the power of his words, yet he frequently singled out writers for abuse, such as Pilnyak, Olesha, Pavel Vasilyev and Smelyakov. When RAPP had been disgraced, he at once attacked the novel *The Driving-Axle* (*Vedushchaya os*, 1932) of Ilyenkov, a leading member of the organisation, on the grounds that it advocated sectarianism,[22] the main charge against RAPP. Although these criticisms were contained in a private letter, it was published in the press just three days after the decision to disband RAPP had been announced.

Meanwhile, he adopted a more orthodox Soviet line on all controversial political matters. He denied the existence of

* Our readers will soon be culturally and ideologically more literate than the writers.

forced-labour camps in Soviet Russia, though in 1918 he had fearlessly denounced the first Bolshevik repressions. In the famine of 1921 he had persuaded the Soviet leaders to let him appeal to the Western powers for help, but he now evaded his friend Romain Rolland's queries about the disastrous famines that had followed collectivisation; he spoke in vague terms of disturbances, a shortage of shoes and cosmetics, and the traditional avarice of the peasant and his envy for the life of the worker.[23] This letter was written from Sorrento, and so it can hardly have been composed with one eye on the Soviet censor. He had once prided himself on being 'a heretic everywhere',[24] but he now inserted frequent references to the Party, 'the one and only altruistic leader of the labouring people'.[25] In 1918 he had rejected the charge of being non-proletarian on the grounds that to boast of proletarian origins was as snobbish as boasting of any other kind, but he now declared:

я всю жизнь чувствовал себя пролетарием, и то что я говорю сейчас, — я говорю, как пролетарий, социалист и революционер.*[26]

The former champion of legality now came out with a denunciation of the accused on the first day of the Prompartiya trial; since he was in Sorrento at the time, the article must have been written considerably earlier than that. He defended the execution without trial of the 48 (they had been accused of organising a famine, i.e. of resisting collectivization) on the grounds that their crimes were too monstrous to be publicised:

Я не знаю мотивов, по которым советская власть не предала суду этих заговорщиков, но я догадываюсь: есть преступления, гнусность которых слишком приятна врагам, и учить врагов гнусностям было бы слишком наивно.†[27]

The lover of literature who had once almost renounced his Soviet citizenship in protest against the censoring of Tolstoy, now opposed the re-publication of Turgenev's famous story

* All my life long I have felt myself a proletarian, and what I say to you today, I say as a proletarian, a socialist and a revolutionary.

† I do not know the reasons why the Soviet authorities did not put these conspirators on trial, but I can guess: there are crimes whose horror would be all too pleasing to our enemies, and to instruct our enemies in these horrors would be too naive.

Bezhin Meadow (*Bezhin lug*) as unfit for modern kolkhozniks;[28] he advised against the publication of the poems of Koltsov because:

по форме они слишком примитивны, а по содержанию совершенно устраняются стихами Никитина, Некрасова. . . . Лирические стоны Кольцова не возбуждают ни гнева, ни ненависти, а нам необходимо воспитывать в молодежи именно ненависть к прошлому, которое, — как мы видим, — буржуазия намерена возвратить и укрепить.*[29]

Gorky's articles are not, of course, his most important works. They are rambling and repetitious. He himself wrote: 'I don't attach any importance to them.'[30] But in the last period of Gorky's life their bulk becomes overwhelming; the articles and speeches of 1929–36 alone fill three large volumes in the thirty-volume set of his collected works. In all this verbiage a few standard themes and examples return again and again: the immense progress of the Soviet Union since 1917, and the corruption of the bourgeois West – homosexualism is explained on the ground that it is cheaper to find a man than a girl,[31] and even contraception is cited as evidence of Western perversion.

It has been suggested that Gorky often did not contribute more than his name to these articles;[32] there is in fact one reference to censorship distortion in a letter of April, 1932:

Очень разрастается интерес к нам среди интеллигентов Европы и Америки, это усиливает, увеличивает и мою корреспонденцию. Пишу — много, а печатают не все, да и то, что печатают — искажают. По этому поводу тоже придется писать.†[33]

It might seem that Gorky is referring to Western attempts to tamper with his writings, but it can hardly be doubted that in such a case he would have protested; throughout this period he showed no hesitation in criticising Western morals. Indeed

* Formally they are too primitive, and in content they have been superseded by the poems of Nikitin and Nekrasov . . . the lyrical moans of Koltsov do not arouse wrath or hatred, and hatred of the past is just what we must inspire in our young people, that past, which, as we see, the bourgeoisie intends to bring back and reinforce.

† Interest in us is growing strongly among the intellectuals of Europe and America, and this has multiplied my correspondence. I write a great deal, but not all of it is printed, and what is printed is distorted. I shall have to write on this topic too.

the very vagueness of the complaint – normally Gorky would give chapter and verse – suggests that he is referring to Soviet censorship, but so far as we know, he did not make any protest. He certainly did not feel strongly enough to withhold publication of his works from the Soviet authorities, although he was abroad at the time and was to spend one more winter in Sorrento before his final return.

In fact the tone of his articles did not change significantly after his return – in the sense that the tone changes in 1927 – and his private letters do not indicate any significant differences of opinion from those expressed publicly. Even allowing for the possibility that a ghost-writer may have touched up Gorky's works, there is no solid ground for doubting that the bulk of his articles and speeches came from his own pen. It is if anything the mistakes and blunders, the blimpishness and long-windedness of these later works that, paradoxically, makes Gorky's authorship more likely. Bertram Wolfe has suggested that he was not responsible for the later revision of the memoir on Lenin:[34] but the evidence would suggest that it was done by Gorky himself during the spring and summer of 1930 which he spent in Sorrento. In August Khalatov wrote to him: 'We have sent your revised manuscript on Ilich [Lenin] to the printer'.[35] Even if Gorky had no hand in the rewriting, his uncomplaining acceptance makes him no less responsible.

It is true that Gorky failed to write any eulogy of Stalin to match his memoir of Lenin, but this does not prove any implied reservations on his part. Even allowing for the possibility that he was not responsible for the adulatory references to Stalin in his articles, several cases can be found even in his private letters; since these were published only in 1955, they are probably genuine enough. The strained relations between Lenin's widow and Stalin were notorious, and it was therefore tactless of Gorky in writing to her on her 65th birthday to congratulate her on having lived into the time of Stalin.[36] To one ordinary Soviet citizen he wrote in 1934:

> А теперь повторю мое пожелание Вам и мужу доброго здоровья и чтоб Вы родили штук шесть хороших сталинцев . . .*[37]

* And now let me repeat my wishes for good health to you and your husband, and that you should give birth to half a dozen good little Stalinites.

In assessing Gorky's last years, we must remember that he was an old man, sick and tired. He suffered from acute arthritic pains, and his bronchial trouble caused him much discomfort. In May 1934 he was severely shaken by the death of his son. It may, therefore, seem harsh to hold his writings and actions against him. But Gorky in these years enjoyed truly fantastic powers and privileges. We are concerned with the way in which he chose to exercise those powers, and the consequences of that choice.

His influence on the development of Soviet literature has been profound. Socialist realism bears many marks of his personality and prejudices. His own extraordinary career had persuaded him that literature can influence life, and it was perhaps understandable that he should have believed that this was its primary function. But the concealment of unpleasant truths on the grounds that they might discourage or even corrupt readers, and might anyway soon cease to be true, was a dangerous principle for Gorky himself to follow; it was disastrous when it was imposed on other writers, whether by Gorky or by the Soviet State. His strong prejudices on the subject of classical Russian literature, notoriously his antipathy to Dostoyevsky and the Symbolist poets, provided unimpeachable authority for the retroactive censorship which he had once denounced. With his elevation to the rank of the 'founder of Soviet literature' and even of 'Socialist realism' all these personal eccentricities were transformed into official dogma, and enforced upon Soviet writers. Even his style and his formal principles were imitated uncritically by countless Soviet authors.

It is customary in the West to criticise such writers as Mayakovsky and Leonov for having prostituted their talents to the requirements of Soviet politics; but for some reason Gorky in his last years is generally regarded as a pathetic victim and dupe, who did what he could. In fact, with his far greater power to influence the course of events, his activities would seem to have been more negative than positive, often actuated by personal bitterness, rather than by his earlier concern for Russian culture. He was undoubtedly exploited by the envious and the malicious. His attacks on Pavel Vasilyev, for example, are now admitted[38] to have been based on false reports; Vasilyev was executed in 1937. There are many other cases. If Gorky, once the great humanist, could use his authority so irresponsibly and so damagingly, he had set a grisly precedent for his less reputable successors. There is little in his record after 1927 of the principles which he had earlier asserted so courageously and obstinately. The fact that Russian literature in the 1930s prostituted itself so abjectly, by comparison with the arts of drama, cinema and music, must largely be laid at Gorky's door.

One of his colleagues tells us that in the summer of 1935 Gorky suddenly admitted to a fear that he had been tricked and trapped;[39] but it must be admitted that he had co-operated perfectly with the trappers. What good is the ennobling lie, if it still remains a lie?

3

The Cultural Scene

The 'great break' of 1928–30 was not confined just to social, political and industrial developments; it was a time when all activities in all fields were finally brought under the control of the State. In the cultural sphere, these changes were achieved by a combination of moral pressures, strong-arm methods and organisational and ideological legerdemain.

The stress on physical effort and achievement, so characteristic of the years of the First Five-year Plan effectively denied the intellectual any recognised place in society. It was a time when the emphasis was all on action; even the word 'objective' acquired strongly pejorative overtones. Where so many were acting out of faith and enthusiasm, the thinkers were out of place, Their way of life seemed provocatively bourgeois, and they were frequently suspected of, and charged with, sabotage. These resentments and suspicions found an outlet in the various show-trials, such as the *Shakhty* case of 1928, and the *Prompartiya* affair of 1930. But these were only the tip of the iceberg. All along the line, the formerly independent associations of artists and intellectuals were either discredited by some kind of smear campaign, disbanded, or simply infiltrated; they were then re-organised under the direct control of the Party.

This can be seen best in the case of philosophy. In the 1920s the disputes between the mechanists and the Deborinites had been finally resolved in favour of the latter's view that dialectical materialism was a science of a higher order than the others. But the triumph of the Deborinites was short-lived. Only two months after the disgrace of the mechanists, Deborin himself was accused of pursuing theory at the expense of practice. He was demoted and compelled to sign confessions which were duly rejected for their 'insincerity'; some of his colleagues were arrested. His place was taken by a man who had graduated in the previous year, but who was of impeccable Party orthodoxy. For philosophy was no longer the concern of the philosophers, whether mechanists or Deborinites, but of the Communist Party and of Stalin, the 'theoretical chief of Soviet Marxism',[1] who were engaged in its practical application. The primacy of politics now had a theoretical justification.

By the end of the 1930s no scholarly work could appear without paying elaborate acknowledgements to the contributions of Stalin to its subject, however remote or abstruse. The task of the intellectuals whether philosophers, scientists or artists, was not just to study the world, but to help 'change' it; in practice this meant to provide confirmation for the wishes and beliefs of the politicians.

This change was accompanied by a re-interpretation of the word 'partiynyy'. In the 1920s the word had indicated a more or less unconscious adherence to the party of one's class. In the 1930s, however, the new emphasis on 'practice' totally altered the meaning and indeed the meaningfulness, of the original idea. It too came to be interpreted in a 'practical', activist way. Any difference of opinion with the Party, however abstract or theoretical, was translated into 'practical' terms and treated as intolerantly as militant counter-revolution. From the Party's point of view, wrong opinions were indistinguishable from wrong actions; while right views were meaningless unless confirmed by right actions.

This new activist interpretation was called 'Leninism', not totally unjustifiably, though it probably went further than he had envisaged. At any rate it took Stalin to put it into effect. Lenin had written in 'Party Organisation and Party Literature':

> Каждый волен писать и говорить все, что ему угодно, без малейших ограничений. Но каждый вольный союз (в том числе партия) волен также прогнать таких членов, которые пользуются фирмой партии для проповеди антипартийных взглядов.*[2]

* Everybody is free to write and say whatever he pleases, without the slightest restriction. But every free association (and that includes the Party) is also free to expel members who use the Party name to propagate anti-Party views.

In the conditions of a one-party State, the implications were ominous. In bourgeois states culture may well reflect the assumptions, prejudices and interests of the dominant class; in the Soviet Union it was now not allowed to do anything else. The controversies of the 1920s, vicious and scholastic as they had often been, were at least discussions between equals; in the 1930s the only categories admitted were 'Party' and 'anti-Party'; there was no third possibility. Politics was all.

This situation led inevitably to the thorough-going exploitation of the arts and sciences for the immediate short-term interests of the ruling elite. The very attempt to break out of the trap of the premature revolution by means of the forcible imposition of 'socialism' has only served to confirm Marx's prophecies of its dangers.

The Intellectuals

The citadel of academic independence in the 1920s had been the Academy of Sciences. In its concern with the humanities and the theoretical sciences, its freedom from censorship, its failure to admit a single Party cell, and its international prestige, it represented a continuing challenge to the ambitions of the Communists.

The campaign against the Academy began in 1927 with the issuance of a new charter. The Academy still retained certain privileges such as the right to elect its members, but the Party recommended that its numbers be increased and assumed the right of nominating candidates for the new vacancies. In the following year the Party unilaterally amended the charter by introducing new Chairs in the social sciences, for which only Marxists were acceptable, thus giving the Party a foot in the door. As a result in 1929, after some feet-dragging by the Academy, more new members were admitted than in all the years since the Revolution put together. The admission of more Party-backed candidates in the next two years left the old Academicians without even a one third representation with which to block unacceptable measures.

With the assurance of a guaranteed majority vote, it became possible for the Communists to move openly. A new charter was introduced, imposing stricter ideological requirements on the scholars, and a censorship on all their publications; even foreign associates of the Academy were required to be in sympathy with the policies of the Communists. In the winter of 1930–1 a series of arrests removed some of the most illustrious Academicians, among them the historians Platonov and Tarle; some were later allowed to return, but others were executed or died in exile. Oldenburg, the Secretary, who during the 1920s had tried to preserve the autonomy of the Academy by co-operation with the Communists (many Academicians had criticised him for conceding too much) was now removed and replaced by a Communist, Volgin, whose arrogance and boorishness became a byword, until he was in turn removed in 1935.

The Party leadership was chiefly concerned to redirect the work of the Academy into channels that contributed positively to the Five-year Plan. Such concepts as 'self-criticism', 'socialist competition' and even 'shock-work' were introduced from other walks of Soviet life. The humanities were now down-graded and given second place to the sciences, and especially to the technological applications of science. Unable any longer to choose its own members, the Academy lost the right even to select its students. The most it could do was to expel the less academic ones who had been foisted upon it and to protect genuine scholars from victimisation.

Finally, when the Academy had been wholly subjugated to the Party's wishes, it was possible to relax; the more co-operative members were richly rewarded with high salaries, luxurious living conditions, and prestige. There was now no more need for the Communist Academy, once intended to supplant it; it was quietly closed down in 1936, and its members were simply transferred to the Academy of Sciences.

The intellectuals were both outmanoeuvred and outgunned, but they put up some resistance. Pavlov had been hostile to the Communists from the first, and he was particularly outspoken at the Party's take-over of the Academy. He used to avoid the Soviet-sponsored Congresses of Physiologists, although in the 1920s he was regularly elected honorary President; in 1930, however, the entire Politbureau of the Communist Party was elected *en bloc* to this post. Yegorov, the mathematician, was openly scornful of dialectical materialism and the harnessing of the sciences to the Five-year Plan, saying that the real saboteurs were those who were imposing a rigid and narrow conformity, not those who were trying to resist it. He was arrested, but his colleagues refused to expel him from their organisation, the Society of Mathematicians; accordingly, it simply ceased to function until after his death in 1931. Some scientists tried to protect themselves by paying lip-service to the Party's commands and pursuing their own studies as best they could; but the Party was only infuriated by this apparent hypocrisy and passive resistance. Faced with a determined and ruthless opponent, there was nothing the scholars could do, except behave with dignity and courage, and in the 1930s this many of them did.

The experiences of the Academy were repeated with variations throughout the academic pyramid. The various scientific societies were first infiltrated and then bullied into submission. It was less difficult and the execution less cynical than in the case of the Academy, inasmuch as in most other institutions the Communists already had a footing. In 1928 all university professors who had been appointed before the Revolution were required to submit to re-examination by their colleagues and students, many of whom were now Party members. In fact, in the majority of cases, they were not seriously challenged, but the precedent was an ominous one.

To meet the lack of technical experts, the universities were required to admit a thousand Communists into their graduate courses in engineering regardless of their lack of previous training. The faculties naturally felt little respect for these uninvited guests, but their numbers were increased in the following years, and unqualified teachers, with good Party records, were introduced to cope. In an attempt to turn out as many as possible, these classes of students were examined and graduated in groups rather than on individual performance. During the First Five-year Plan the student body trebled, and the number of teachers doubled. As at the Academy of Sciences the older generation was submerged in the flood.

In 1932, however, the line suddenly changed; Stalin and Molotov began to advise Communist students to treat scholars with respect; the mere fact that an engineer or an academic was middle-aged did not after all mean that he was necessarily a criminal or a wrecker. The excesses of some enthusiasts were deprecated in fields ranging from engineering to ichthyology. The use of shock-brigade tactics in the sciences was now condemned; academic excellence became once again the chief criterion; the cramming of graduate groups through courses of higher education now gave way to more conventional methods.

At the beginning of 1933 the tables were finally turned. It was now the Communists in higher education who were purged and forced to apply for re-admission. But the academics had learnt their lesson; only a few Communists lost their posts in this way. The Party had established its control of the academic institutions, and it had given clear indications of its determination to maintain this control by any means, including terror. In this situation non-Party experts could be left in charge of university departments reasonably safely, and they could even be allowed to pursue their own subjects in their own way. This was, after all, a more likely method of extracting useful work from them. Thus, though in principle the scholars and scientists seemed to have lost their freedom as effectively as any other group in Soviet society, the scientists, with some exceptions, were in fact able to retain considerable autonomy within the limits imposed. The Party would occasionally remind them of their priorities, as for example in 1937, when *Pravda* chose to denounce 'alien, hostile, diversionist wrecking in astronomy',[3] but on the whole scientists in the less controversial fields, particularly physics and chemistry, were largely left to themselves until after the war.

Certain subjects were particularly vulnerable. Statistics, which had been developing promisingly in the 1920s, ceased to exist as an objective study in the 1930s. In 1930 the Institute of Statistics was closed down; the leading statisticians were arrested soon afterwards; those that survived were employed in cooking rather than collecting the figures. Industrial and agricultural statistics were falsified for propaganda purposes. Social statistics, on the other hand, the figures for crime, illiteracy, venereal disease, and social problems of every kind, were either not collected or suppressed. The job of the statisticians was not merely to be content with the passive recording of information, but to play their part in the dynamic transformation of Soviet reality. The preference for 'ennobling falsehoods' had spread to scientific fact.

Historiography was another casualty. The Soviet Marxist historian Pokrovsky (he had died in 1932), who had treated Western and Tsarist colonialism as equally reprehensible, was suddenly denounced in 1934 as unpatriotic; it was now asserted that some Russian Tsars, notably Peter the Great and Ivan the Terrible, had played a progressive role, in that they had assisted the coming of the proletarian revolution. (In itself this judgment was more consistent with Marx's view of history, but here it was dictated primarily by the need to find a historical basis for the very similar ambitions of Stalin.) This led to a glorification of the colonialist policies of Imperial Russia towards the non-Russian nationalities. It was not particularly difficult for the Russians to adjust to the new line, but it had serious repercussions for the nationalities involved. Inevitably, their national heroes had made their name at the expense of the Russians, while the collaborators were either forgotten or execrated as traitors. In 1937, however, such resistance to the progress of history towards 'socialism in one country' and still more the expression of any sympathy with this resistance was denounced as 'bourgeois nationalism'. The traditions of these nationalities had to be torn up and new ones hastily substituted. Naturally this led to resentment and so to further Russian repressions.

By a curious oversight the linguistic theories of Nikolay Marr were not renounced during the 1930s. An outstanding scholar, particularly in the Caucasian languages, Marr had tried to apply the theories of Marx to linguistics. Since language did not form part of the socio-economic basis of society, he argued that it must therefore belong to the superstructure. It followed that, after any social upheaval or revolution, the language must necessarily be transformed as radically as the society. Marr believed that a new socialist language would emerge in the Soviet Union, a fore-runner of the universal world-language of Communism.

Accordingly Marr was passionately interested in the experimentalism, the neologisms and the dialectalisms of early Soviet literature, in which he discerned the embryo of the new language; in this respect he was utterly opposed to the traditionalists, whether of the October group, or among the *poputchiki* such as Gorky. He envisaged the same processes working themselves out in the non-Russian languages, and so he was a firm supporter of the early altruistic Soviet policies towards the national minorities.

Although established as the leading Soviet authority on linguistics at the time of his death in 1934, Marr thus provided little support for the new colonialist line. However, his negative views on linguistic conservatism were quoted out of context to show that the preservation of the minority languages and their resistance to the incursions of Russian were only a fad of reactionaries, while his views on the future international language of socialism were twisted to suggest that he had always envisaged this role for Russian. It was only at the end of 1950 that Stalin chose to bring linguistic theory into line with practice by his decision that language was a special case, neither basis nor superstructure. Marr's posthumous dictatorship in linguistics was then denounced and rooted out from all texts as ferociously as if he had still been alive.[4]

The deepening isolationism of the Soviet Union affected Soviet science too. In the 1920s the scientists had travelled freely, they could subscribe to Western publications, and contribute articles to them. But with the introduction of terror against them from 1930 onwards, the regime naturally became less confident of their loyalties. In 1933, the distinguished theoretical physicist Gamov refused to return to the Soviet Union. When Petr Kapitsa, the world's leading authority on low-temperature physics, revisited Moscow in 1935 after several years at the Cavendish Laboratories in Cambridge, he was detained and prevented from returning to the West. After 1935 Soviet scientists were prevented from participating in any further international scientific gatherings; they were even criticised for publishing their works abroad.[5] This chauvinism was to be modified during the war, only to re-appear with greater virulence and absurdity afterwards in the period of Zhdanov and Lysenko.

These developments are clearly reflected in the literature of the 1930s. Gorky's play *Somov and Others* (*Somov i drugiye*, 1931), his only play set in the Soviet period, links the bitterness against the intelligentsia characteristic of his last years with the usual charges of sabotage and treachery. More interesting is

Afinogenov's play *Terror* (*Strakh*, 1930), which deals with an ageing scientist (supposed to have been modelled on Pavlov).[6] The hero has been studying the role of external stimuli on human behaviour and comes to the conclusion that eighty per cent of Soviet citizens act primarily out of terror. Believing in the value of objective truth, he is easily tricked by some foreigners into publishing his results; when the counter-revolutionary implications of his action are pointed out to him by a young Communist scientist, he is appalled, and admits that Party guidance is essential in the sciences.

Leonov's novel *Skutarevsky* (1932), later adapted for the stage, depicts a loyal physicist working on the wireless transmission of electricity. He is devoted to the regime since Lenin has personally backed his projects; but he fails to understand that he is surrounded by spies and counterrevolutionaries even within his own family. He regards them as misguided rather than anti-Soviet, and, anyway, he mistakenly fancies that one should be loyal to one's kith and kin. Even when his son is suspected of sabotage Skutarevsky still hesitates to denounce him; only after the boy's suicide and some ideological guidance from a young Communist does he perceive the limitations of his narrowly scientific outlook on life:

> Должно быть, политика делит мир совсем на иные молекулы, чем делим его мы, механисты, так сказать, физики и химики...*[7]

As in *Terror* we see how a good and loyal but apolitical scientist almost falls into the arms of the counterrevolution; political awareness must therefore be the first duty of the intellectuals.

In the concentration of all resources and energies on the Five-year Plans, the accent was entirely on practical applications, not on research. In some cases departments of theoretical physics and chemistry were closed down. The consequences for such subjects as psychology, law and genetic biology were even more far-reaching, and mark a revolution in Soviet thinking which has lasted to the present day.

In the 1920s Pavlov's interpretation of human behaviour as a response to external stimuli had dominated Soviet psychology. But the Party was now applying the science of Marxism to the

* Politics, then, must divide the world into quite different molecules from the ones that we, so to speak mechanists, physicists and chemists divide it into.

reconstruction of the environment in the Five-year Plans. It was calling not for reaction, but for positive action. The emphasis was all on the role of the individual in changing the world, on the ability of man to become master of his fate. If man was susceptible to external stimuli, then these should be, not events in the past, but the goals of the socialist future. (The same assumptions can be seen in Soviet advertising as opposed to the Freudian-based techniques of the West.) The responsibility of the individual, the importance of the will and consciousness were now emphasised. This fundamental reappraisal of man's role in the world was inherent from the first in the premature revolution. Though technically unMarxist, it was Leninist in every sense of the word, and it certainly matched the needs and the mood of the time. It effectively brought psychology into line with current Soviet practice elsewhere. The Freudian concept of the 'unconscious' was now banned altogether. It was sufficient simply to pose the rhetorical question: 'Does the Freudian man meet the demands of the task of socialist construction?'[8]

In the field of law, the persistence of crime and the vast increase in the numbers of prisoners in the labour-camps also required a rethinking of Soviet legal principles. If the environment was being re-planned under the direction of the Party, and by the efforts of countless loyal workers, by the same argument, it was the individual who was guilty of uncooperativeness for any failures or backsliding. The earlier idea of the redeemability of human nature now gave way to a more pessimistic view of man's essential inability to act as a conscientious social being. The idea of punishment replaced the idea of correction; heavy sentences were now imposed for all crimes, and the accent shifted from 'corrective' to 'forced' labour. Pashukanis, the guiding spirit behind the reforms of the 1920s, was arrested (and probably executed), apparently because the sentences he had recommended for the new constitution were unacceptably mild.[9]

The most notorious case of the State's intrusion into the sciences occurred in genetic biology. If in the 1920s Soviet objections to classical genetics had been mainly theoretical, in the 1930s they were more practical. The very idea of genetic processes occurring without the possibility of human intervention now seemed quite intolerable. With the current demand for quick results, Vavilov's painstaking procedures of selection and breeding seemed unacceptably slow; it was even suggested that he was deliberately holding back the development of Soviet agriculture.

Lysenko's theories on the subject were, from the point of view of the Soviet leadership, far more satisfactory in every way. Lysenko assumed that heredity was a natural property of organic matter, and that changes were a product of interaction between the organism and its environment. (This hypothesis had the advantage over classical genetics of providing a kind of dialectical explanation.) If heredity was a property of matter, it followed that these changes could be transmitted hereditarily. To meet the obvious objection that, say, sunburned parents do not produce tanned children, the new school of Soviet biologists posited some kind of ability of the organism to select or reject changes for hereditary transmission. This attribution of free-will to cells of organic matter might seem 'idealistic', but it was an illustration of the pervasive belief in the Soviet Union of the 1930s in the ability of will-power to remake the world. Lysenko accused Vavilov of preaching bourgeois conservatism by his theories, but the social and political fashions of the time were of course very much more obvious in his own work. It is perhaps the clearest example of the wishful thinking inherent, if not in Marxism, then at least in the theory of the premature revolution.

Lysenko's theories seemed to offer the possibility of dramatic improvements in agriculture. He claimed various successes for his own methods; by treating seeds in a particular way, he was able to speed up the germination process, and enable crops to be grown further north, where the growing season is shorter. (This practice, known as vernalisation, has nothing to do with genetics. It had been known to Western farmers since the middle of the nineteenth century; but it had since been discarded because the use of genetics to produce new varieties had obviated the need for it.) By changing the foodstuffs of animals, the soil conditions of plants, and by the use of grafting, he even claimed to be able to change one species into another; in 1950 he was to assert that he had successfully changed wheat into rye. Lysenko's theories, however, were based on a handful of isolated experiments, without any adequate controls; his results have never been confirmed by experimental investigation anywhere outside his laboratories or those of his followers. This was partly due to his scientific incompetence, but chiefly to deliberate falsification.

Throughout the 1930s the pressures mounted against Vavilov; some of his colleagues were arrested, but this made little impact on the outside world. An international Congress of Geneticists was actually scheduled for Moscow in 1937 as a tribute to Vavilov and his associates. At the end of 1936, however, the Russians postponed the Congress indefinitely; when it was re-arranged for Edinburgh in 1939, Vavilov accepted the invitation to take the presidency. But in the event neither he nor any other Soviet geneticist was allowed to attend. He was eventually arrested in 1940 on an expedition to Soviet-occupied Poland, and charged with espionage and plotting to flee to the West. He died in captivity in January 1943. His brother, who had been forced to join in the chorus of denunciation, was later elected to the Presidency of the Academy of Sciences.

The results for Soviet agriculture were particularly harmful, both in the production of grain and the development of livestock. Total disaster seems to have been avoided by local officials ignoring the theories of Lysenko for practical purposes, while being careful to credit his methods with all the successes that they achieved. Lysenko survived the failure of his policies thanks to this tacit co-operation, and also to the liberal use of arrests among those who failed to achieve the desired results; he seems to have been, like General Vlasov, one of the few men that Stalin really trusted. Even when his falsifications were finally admitted in 1956 no legal proceedings were instituted against him; he has retained many of his positions and all of his Stalinist awards. When Zhores Medvedev tried to publicise the facts of the case in 1962, his book was suppressed,[10] and he himself confined in a lunatic asylum. Even in the case of Lysenko's criminal activities, his scientific falsifications, his sabotage of Soviet agriculture, his part in the murder of Soviet scientists, all to further his own career, it is difficult for the Russian Communist Party to face the truth. By its own interference in scientific matters, it is even more to blame than any of the quacks and charlatans that it has fostered.

The politicisation of Soviet life, the tendency to judge all issues, even matters of scientific theory in terms of the crudest black and white, the identification of the wishes and ignorant guesses of political theorists and practitioners with objective truth, led to a denial of the spirit of free enquiry and so to the stultification of intellectual life. While supposedly practice led theory, in practice it was totally determined by the most abstract and artificial theoretical considerations, with absurd and often tragic consequences.

In the humanities, historiography, jurisprudence and social theory, the results were dictated almost wholly by the Party line of the moment. For the scientists, life was slightly easier; forced to concentrate on the practical applications of their knowledge, they were able to live off the theoretical research of earlier years; and, provided they took the precaution of framing their findings in dialectical materialist terminology, they enjoyed considerable freedom. In the case of statistics and genetics, however, ideological and political interference succeeded in destroying established and essential branches of scientific knowledge, both theoretical and practical. The short-term effects for agriculture and administrative planning and decision-making were ruinous. The long-term consequences are just now beginning to emerge in the new spirit of criticism and opposition originating in the modern Soviet scientific community.

Literature

The campaign against the intellectuals led naturally to a sharpening of the attacks on the *poputchiki* of the literary world. This started with a deliberate attempt to discredit two of their leaders, Zamyatin and Pilnyak. They were accused of having published anti-Soviet works in the Western press. Zamyatin's novel *We* had been published in a pirated edition without his knowledge or consent; Pilnyak had had his story *Mahogany* (*Krasnoye derevo*, 1929) published in Berlin, the usual way of securing foreign copyright for a Soviet author. For good measure Erenburg, another prominent *poputchik*, was also accused (rather more justly) of having issued his novel *The Grabber* (*Rvach*, 1924) in two versions, one for Soviet and the other for non-Soviet consumption. Since, however, Erenburg was living in Paris at the time, these charges meant very little and they were soon dropped. But the campaign against Pilnyak and Zamyatin continued: Pilnyak soon capitulated, and undertook to rewrite *Mahogany* in a more satisfactory way; the result was the novel *The Volga Falls into the Caspian Sea* (*Volga vpadayet v kaspiyskoye more*, 1930), but this too was soon banned in the Soviet Union. Zamyatin, however, fought back; he wrote to the press (his letter was printed in *Literaturnaya gazeta*, 7 October 1929) proving his innocence, and protesting against the abuse and misrepresentation to which he had been subjected. Finally, he protested directly to Stalin, and, after the intercession of Gorky, he was allowed to emigrate. As for Pilnyak, he was to remain under suspicion for the rest of his life. For all his attempts to prove his loyalty, nothing succeeded; he was finally arrested, and executed, probably in 1938.[11] Erenburg on the other hand, survived into the Khrushchev era to become one of the grand old men of Soviet literature.

The campaign was clumsily handled, but the Soviet authorities had made their point. They had aimed to shake the prestige of two of the most prominent *poputchiki*, and they had succeeded. One writer had surrendered and another had fled to the West. Even if this did not affect their literary achievements, it had at least discredited them politically. For the next four years, writers, like scholars and scientists, were subject to continuous intimidation, both physical and moral, from the RAPP-dominated Federation of Organisations of Soviet Writers.

In keeping with the currect subjection of theory to practice, the writers too were now bound by the requirements of the Five-year Plan. If literary production by itself was hardly of the same practical value as manual labour or applied science, it could nevertheless be harnessed for propaganda purposes. Literary accounts of industrial achievements in one area could set the pace or provide incentives for workers in another; by describing the proletarian paradise on the other side, they could help to reconcile the man in the street to overwork and poor living conditions in the present. At the same time the picture of unrelieved triumph along the industrial front could serve as a valuable advertisement for the Soviet Union in the eyes of her well-wishers abroad. Like the workers, the writers also had a part to play in helping to change, or 'remake' life; literature too could fulfil the Marxist ideal.

The writers were in fact treated in the same sort of way as the other sectors of the economy; mass-production and the head-on assault seemed to be guarantees of success in literary as in industrial production. Accordingly, they were organised into small groups or 'brigades' (usually designed to cut across the previous literary groupings), and sent to study all sorts of enterprises: industrial, such as Magnitostroy; military, such as the exercises of the Baltic Fleet; or social, such as the construction of the White Sea Canal by corrective labour teams.

For the writers the choice was not simply between artistic integrity and compromise. In retrospect they may seem to have sold out all too easily, but at the time their co-operation was not unreasonable. They were aware of the gulf that still separated them from the masses, and they welcomed this opportunity of seeing their country's achievements for themselves; the socialist ideal of intellectuals and workers mutually inspiring and sustaining one another seemed to be almost within reach. Even the demand for propaganda rather than literature did not seem so reprehensible in the years after 1928, when the rigours of collectivisation were threatening to spark off another civil war, and the headlong drive to industrialise the country was antagonising many of the workers. To insist on one's artistic independence when Communism itself seemed to be at stake would have required extraordinary courage in the overheated atmosphere of the times.

The books devoted to the First Five-year Plan represent the first response to a compulsory 'social commission'. E. J. Brown, in his study of the period, has called it 'the proletarian episode in Russian literature', but this is misleading insofar as it suggests a revival of the Proletkult and its ideas. True, the titles of the novels, *Energiya* (1930), *Magnitogorsk* (1930), *Gidrotsentral* (1931), *The Great Conveyer Belt* (*Bolshoy konveyer*, 1931), *The Driving Axle* (*Vedushchaya os*, 1932) sound as proletarian as *Cement* and *The Blast Furnace*; but the aims and assumptions of this new literature are different. In the early 1920s the practical motivation was coloured by a sense of romance; the victorious class, the international proletariat, was about to enter into its birthright. At the end of the decade, by contrast, industrialisation had become the declared priority of the ruling party of a single country; it was tied to the prestige of the Communist Party and of Soviet Russia. The revolutionary overtones are replaced by more nationalistic, even loyalist, sentiments. The power generated by a factory moving into full production frequently serves as an image of Russia moving into the front rank of modern powers.

The new virtues are not those of the classless or proletarian Utopia, but those of the Party bosses, fulfilment of the Plan, and obedience to the Party's commands. The new heroes are usually managers and Party commissars. The action shifts from the shop floor to the committee rooms; from manual labour to political and administrative problems. In the works of the Proletkult man and machines had conducted an ecstatic love-affair. During the Five-year Plan, however, machines were seen as objects to be exploited and discarded as soon as they had served their purpose.

The plots of these novels are very similar. They are constructed around an allotted task, such as building a new factory, overfulfilling a target, or breaking an industrial record. The action takes place on the site or factory where the heroes live and have their being. Personal lives are secondary, and are sometimes ignored altogether. Most characteristics that cannot be harnessed to the task of raising productivity are regarded as weaknesses, and take the place of moral vices in conventional novels. Even love has to play its part; the girls are usually dressed in boiler-suits and are handy with pick-axes. Love scenes, if any, take place in the office or on the shop floor, and they are depicted not as distractions from work, but stimulating industrial competition between the sexes.

Love, however, is in some cases a source of conflict, as, for example, where the hero falls in love with an unsuitable heroine. In the Proletkult novels, the problem had been solved by the class allegiances of the characters involved; now the decisive factor is age. The young people usually rise to the occasion (Safonov in Erenburg's *The Second Day* (*Den vtoroy*, 1932), is an exception), by rejecting the bourgeois or suspect partner. The old are less successful; they are still blinkered by their bourgeois indoctrination and prejudices; but their failure is not too serious because they will soon be dead. Solutions vary with the middle-aged, who often provide the main interest in these books;

predictably they vacillate, but there can be no neutrality; by the end they are either unmasked as saboteurs, or else throw in their lot with the Communists. In such cases the usual criterion is usually the usefulness of the hero's speciality to the industrial effort.

The novels end in triumph: the building is completed, the plan overfulfilled, or the record broken. Nor has there ever been any doubt; for the moral of these books is that history, in the form of the young heroes and general success, is with the Communist Party. Failure is therefore out of the question. A disappointing result or even excessive difficulties encountered on the way to success could be interpreted as a discouragement rather than as an inspiration or incentive. In the crisis atmosphere of the Five-year Plan such discouragement was easy to identify with pessimism; pessimism with defeatism; defeatism with subversion; and subversion with treason. Most writers preferred to moderate the conflicts of their works rather than run any risk of this slippery slope. After all too weak a conflict could produce nothing more damaging than a bad novel.

In general Soviet authors chose to depict two types of conflict. In its cruder forms the opposition could come from saboteurs or foreign agents. This solution had the advantage of appealing to popular sentiments, which naturally grudged the bourgeois technical experts their high salaries and comfortable living conditions. It carried the useful moral too that ordinary Russians should be suspicious of having any dealings with foreigners. But it was not easy to devise a plot which would both create tension and not incur the charge of defeatism. Most authors settled for grotesquely stagey villains, bordering on the comic, such as Polovtsev in Sholokhov's *Virgin Soil Upturned* (*Podnyataya tselina*, 1931).

Alternatively, the opposition could be assigned to the natural elements in the form of gales, floods or extreme cold. This provided an opportunity for showing the heroism and endurance of Soviet workers, but again at the risk of overdoing the setbacks. From the artist's point of view, however, this struggle with the natural elements could serve as an image for the conflict within man, and so as a device for introducing psychology into an otherwise flat range of characters. Since the creation of a new Soviet man was supposed to be one of the by-products of industrialisation, a certain amount of psychological development was justifiable, although the critics usually treated it with scepticism. Bruno Yasensky called his novel *Man Changes his Skin* (*Chelovek menyayet kozhu*, 1932), and Leonov's *The River Sot* (*Sot*, 1930) ends with the words:

Изменялся лик Соти, и люди переменялсь на ней.*[12]

(In later editions the words were made even more emphatic: '. . . the people there *had* changed'.)[13]

The literature of this period contains no masterpieces, but it can boast several ingenious and readable novels. Though, significantly, the better works came not from proletarians or even from Party loyalists, but from the former *poputchiki*. Within the limitations imposed by their subject matter they contrived to show considerable variety of technique and formal approach; they turned their minds to the problem of incorporating technical descriptions into their fiction conscientiously, and though they did not always master their material completely they at least did their best to make it intelligible to the layman.

The skills that they had acquired during the 1920s stood them in good stead in the changed conditions now prevailing. In the NEP period they had been interested in the subtleties and paradoxes of human behaviour; but now individualism was discountenanced and the collective mentality was advocated in its stead; the man of action replaced the man of conscience or reflection. Moral problems and spiritual development gave place to material achievements; the intellectual heroes of the previous decade became the disillusioned misfits and saboteurs of the Five-year Plan, and, after one or two psychological twists, to keep the author's hand in, they were usually dispatched without sympathy (though Erenburg later declared that his Volodya Safonov was the true hero of *The Second Day*).[14] But it was still the *poputchiki*, not the proletarians, who were best equipped to turn these themes into literature. The period of the Five-year Plan effectively resolved the dilemma of the premature revolution: how does a socialist-proletarian culture supplant its bourgeois predecessor? The *poputchiki* had accepted the challenge of socialist themes, and the other writers were now left to fend for themselves – or become critics. As in the scholarly world,

* The face of the Sot was changing, and the people too were changing.

so in the arts, the Party had got its way; the screws could be relaxed.

The RAPP era in Soviet literature was brought to an end abruptly. On 23 April 1932, a *Pravda* editorial accused the RAPP leadership of having abused their position for factional interests; they were charged with having advocated a proletarian culture, just when Soviet society was entering the classless socialist stage; the literature which they had dictated was called illiterate. The RAPP leaders had indeed been intolerant and dictatorial, but there was an ominous note in the way in which *Pravda* assumed that literary standards justified political action. At the time, however, this was largely ignored in the general euphoria with which creative artists welcomed the decision.

The aftermath of the RAPP affair shows clearly that the whole campaign was engineered by the Party. Under RAPP the *poputchiki* writers had been cowed and conned into submission. The Party was now able to step in and pose as their liberator. But the apparatus of power in the literary world was not altered in any way; indeed many of the RAPP leaders were back in print before the end of the year. Even if there was a certain satisfaction in seeing RAPP now being harried with its own tactics, it can hardly have reassured the more thoughtful writers who were simply hoping for a period of greater cultural freedom.

There ensued a comparatively liberal period, which culminated in the Congress of Soviet Writers, from 18 August to 1 September 1934. The immediate purpose of this Congress was the formal inauguration of the Union of Soviet Writers, now purged of its 'undesirable' elements, the ratification of the Code of the Union, and the installation of Maksim Gorky as its first President. But it was much more than a purely literary occasion. Sailors, collective farmers, students, miners and factory workers all spoke from the platform. Prominent politicians such as Bukharin and Radek spoke on the importance which the Party attached to literature, and the demands that socialism made on the Soviet writer. Foreign guests, such as Louis Aragon and André Malraux, gave the proceedings their blessing; Bernard Shaw sent his good wishes.

Such an occasion was hardly the time for a discussion of

the real issues confronting Soviet literature, and most writers contented themselves with expressions of loyalty and gratitude for the assistance they had received, and for the creation of a literate reading public far wider than their predecessors had dreamed of. They took good resolutions to make their works more generally accessible, to bear the interests of the masses in mind, to be conscious of their duties to new readers, and they all affirmed their devotion to the new ideals of socialism. Even such sophisticated writers as Babel, Olesha and Pasternak spoke, no doubt sincerely, of their desire to play their part. They pointed out that artists naturally wished to contribute something to society, and to feel that they were read and appreciated, but they warned too that they should be wary of surrendering their own individual visions and style in the process. Artists were bound to experiment and to make mistakes, and they asked for the Party's tolerance in such cases. They appreciated the Party's desire to encourage Soviet culture, but they asked that the Party should not dictate content and method as it had done in the recent past.

At the time, these speeches may well have represented realistic hopes, but in retrospect, they seem tragically prophetic. So many of the speakers at the Congress, writers, politicians and ordinary working-folk were to disappear from Soviet life during the next five years that even the book containing the proceedings was later suppressed – like the records of the Seventeenth Party Congress. Nothing came of the undertaking to hold a Congress every three years; the next one did not take place until after Stalin's death. The most durable product of the occasion proved to be the doctrine of socialist realism, which was formally accepted as the method of Soviet literature, and which is still officially prescribed for all Soviet writers.

The NEP and the First Five-year Plan had failed to evolve a socialist culture; it would therefore have to be created by an effort of will. Hence the call for '*partiynost*', in its new meaning, in literature too. If the scholars were under pressure to produce the required results, the artists could hardly hope to escape; socialist realism was the formula for the creative arts. The word 'socialist' reflected this new activist, Party-directed attitude; it was both a prescription for the artist, and a criterion for the critic in evaluating the extent to which a work of art contributed to the establishment and consolidation of socialism in one country.

The other half of the phrase, 'realism', has a rather longer history. Engels had regarded realism as the highest stage in the development of art; largely because it seemed to provide the nearest artistic equivalent to the scientific method. But the term is also strongly coloured by traditional Russian aesthetic thinking.[15] In the nineteenth century such social critics as Belinsky, Chernyshevsky and Dobrolyubov had used the medium of literary criticism as a device for circumventing the Tsarist censorship. They had assumed that contemporary literature was a mirror of Russian society, and so, by criticising the social reality depicted in fiction, they expressed their dissatisfaction with the state of contemporary Russia, and their hopes for a new type of socialist, rational man, the 'positive hero', who would change it. Thus the central concept in their criticism was 'realism', for if literature was not a mirror of society, then the crucial step from literary to social criticism was lacking and the whole argument fell to the ground. As a result 'realism' as a term of literary criticism in Russia came to mean not merely the objective depiction of reality, but a critical attitude towards it. This helps to explain why Russian critics have often described as 'realistic' works which non-Russian critics would call 'grotesque', 'symbolic', or even 'fantastic'. This special view of realism is so characteristic of Russian criticism that it was not until the Soviet period that it was defined as 'critical realism' to distinguish it from the new 'socialist realism'. In both cases realism is defined not in terms of *method*, but of *content*.

Socialist realism was introduced at the Congress by Zhdanov, Stalin's spokesman for cultural matters. His speech was confused but the following passage from it is generally considered by Soviet and Western commentators to contain the heart of the matter.

Это значит, во-первых, знать жизнь, чтобы уметь ее правдиво изобразить в художественных произведениях, изобразить не схоластически, не мертво, не просто как 'объективную реальность', а изобразить действительность в ее революционном развитии. При этом правдивость и историческая конкретность художественного изображения должны сочетаться с задачей идейной переделки и воспитания трудящихся в духе социализма. Такой метод художественной литературы и литературной критики есть то, что мы называем методом социалистического реализма.*[16]

These definitions only carry the traditional Russian confusion over 'realism' a stage further. Socialist realism claims to be both a 'scientific' account of the real world, and a partisan statement of how it is changing and how these changes might be accelerated. Socialist realism too is a child of the premature Marxist revolution.

The ideal of recording society in the process of change, whether one calls it the dialectic, or 'revolutionary development', or just 'social realism', is one to which most novelists, whatever their political sympathies, probably aspire. The peculiar feature of *socialist* realism in the Soviet Union lies in the involvement of the ruling Communist Party in the realisation of this prescription. The ideals of the Russian radicals of the nineteenth century, and of the October critics of the 1920s: clarity of form and style, sharp distinctions between good and bad characters, the optimistic ending and the creation of a model 'positive' hero, were now no longer prompted by the particular vision of an individual artist, or by the requirements of mass-accessibility, but by the Party's demand for the writer's active co-operation in executing its policies. As Blok had warned, the voices of Belinsky and Benkendorf were no longer opposed to one another, but in alliance, with no possibility of manoeuvre between the two.

This doctrinaire view of art effectively prevented the writer from writing truthfully about the present or imaginatively about the future. In practice, therefore, socialist realism worked out as glossy propaganda for the present state of affairs, as if it were immutably fixed. Instead of tracing the painful process of the dialectic at work, writers were required to assert the stability of the *status quo*. But since even the *status quo*, as presented in these books, had little existence in reality, no dialectic or revolutionary development could possibly emerge. Far from establishing dialectical truths about the progress of Soviet

* This means, firstly, knowing life, so as to be able to represent it faithfully in works of art, to represent it not scholastically, not lifelessly, not just as mere 'objective reality', but to represent reality in its revolutionary development. At the same time, the truth and historical concreteness of artistic representation must be combined with the task of ideological re-making and education of labouring people in the spirit of socialism. This is the method of literature and literary criticism that we call the method of socialist realism.

society towards Communism, writers were simply condemned to retail falsehoods about the contemporary scene.

Socialist realism is thus defined in theory and in practice entirely in terms of content; it was argued, logically enough, that the new content of Soviet art would in time generate its own forms. But in practice, the freedom to innovate and experiment with new forms was limited by the ban on 'formalism'. This meant that writers were condemned to remain within the forms and techniques of the nineteenth century, which had become so familiar that they were not felt to be 'forms' at all; anything more recent was dismissed as 'decadent', 'modernist', or 'formalist' (the terms were deliberately confused). This instinctive orientation by the past is confirmed by the fact that, although most works of Soviet fiction since 1934 are socialist realist in intention, remarkably few have been claimed as models of the method. Apart from the best known of them, Sholokhov's *Quiet Don* (which in fact defies some of the basic requirements), Soviet critics are usually happier with works written before 1934, such as Gorky's *Mother* (1907), the post-revolutionary poems of Mayakovsky, and Fadeyev's *The Rout* (1927). The Soviet writer is not only required to depict 'reality in its revolutionary development', but to do so within the conventions of literary styles and genres established long before socialist realism was ever thought of.

Although socialist realism makes certain demands of the writer, it makes none of the critics. The consequence was to give the critics almost unlimited power, for when a writer is a State employee, even purely literary faults can be construed, if so desired, in a political way. The distinction between literary criticism and Party discipline disappeared. The critic assumed the role of an inquisitor scrutinising the work of his inferiors for heresy; many critics were no better than informers. Perhaps, as Blok had suggested, bureaucrats are naturally hostile to art.

The establishment of socialist realism as the method of Soviet literature was paralleled by the monopoly now given to the Union of Soviet writers, a body which, through political appointments to the various committees, and the existence of a vigilant censorship, remained totally subservient to the decisions of the central government. The possibility of any literary organisation or indeed literature appearing independently of the Union of Soviet Writers was now excluded. For writers who conformed the rewards were tempting; there were Government subsidies and Government housing, and the massive resources of the State Publishing House. The writers were paid, as in the nineteenth century, by bulk; the size of the editions was fixed, not by popular demand, but by a political decision. This meant that while certain writers could not be published at all, or only in strictly limited editions, others enjoyed the profits and prestige of large editions and frequent re-issues regardless of sales or literary merit.

All these features conspired to make the literature of socialist realism conservative to the point of reaction. Artists were given every incentive *not* to innovate. The privileges which they enjoyed, and the appalling consequences of a fall from grace, made them unwilling to take any risks which might endanger their position. Inevitably, too, their official status imposed bureaucratic mannerisms and intonations upon their writing. Both in form and in content, they followed established models. Far from creating a new socialist culture, the system served only to encourage shoddy workmanship, and a cynical indifference to real issues and unvarnished truths. It led inevitably to the creation of a cultural elite as morally compromised as the political leaders, and with the same vested interests in the perpetuation of the *status quo*.

Two novels that came out soon after the official promulgation of socialist realism may be seen as different responses to the problems it posed. Although Nikolay Ostrovsky's *How the Steel was Tempered* (*Kak zakalyalas stal*, 1934) was completed before the Congress of Soviet Writers, it is one of the few Soviet works that genuinely merits the description of socialist realist. (It was begun in 1932, about the time when socialist realism was first being discussed.) *How the Steel was Tempered* has become the most popular of all Soviet novels, and one of the most influential; some forty million copies have been printed, and it is even studied in schools. The novel is a thinly disguised autobiography in which Ostrovsky appears under the name of Pavel Korchagin; it is his steel that is tempered in the course of the book. His life is a model of Communist devotion; as a boy he fights in the Civil War, and he is one of the first to join the Komsomol when it is founded; then he serves in the Cheka and the frontier guards, two of the most unpopular wings of the Soviet armed forces. Nothing is allowed to interfere with his ideal of service to the Party. He rejects his first girlfriend because she is of bourgeois parentage, and when he later falls in love with a Communist girl they agree to postpone life together until the world revolution has been successfully completed. But eventually the years of deprivation, self-denial and overwork take their toll; Korchagin's various ailments culminate in general paralysis and blindness. Even so, he continues his Party work to the very end. He studies *Das Kapital* which he had not had time to read before, he helps to train young members of the Komsomol from his deathbed, and finally he passes on his experiences to posterity by dictating his autobiography.

To the uncommitted observer Korchagin is likely to appear as a prig and a fanatic. He is never prey to any doubts, he is never confronted by any dilemmas, and he is never at a loss for an answer. His advice is always taken and it invariably proves to be right. Reality is shown from the angle of a man for whom the Communist goal justifies all means, which is a plausibly Leninist interpretation of 'revolutionary development'. At the same time *How the Steel was Tempered* provides an answer to the most difficult problem posed by socialist realism, namely how to present a hero who is both realistic and a paragon of Communist virtue, without him ceasing to be a credible character. Korchagin really does embody both extremes; in conventional fiction his conduct might well be incredible (though it is usually termed 'typical' by Soviet critics), but this objection is irrelevant in face of the transparently autobiographical nature of the book. This naive overlap of two genres, fiction and autobiography, not only contributes to the total effect, but actually founds a new form, which by the nature of the case can hardly be imitated. Finally, no Soviet book has done so much towards the re-making of life; Korchagin's cult of stamina and willpower, the suppression of all individuality in the name of the Party, were to set a life-style for countless thousands of young Communists.

Leonov's *The Road to Ocean* (*Doroga na okean*, 1935) which came out in the following year displays several superficial parallels with *How the Steel was Tempered*. In both novels the hero is a Party member working on the railways, and in both the hero finally dies; but there is a world of sophistication between them. Leonov's Kurilov begins as a conventional Soviet hero: he is a commissar; he has fought in the Civil War, and he represents an ideal synthesis of brain and brawn, 'the shoulders of a stevedore and the brow of a Socrates'.[17] But it soon transpires that he is suffering from cancer of the liver; he is a sick man, and he finally dies after an unsuccessful operation, having completed none of the tasks that confronted him in the opening pages.

Such a plot is unique in Soviet fiction, where Communists are customarily shown in action, invincible and indefatigable. By emphasising this unusual course of events, Leonov raises much deeper issues. On the philosophical and aesthetic level he questions whether socialist realism is compatible with tragedy. More particularly, he asks how Communism accounts for accidental illness and death; in the work-oriented society of Soviet Russia what happens to a Communist who is unable to work? does he become useless and expendable, or is he just to be pensioned off in recognition of past services? Such solutions are all unsatisfactory for they show Communism entirely in terms of its demands on men, and giving them nothing in return. Communism can hardly be content to offer them less than the religions and creeds it claims to have superseded.

Leonov's solution is to show the deepening humanity of his hero. Like Korchagin, Kurilov is suddenly presented for the first time in his life with unlimited leisure; but unlike Korchagin he spends it on an idyllic holiday with a girlfriend in a sanatorium. He begins to enjoy himself talking, drinking, and finally falls in love. The humanisation of a political machine is in itself, of course, not socialist realism, but Leonov tries to suggest an extra dimension to Kurilov by excursions into the atrocious capitalist past and the distant Utopian city of Ocean. Kurilov still carries the germs of the past within him in the form of his cancer (caused by torture in the Civil War), but he also bears within him the seeds of the future; the excursions into Ocean are realisations of his dreams, visions of a future to which he already belongs. He 'was like a bridge and people crossed over him into the future.'[18] Leonov has attempted to answer the same problems as Ostrovsky, but by more literary means. His Kurilov is described realistically, and he is measured against an ideal seen in philosophical terms, though its attainment is none the less assured. But where Ostrovsky aspires to the state of 'steel', the Soviet ideal of the 1930s, Leonov has tried to imagine the oceanic fluidity and fullness of the Communist man foreseen by Marx.

Leonov's intellectual response, fascinating though it is, does not carry complete conviction; the tone falters painfully in the trips into the future, and the central figure of Kurilov never attains the stature that Leonov intended. But it has a good claim to be considered the most ambitious and serious Soviet novel of the Stalin period. Unfortunately, in the atmosphere of 1936 *The Road to Ocean* was not appreciated. After favourable comment on the early chapters, critical opinion turned against the novel, and within a year of its first appearance it was virtually suppressed. It was naturally compared with *How the Steel was Tempered* and one critic neatly summed up the principles of socialist realism as applied in practice, when he remarked that no doubt Leonov's novel was superior in purely *literary* merit, but that this was quite different from *artistic* merit.[19]

The triumph of *How the Steel was Tempered* and the discomfiture of *The Road to Ocean* were symptomatic of a new stage in Soviet literature. With the outbreak of the great purges, the situation of the Soviet writer became intolerable. It is still not known how many writers disappeared in these years; in 1956 some six hundred were posthumously rehabilitated, but even this number was far from complete.[20] It was clearly impossible to deal realistically with the contemporary situation – in 1937 *Novyy mir* did not even print the usual index to the year's contents in its December issue – too many of the contributors were now un-persons. Social questions disappeared from literature completely; they were far too dangerous to be risked. Within two years the doctrine of socialist realism had led to a total separation of art from life.

Some genres were particularly affected by socialist realism. For example, satire could hardly flourish if it was required to be affirmative. Theoretically, writers could condemn the evils of bourgeois societies, or mock the shortcomings of Soviet life (once they had been officially recognised and denounced), and balance this negative tone with a demonstration of the progress made in the Soviet Union and the wisdom of the Communist

Party. But this is hardly satire: satire only really bites when the author is ahead of his time and is prepared to question accepted values; in the conditions of the late 1930s no Soviet author could afford to do this. Only in the plays of Yevgeniy Shvarts, *The Shadow* (*Ten,* 1934), *The Naked King* (*Golyy korol*, 1940) and *The Dragon* (*Drakon,* 1943), are the absurdities of Soviet Russia mocked. Ostensibly satires on Nazi Germany, these plays contain countless reminders of Stalin's Russia, the megalomania of the leaders, the sycophancy of their entourage, the banning of books, the persecution of gypsies, etc. Paradoxically the very enormity of this parallel was enough to deter the censors from acting, for even to see such a similarity was dangerous.

On the other hand, the historical novel came into its own in these years. In many ways it is the logical culmination of socialist realism. The present and the future had become too dangerous to handle; but the new patriotic line in historiography seemed one of the few likely permanencies in a very impermanent world. The great names of the past, Tsars, poets, generals and rebels all provided tailor-made 'positive heroes'. The correct interpretation was already available in the new history books, and the writer needed to do little more than put a literary veneer on the top.

Translation attracted many poets. It offered a way of keeping one's hand in, while avoiding the obvious dangers of expressing one's own thoughts in one's own name. In this respect the translators were reviving a classical Russian tradition. The standard of Russian translations, already high in the nineteenth century, was raised to new heights in the Soviet period – perhaps Lozinsky's translation of *The Divine Comedy* is outstanding – but gifted poets, Akhmatova, Aseyev, Martynov, Pasternak, Tikhonov, Zabolotsky and many others generously bestowed on foreign poetry the gifts they could not use at home.

Other writers turned to scholarly work. The high standard of such studies in the 1930s owes much to the peculiar circumstances of the time. There was naturally a certain selectivity in this approach – Dostoyevsky, for example, was virtually ignored – and the interpretations were frequently tendentious. For the most part, such scholarship was confined to work on the distant past, the eighteenth century or the age of Pushkin, but there were also published valuable studies of the symbolists, and the year 1940 was remarkable for new editions of Khlebnikov's works and Bely's correspondence.

Some Soviet writers turned to children's literature, a genre which had been encouraged from the beginning by the Soviet regime, for its importance in education. Here too they were continuing a distinguished pre-revolutionary tradition, to which most of the Russian classics had contributed. Even so the standards of Soviet children's literature have always been high, and the names of Chukovsky and Marshak are justly famous. The attractions of telling a good story with a minimum of ideological stuffing naturally attracted such sophisticated story-tellers as Veniamin Kaverin, the author of *Two Captains* (*Dva kapitana*, 1938–44) and Valentin Katayev with his *A Lone White Sail* (*Beleyet parus odinokiy*, 1936).

Socialist realism was imposed in varying degrees on the other arts. In painting and sculpture, the combination of academic representation and propagandist moral proved fatally easy to apply and evaluate. Paintings and busts of Party functionaries, groups of happy workers and peasants, and, in Solzhenitsyn's phrase, 'realistic fifteen-foot-high portraits of Stalin',[21] sprang up like mushrooms. In music, an attempt to impose the doctrine was begun with the attacks on Shostakovich's opera *Lady Macbeth of Mtsensk* (*Ledi Makbet Mtsenskogo uyezda*, now revised as *Katerina Ismaylova*); in its place Dzerzhinsky's opera *The Quiet Don* (*Tikhiy Don*, based on Sholokhov's novel), consisting of a string of folk-type melodies, was temporarily held up as the model for Soviet composers to emulate. At the end of 1937, however, Shostakovich returned to favour with his Fifth Symphony, and this won Soviet composers a breathing space until 1948, when a new round of decrees reduced them to the level of their colleagues in painting and sculpture. In these ten years, however, Shostakovich's piano quintet and Eighth Symphony, Prokofyev's Sixth, Seventh and Eighth piano sonatas, and Sixth Symphony succeeded in gaining a world-wide reputation before being banned in their own country.

The spell of the late 1930s was broken by the cataclysmic experience of the German invasion.

Pasternak described it thus in *Doctor Zhivago:*

И когда возгорелась война, ее реальные ужасы, реальная опасность и угроза реальной смерти были благом по сравнению с бесчеловечным владычеством выдумки, и несли облегчение, потому что ограничивали колдовскую силу мертвой буквы.*[22]

The repetition of the word 'real' is the key to the passage. This was no time for bogus villains and problems, but for real people, and real responses to real situations. There was no need to construct the artificial virtues of the 'positive hero', when so many ordinary Russians, and not just Party members, were fighting heroically and selflessly. After all the trumpetings of Soviet unity in previous years the literature of the war-period demonstrates it far more convincingly, by never pointing it out – it could be taken for granted.

Ironically, the power of the censorship was relaxed once the war had started. Soviet writers were given virtually a free hand in their treatment of the war; they were even exempted from military service; the older ones were evacuated to safety in the Urals or Central Asia. Many writers, most notably Simonov and Tvardovsky, did of course serve in the army; of the older writers many became war correspondents – Erenburg and Aleksey Tolstoy, in particular, played an important part in raising morale during the reverses of the early years.

The writers still tended naturally to play down such topics as the separation of soldiers from their wives, the hardships of the civilian population, or the ethical problems raised by war. They of course avoided such sensitive issues as criticism of the political and military leadership for their part in the debacle of the early months. It was to be many years before Soviet writers could hope to deal at all freely with events so closely involved with Stalin's personal prestige. Since his death Simonov's *The Quick and the Dead* (*Zhivyye i mertvyye*, 1959) and *Soldiers are Made, not Born* (*Soldatami ne rozhdayutsya*, 1964), and the novels of Baklanov and Bykov have attempted a reasonably objective account of the early days of the war, Stalin's blunders, the large-scale panics at the front, and the still surviving suspicions of treason and espionage from the previous decade; but these works belong to another epoch of Soviet history.

* When the war flared up, its real horrors and real dangers, the threat of real death seemed a blessing after the inhuman domination of falsehood, and actually brought some relief insofar as they checked the power of the dead letter.

The greater part of Soviet war literature shares the weakness of war literature everywhere else. The tensions and oversimplifications of wartime, the temptations to write passionate but ephemeral propaganda, the tendency to identify the cardinal virtues as hatred and vengeance, seem to be universal. Perhaps the most attractive of the works directly inspired by the war is Tvardovsky's *Vasiliy Terkin* (1941–5), a long narrative poem which came out in serial form. The language is direct and expressive, and the trochaic rhythms catchy and memorable. The hero, Terkin, is a private in the Red Army. He is shown as a simple, but stubborn character, with a sharp tongue and a racy sense of humour, fond of his food and family, and heroic by accident rather than by intention. For the most part his adventures are realistic and commonplace, but even in the famous episode in which Terkin is left for dead but refuses to die, Tvardovsky maintains the mood consistently, and avoids making his hero a superman, or his theme merely whimsical.

From a literary point of view, however, the most remarkable feature of the war period was the re-appearance of writers who had been silent for many years. Pasternak's poems began to be printed again from 1941 onwards, and a new book *Early Trains* (*Na rannikh poyezdakh*, 1943) was allowed to appear. Even more important was the re-appearance of Anna Akhmatova. Her rehabilitation had begun in 1940, when some new poems of hers were published, and even a book of poems, the first to appear for eighteen years. Much of her war poetry is undistinguished (though it is often included in anthologies), but her major work of these years is one of the masterpieces of Russian literature. *Poem without a Hero* (*Poema bez geroya*, 1940–66) is a long complex, even cryptic poem which surveys the tragic events of her personal life and of Russian history over a span of some thirty years. In its treatment of the great issues of the century, its originality of form, its mingling of surrealism with real names and events, and its progression from the individual to the universal, Akhmatova's poem stands for all the artistic qualities that had been excluded by socialist realism. It has still not been published complete in the USSR.

Even more unexpected at the time was an autobiographical work by Zoshchenko, *Before Sunrise* (*Pered voskhodom solntsa*, 1942–3), which was printed in the most conservative of all

Soviet literary periodicals, *Oktyabr*. Here Zoshchenko put aside his usual farcical manner to write an intensely personal and introspective work; he tried to recreate his youth, childhood and infancy in the hope of uncovering the causes of his melancholic and hypochondriac disposition. His intention was, allegedly, to show his eventual cure, and transformation into a happy Soviet citizen; but only two instalments were published before the censors intervened. It is not even known whether Zoshchenko completed the work.

All three writers were to pay heavily in 1946 for this brief rehabilitation; they were publicly denounced in the most scurrilous terms by Zhdanov; the periodicals in which their works had been published were severely reprimanded. It was the sign for the re-introduction of Party controls in all their rigour. Any hopes that the common victory over the Nazis might lead to greater liberalism at home were shattered in a few weeks. The reinstatement of the old atmosphere of Philistinism, chauvinism and terror was to last without interruption until Stalin's death.

The Theatre

The story of the Soviet theatre in the 1930s reflects credit on the artists involved. Subject to the same pressures, political and physical, as the writers, they showed greater courage and determination in their loyalty to their traditional values, both personal and artistic.

The first step in the Sovietisation of the theatre was to increase the number of Soviet plays in the repertoire. Competitions and prizes were instituted to stimulate their composition, with some success. If in the mid 1920s, contemporary Soviet plays had constituted only a small minority (about twenty per cent), by 1933 they comprised over fifty per cent.[23] Even the senior 'academic' theatres were now required to add a quota of Soviet 'classics' to their standard repertoire. These directives were backed up by administrative measures. Hitherto the Party's control of the theatres had been exercised through representatives of the Soviets and the Party, but these functionaries had been ignorant and shy of interfering in the theatre's affairs. The passage of time, however, had produced Party members qualified in theatrical matters; there was even a special Party school for this purpose. With the infiltration of the Party into theatre administration, the artistic director was outnumbered and outgunned. Policy was now determined entirely by the Party, and even the artistic side of the productions came under careful scrutiny.

As a result Soviet plays began to fall into recognisable patterns, classifiable by specific themes: the Five-year Plan, the politicisation of the intelligentsia, the corruption of the West. The canonisation of Gorky led to innumerable performances of his plays, especially *Enemies* (*Vragi*, 1907) and dramatisations of his novels and short stories. But it is only fair to add that the finest of all his plays, *Yegor Bulichev and Others* (*Yegor Bulichev i drugiye*, 1931), was written and produced in these years. Many stage productions took the cautious line of adapting contemporary novels that had already been approved in book form. Contemporary Western plays were virtually ignored after Zhdanov had dismissed them all as pornography in 1934. There remained the classics, both Russian and foreign. These were limited to a certain percentage, and required some ideological updating at first. For example Akimov's *Hamlet* (1932) declaimed 'To be or not to be . . .' while contemplating the crown; in a production of *Romeo and Juliet*, the love of the protagonists was completely overshadowed by the 'class-war' between the Capulets and Montagues.

With the coming of socialist realism, however, the stress shifted to a more 'positive' approach to the classics. It was no longer required to turn them inside out, but to present them in a traditional manner, while nonetheless extracting a Soviet moral from them. If Hamlet was no longer guyed, he was not to be depicted as a vacillating intellectual either; instead he was shown as a strong character who conscientiously performs his duty, and is destroyed in the process by the reactionary society around him. It is sometimes thought that a 'strong Hamlet' is Pasternak's idea; in fact, the idea was already a cliché of the Soviet stage, when he elaborated it in his *Notes on Translating the Shakespearian Tragedies* (*Zametki k perevodam shekspirovskikh tragediy*). In the same spirit Tairov depicted Madame Bovary as an outstanding example of noble feelings victimised by her bourgeois environment.

Only Vsevolod Meierhold remained obstinately outside the prevailing Soviet orthodoxy. His productions of Soviet plays consistently ignored the current line. He followed up his sensational productions of Mayakovsky's satires with Olesha's *List of Blessings* (*Spisok blagodeyaniy*, 1932), in which the heroine finally chooses life in Russia rather than in the West, but only as the lesser of two evils. This half-hearted tribute was denounced as libellous, and the play was soon taken off. Meierhold refused to stage any of the works of Gorky, or even the approved Western classics. In 1934 he staged Dumas' *Lady with the Camellias*, the most classical of all his productions, and one of his greatest successes, although it was violently attacked in the press. His final work was his superb production of Tchaikovsky's *Queen of Spades* (*Pikovaya dama*, 1935), in which, true to his practice, he combined Tchaikovsky's opera with other Pushkin themes, such as *The Bronze Horseman*. However it was denounced in the general onslaught on music, in early 1936.

As a concession to socialist realism Meierhold tried to stage two Soviet works, dramatisations of Seyfullina's *Natasha* and Ostrovsky's *How the Steel was Tempered* (adapted as *One Life*). Both, however, were banned when they reached the dress rehearsal stage. Meierhold's contracts for producing more operas were cancelled. His theatre was closed down in 1938, and the long-promised grants for his new theatre were stopped. (It was later built to a modified version of his plans, and is now known as the Tchaikovsky Hall.) Meierhold himself came under attack. However, the theatrical world, except for the party stooges in its midst, still refused to join in the ritual of denunciation; Stanislavsky promptly found him employment in one of his studios. Meierhold survived unscathed until June 1939. It is possible that he was on the point of being restored to favour, but instead of public penitence, he launched into a fiery denunciation of Soviet policies towards the arts. He was arrested two days later, and disappeared from Soviet life – different Soviet works today are still not agreed as to the date of his death.

The Moscow Arts Theatre, after a long period in the political doldrums, emerged in the 1930s as the leading Soviet theatre. In 1937 it was awarded the order of Lenin, and declared to be a model for all other Soviet theatres. Stanislavsky, however, although officially honoured, played less and less part in the productions. The earlier aesthetic ideals gave way to the new ideological pressures. The change was symbolised by the shift of loyalties from Chekhov to Gorky – Gorky's name was even taken into the theatre's official title. Even in its productions of Chekhov's plays the Arts Theatre now tried to bring out the forward-looking optimistic elements.

This trend had the effect of reducing all Soviet theatres to a common level. The 'realistic' approach of the Arts Theatre now spread to all the others, and the individuality of their directors counted for less. Their productions became less bizarre and shocking, but also less inventive. Some theatres were forced to amalgamate; others were sent out to the provinces, while some were just closed down, such as the famous Second Studio of the Moscow Arts Theatre, on the grounds that it was no longer worthy of the name.

The immediate pre-war years saw a great increase in the number of Soviet plays written. Many of them are constructed round a Soviet family, usually a large one, whose various members follow different careers, predominantly in the armed forces. This unity is temporarily threatened by an intruder, either a survivor from the pre-1917 past, nourishing the vain hope of a restoration, or a foreigner, in which case he usually speaks with a German accent; in some cases he was even made up to resemble Hitler. After the Molotov-Ribbentrop pact, this was quickly changed; fortunately for the theatres this historic event fell outside the theatre season.

During these years (the outbreak of war only increased this tendency) the Russian past was glorified shamelessly, on the stage as in historical fiction. This trend extended to the Soviet period; Pogodin composed plays round the figure of Lenin, *The Man with a Gun* (*Chelovek s ruzhyem*, 1937) and *The Kremlin Chimes* (*Kremlevskiye Kuranty*, 1939). Many plays culminated in the adulation of Stalin.

In the wake of the Allied victory over the Nazis, the immediate post-war period witnessed a brief revival of light comedies and foreign plays; Soviet plays dropped to a mere twenty per cent of the repertoire.[24] But in August 1946, with the general crack-down in all fields of cultural life, the campaign against the theatre was re-opened with the *Pravda* article, '*O repertuare dramaticheskikh teatrov i merakh k yego uluchsheniyu*' ('On the

Repertoire of the Dramatic Theatres and Measures for Its Improvement'). This was the final blow, and the Soviet theatre was to show no signs of life again until after Stalin's death.

The Cinema

It was in 1930 that the Soviet cinema began to experience the effects of the Party's new policy of active interference in artistic matters. Film production was now subjected to the same controls and plans as all other sectors of the economy. The current political line was imposed on both the content and the formal techniques of the film; the methods of Eisenstein and Pudovkin were alike dismissed as bourgeois formalism. For the next eight years the Party bureaucrat, Shumyatsky, was to browbeat, obstruct and blackmail Soviet film makers.

As in the other arts Party interference was marked by a growing conservatism. Original artists now tended to avoid the cinema. The most brilliant of Meierhold's disciples, Okhlopkov returned to the theatre after his frustrating experiences with *The Way of the Enthusiasts* (*Put entuziastov*, 1930), a film which was finally never released.[25] For the most part Soviet cinema confined itself to reflecting the Five-year Plans in industry, in films such as *Entuziazm* (1931, translated into English as *Symphony of the Donbass*); or else screen versions of plays and novels: Fedin's *Cities and Years* (*Goroda i gody*, 1930), Dostoyevsky's *House of the Dead* (*Mertvyy dom*, 1932) and Sholokhov's *The Quiet Don* (*Tikhiy Don*, 1931).

The sound film was introduced late to the Soviet Union. The leading film makers had regarded it with distrust because they saw it as weakening the visual element, and as a return to the form of the theatre which they had repudiated from the first. Eisenstein and Pudovkin had envisaged ways in which sound could be used creatively, commenting on or counter-pointing the visual side, but they feared that the natural trend would lead to the domination of spoken dialogue and conventional background music. The backwardness of Russian industry and the shortage of foreign currency however, held back this development, and sound became standard in Soviet films only from 1930 onwards. This meant that Russian films avoided the garrulity of the first Western sound films, but in view of the political exigencies of the period and the absence or silence of the more creative minds, sound was used unimaginatively, mainly as a way of spelling out the ideological message of the films.

The one major new talent of the decade was Aleksandr Dovzhenko, the most poetic of the great Soviet directors. His film *Arsenal* (1929) was devoted to the Ukraine in the years of Civil War. Although he followed the Party line uncritically on such matters as 'Ukrainian nationalism', the complexity of the interweaving threads and the sense of passionate involvement and conviction far outweigh the political distortions. This film was surpassed by its successor, *Earth* (*Zemlya*, 1930), superficially a conventional Party documentary on collectivisation, with unrelievedly good 'poor peasants' and wicked *kulaks*. Underneath this propaganda surface, however, Dovzhenko's concern with philosophical questions, and his characteristic interest in death attained their most poetically realised expression. *Earth* was angrily denounced in the Soviet press; it was heavily cut before it was released for general circulation. Like so many other works of Soviet art, it was only after Stalin's death that it became accepted as a masterpiece of the Soviet cinema, and that largely due to Western advocacy.

The other notable film of the decade, Ekk's *Ticket to Life* (*Putevka v zhizn*, 1930), the first Soviet sound film of any merit, deals not too sentimentally or melodramatically with the problem of reclaiming juvenile delinquents. Of the other popular films, the Vasilyev brothers' *Chapayev* (1934) and Mark Donskoy's trilogy on Gorky's autobiographical sequence, *Childhood* (*Detstvo*, 1938), *Among People* (*V lyudyakh*, 1939), *My Universities* (*Moi universitety*, 1940) have been overpraised. They reveal the increasing tendency to rely on literature for cinematic subject matter, and the content of the works has been clumsily distorted to fit the new ideals of socialist realism. Furmanov's *Chapayev* had been a solid documentary novel, achieving its effect through its painstaking honesty. In the film version Chapayev is romanticised into a conventional partisan hero, coarse but with a heart of gold. The diffidence of Furmanov's original has been replaced by the arrogant dogmatism of the Party in the 1930s. In the Gorky films too frequent liberties are taken with the text and its spirit. There is a banal theme song and the boy Gorky is played as a budding 'positive hero'.

The objection to these screen versions is not so much their simplifications and distortions – these are inevitable in the transference to a different medium operating in different dimensions, and even essential if a genuine work of art is to emerge as a result. The truth is that these changes were dictated not by artistic but by political considerations.

As in the other arts, socialist realism in the cinema led to a large number of historical pictures, Petrov's *Petr I* (from Al. Tolstoy's novel, Part I, 1937, Part II, 1939), Eisenstein's *Aleksandr Nevsky* (1938), Dovzhenko's *Shchors* (1939), Pudovkin's *Minin i Pozharsky* (1939) and *Suvorov* (1941); Lenin and Stalin too were frequently depicted, as in Romm's *Lenin in October* (*Lenin v oktyabre,* 1937), *Lenin in 1918* (*Lenin v 1918 godu,* 1939), Yutkevich's *Man with a Gun* (1938, from Pogodin's play); these tendencies were to become even more pronounced with the outbreak of war.

The purges hit the Soviet cinema too. Even though none of the leading figures was actually liquidated, the Soviet film industry was running into increasing difficulties. The timelag between the first submission of a script and the completion of the film in these uncertain times discouraged any ambitious or even original projects being undertaken. Figures of film-production compared most unfavourably with the 1920s. 157 full-length films had been completed in 1924. In the 1930s this figure, still less the official target of 300, was never approached. Of 120 films planned in 1935 only 43 were completed, of 165 in 1936 only 46 and of 62 in 1937 only 25 (and of these eight were never released).[26] All in all, there is some justification for Khrushchev's remark in 1956 that the Soviet cinema had been particularly abused by Stalin.

This is shown by the continuing case of Eisenstein. On his return from America in 1932, Eisenstein found himself surrounded by mounting distrust and even hostility. Thanks to Shumyatsky's scheming behind his back, Eisenstein failed to get the film of his projected epic on Mexican history ('Que Viva Mexico!') back from the Americans. When he heard of the American arrangements of his material, *Thunder over Mexico* and *Time in the Sun,* he repudiated them angrily. He was now subjected to a series of petty humiliations. We know of several films that he intended to make in these years (he was particularly interested in the possibilities of Joyce's Ulysses); but none of them came to anything. Eisenstein devoted himself to theoretical work and to lecturing in the Moscow Film Institute. His next film *Bezhin Meadow* (*Bezhin lug*) on which he worked from 1935 to 1937 was to be constructed on the contrast between the past of the Russian peasantry (based on Turgenev's famous story) and a recent event in which a boy had been killed by his father for his opposition to the *kulaks*. Work on the film was interrupted first by Eisenstein's illness and then by Shumyatsky's demands for revision. Finally Shumyatsky suspended work on the film and publicly attacked it for formalism. Eisenstein seems to have been temporarily broken by this setback, and he wrote a letter of abject self-criticism. The film was destroyed during the war, and now only a few stills survive.

In the following year, however, after the fall of Shumyatsky, Eisenstein was invited by Stalin as a mark of clemency to compose a film on Aleksandr Nevsky. It is executed in the style of the other historical pageants of the time, brought up to date with the contemporary anti-German mood; it contains little of Eisenstein's usual startling juxtapositions or his sardonic humour. However, it has always been the most popular of Eisenstein's films in the Soviet Union; even the fact that it soon had to be suspended again because of the Hitler-Stalin pact was not held against him personally.

Eisenstein's next projects, on the Civil War, on the Fergana Canal and on Pushkin[27] all came to nothing. His final film, the uncompleted *Ivan the Terrible* (*Ivan Groznyy*, Part I, 1944, Part II, 1946), is perhaps the most ambiguous of all his films. Here the surface portrayal of Ivan the Terrible as a prototype of Stalin, cruel, but devoted only to the greater glory and security of Russia, is undermined (particularly in Part II) by the neurotic atmosphere, the twisted bodies and the gigantic shadows. The first part was awarded a Stalin prize, but the second was banned immediately after its preview; it was not finally released until 1958. Eisenstein was in hospital during the Zhdanovite denunciations of the film. He made no more films, and he died in 1948 of a heart attack, on hearing of the new round of attacks on Shostakovich. His last project is rumoured to have been a film on Nero.[28]

The onset of Zhdanovism practically killed the Soviet cinema. Only a handful of films, all worthless, were released in the remaining years before Stalin's death.

The history of the Soviet cinema may seem to be less horrific than the bloody record of Soviet literature or Soviet science; but the tragic story of Eisenstein, the degradation of Kuleshov, Pudovkin and Dovzhenko into Party hacks, is not just a pale reflection of the fate of other artists and intellectuals. Of all the arts which grew up with the Soviet regime, none was less a child of the old world than the Russian cinema. The films of the great directors indicate no murmur of opposition to the wisdom of the Party (except perhaps in *Ivan the Terrible*, Part II); from the first their skills were directed to the service of Russian Communism. Yet their art, which, above all, good Marxists might have heeded as the voice of their times, was denounced, now as bourgeois, now as formalist, now as counter-revolutionary.

This chapter may suggest that it was not the intellectuals and artists of Soviet Russia who suffered from these failings, but the leadership of the Russian Communist Party.

4

The Peasantry

History

The problems that confronted the makers of Soviet agricultural policy at the end of 1927, the inefficiency of agriculture, the widespread practice of individual small-holdings, the continuing distrust between town and country, were direct consequences of the premature revolution, aggravated by the Bolsheviks' policy (or slogan) of 'All land to the peasants' in 1917. It now had to be admitted that the hopes of voluntary collectivisation had failed, and since it was anyway now only the poorer peasants who had any interest in forming collectives, their prospects for the future looked none too bright.

One solution might have been to give greater encouragement to the more successful farmers, in order to create an incentive for forming larger and more efficient agricultural units. The Government, however, could not easily make such a concession because of the resentment that would result among urban workers. But the crucial factor in the debate was the decision to follow the policy of all-out industrialisation. The capital required for its implementation was not forthcoming from the West; it would therefore have to be raised at home from the peasantry. By bringing agriculture under complete control, the State could dictate both the prices paid to the peasants and the prices paid by the consumer; the profit would be the State's. With the resulting increase in efficiency, labour would be freed for the industrial work-force. Above all, there was the tempting prospect of extending the Party's control over the countryside at long last. Thus ideological, economic and political motives all came together.

In December 1927 the Communists took the first cautious steps towards collectivisation. Naturally there was opposition from Stalin's former allies, the Bukharinites, and when Stalin demanded 'emergency measures' for extracting grain from the peasantry, the local Communists were afraid of carrying them out, because such practices had only just been denounced as 'Trotskyite excesses'. Just as ten years previously, the Communists hoped to impose their will on the peasantry by dividing them among themselves. Throughout 1928 the pressure mounted on the *kulaks*, while every attempt was made to woo the poorer peasants to the Party's side; the middle peasants, the vast majority, were handled cautiously; on the one hand they were potential *kulaks*, on the other their co-operation was essential to the success of the plan.

In April 1929 the Government announced its intention of collectivising twenty per cent of Russian agriculture by the end of the First Five-year Plan. In December it called for 'the liquidation of the *kulaks* as a class'; their property was confiscated to form the basis of the new collectives; the men with their families were dispatched to work on building sites or in labour camps. In January 1930 Stalin abandoned his former target of twenty per cent and instead demanded the collectivisation of the 'enormous majority' of peasant households. The campaign was spearheaded by 25,000 Party stalwarts from the city organisations and the OGPU. In the three months from December 1929 to March 1930, the proportion of peasants under collectivisation rose from four per cent to fifty-eight per cent.

There was no longer any pretence of voluntary collectivisation. It was imposed by force, in an atmosphere recalling that of the Civil War; there were frequent cases of looting and debauchery by the invaders. Many communities accepted the inevitable, and so managed to avoid any great convulsion; but in others the brutality of the invaders inspired desperate resistance, even among the poor peasants. They burnt their crops, slaughtered their livestock and smashed their machinery rather than lose them to the enemy. In these cases collectivisation was imposed by the bayonet and the machinegun; whole villages were destroyed in the process. The vague definition of the '*kulak*' led to the 'dekulakisation' of anyone who objected to the brutality and slaughter.

For the bloodbath of collectivisation (Stalin later admitted that the loss of life approached that of the Second World War)[1] the Party must take the responsibility. Even granted that there were ideological and economic justifications for accelerating the campaign it was disastrously mishandled. Little attempt was made to explain to the peasantry the advantages of collectivisation. They were ignorant and distrustful of the central government as they traditionally always have been. The strange word '*kolkhoz*' and the wild rumours that circulated, were magnified, not diminished, by the Party's intolerant and brutal actions. The inexperience and ignorance of the industrial Party workers sent into the countryside only led to further losses of grain and livestock even after they had been collectivised. All this added fuel to the fears and resentment of the peasantry.

The crude execution of collectivisation had far-reaching consequences for Soviet agriculture. The definition of the *kulak* in terms of his possessions, rather than by his socio-economic function in the rural community, meant that many peasants who had established themselves by hard work since the Revolution were now victimised; when these peasants were executed or dispatched to the labour camps their industry and know-how were lost. Conversely, the poorer peasants, who supported the collectives, included not just the unfortunates of rural society, but also the incompetent and the good-for-nothings; they were rewarded with administrative and responsible posts in the newly-formed collectives. Here too the colossal and unnecessary wastage of collectivisation, as it was actually put into effect, was to cripple Soviet agriculture for decades.

The chaotic three months of the first phase of collectivisation ended in March 1930, when Stalin in his 'Dizziness from Success' speech denounced the 'excesses' of collectivisation (which he had himself only just been demanding). This was partly a recognition of the fact that collectivisation had got out of hand; but primarily it was a tactical move to ensure that the peasants would have some incentive to sow their crops, and, as it happened, 1930 produced a good harvest.[2] During the year the proportion of peasants under collectivisation dropped from fifty-eight per cent to twenty-one per cent; but once the harvest was in, the pressures were resumed under the guise of further de-kulakisation. The disadvantages of remaining outside the collective were steadily increased in the forms of heavy taxes, administrative discrimination and sometimes strong-arm methods; the expansion of collectivisation thereupon proceeded steadily. The peasantry accepted the inevitable and made the best of a bad job. Even so the brutality of collectivisation was a severe shock to many Party members; there were resignations and suicides. It was even rumoured to have caused the suicide of Stalin's wife Nadezhda Alliluyeva.

The collective farms which now absorbed the mass of the Russian peasantry differed in several essentials from the State farms (*sovkhozy*) which had previously been the Marxist ideal. The *sovkhoz* treated the peasant like an industrial worker: he was required to work at a definite job, and he received a fixed wage. The collective farm, on the other hand, was regarded as an inferior, less socialist, form of organisation. It was intended, theoretically, to finance itself out of its own sales and profits; the proceeds would then be divided up among its members according to their contributions. In practice, the *kolkhoz* was strictly controlled. It was required to contribute a fixed amount of its produce to the State at purely nominal prices, and only when it had satisfied the State's exactions could it begin to provide for its own members.

This system of extracting pre-determined quantities of produce from the collective farms, whatever the harvest, served to maximise the contrast between good harvests and bad harvests, between successful and struggling *kolkhozy*. In good years the more fortunate farms could provide a decent living for their members, and invest savings in further improvements; but for the others the good years provided only a meagre subsistence level, and the worse years reduced them to starvation. This was especially so in the terrible famine of 1932–3, which was caused not by a crop failure (the harvest was only slightly down), but by the insistence of the State on maintaining the level of its own exactions. This enabled food supplies to the cities and the quantity of grain exported for foreign currency to be kept at existing levels. The famine's existence was for many years officially denied; even Gorky, as we have seen, played his part in concealing the facts. About five million peasants are reckoned to have died. It finally broke the back of peasant resistance, but their sullen resentment was to act as a brake on the full recovery of agriculture for many years.

The peasant's work on the *kolkhoz* was assessed on a piecework basis, in terms of the labour day, an artificial unit with no necessary relation to a day's work, and quite insufficient to live on. The only concession to the peasant's desire for land was his right to a small plot on which he could grow fruit and vegetables or keep a few animals. It was hoped that this system would serve to reconcile the peasant to the *kolkhoz*, while he was acclimatising himself to the idea that collective farming was more advantageous, and that the private plot would in time cease to have any appeal for him. Instead the reverse has happened. The peasant's nostalgia for the old way of life has led to him lavishing far more care on his own plot of land than on the collective. A disproportionate amount of the country's total agricultural produce has come from this minute fraction of the total land available; and, if anything, this disproportion has tended to increase over the years. The yield per acre has been several times greater, the quality of the produce much higher, the condition of the livestock far superior, by comparison with the collective farm on which the peasant spends the greater part of his time. The private plot is now not only essential to the livelihood of the peasant, who finds it a more reliable support than his share in the *kolkhoz* profits, but it is also essential to the food supply of the cities.

It had been envisaged that the *kolkhozy* would be supervised by trained agronomists who would bring their scientific knowledge to reinforce the local experience of the peasants; but from the first there were very few of these qualified men, and during the purges the rural intelligentsia were particularly hard hit. Instead, orders were usually issued from Moscow by plan-conscious bureaucrats, with no knowledge of local conditions. The men on the spot disobeyed these instructions only at their peril.

In the same way the institution of the Motor Tractor Stations (MTS) was originally a sensible way of overcoming the shortage of tractors, combines, etc., by hiring them out to a ring of *kolkhozy*, thus maximising the work which each tractor could do. At first the MTS were financed by the State, but before long the State required the peasants to pay for these services in kind out of their produce; often these charges were exorbitant, and served merely as another means of extorting supplies from the peasantry. Thus the MTS soon became an instrument not of co-operation, but of coercion. Its power to grant or withhold the loan of machinery gave it immense power, and it soon became the centre of Party organisation in the countryside.

Thus the *kolkhozy* were completely controlled by townsmen who were naturally out of touch with village conditions. If they often demanded the impossible, they were also liable to be duped. Many of these outsiders were conscientious men, but their presence was naturally resented; their superior living conditions, and their generous allowance of labour days made them seem like parasites; and of course some of them were.

Like the industrial workers, the peasants were subject to Draconian laws. The theft of *kolkhoz* property was punishable by death or exile to the labour camps. Peasants who left the *kolkhoz* were banned from owning any land. But the most discriminatory measure of all was the decision not to give the peasants internal passports. This meant that their movements were severely restricted, and they could visit the cities for only a few days at a time. In this way the peasants were reduced effectively to the status of nineteenth-century serfs.

As in the nineteenth century too, the peasants had to rely on their traditional skill in circumventing the wishes of their masters. They bent and stretched the regulations to extend their private plots and to sneak hours from the *kolkhoz*. In 1939 the Party was forced to introduce new regulations and stringent penalties in an attempt to put the peasant back in his place.

The war brought some relief to the peasantry, though they of course suffered from the same hardships as the rest of the population. At the front they were used as cannon-fodder, and so sustained the bulk of the colossal war losses. In the Western regions the peasants were at first sympathetic to the Germans. They hoped for an end to the *kolkhoz* system and the restoration of private farming. The Nazis, however, requisitioned the livestock and removed all the able-bodied men to Germany; by their brutality and arrogance they soon alienated any remaining traces of goodwill. Meanwhile, in the unoccupied areas, Soviet counter-propaganda hinted that the collective system might be reformed at the end of the war, and agriculture was allowed to evolve a certain independence. Food was more important than ideology and prices reached a fairer level.

Thus many of the peasantry profited out of the war. With the coming of peace, it was one of the Government's first priorities to reimpose its control over the peasantry. It re-introduced the measures of 1939; the famine of 1946–7, even more severe than its predecessors in the 1920s and 1930s, and again ignored by the central authorities, completed the crushing of the peasants' short-lived independence.

The peasants have been the main victims of the industrial progress achieved by the Soviet Union since 1928. They are second class citizens; they do not enjoy the industrial benefits, pensions, sickness compensation, subsidised holidays enjoyed by the workers. The State spends far less, man for man, on the rural inhabitant than it does on the townsman. Facilities are poor, libraries and even radios are limited; mechanisation and electrification are still lamentably inadequate. With these drawbacks there has been little to attract skilled men into the countryside. As a result the peasant has fallen far behind, not only in the external signs of material progress; his opportunities for education and decent health have been curtailed too. The tough measures employed by the Soviet Government may have had some economic justification in attracting the young and able-bodied into industry, where there has always been a shortage of labour, but the indiscriminate and ruthless measures employed have now led to a situation where the farms are manned largely by the elderly, the women and children. The continuing weakness of Soviet agriculture is the other face of the technological triumphs inaugurated by the first Five-year Plan. It is the most embarrassing reminder of the cost of the premature revolution.

The Peasantry in Literature

The growing control of the Party over literature is reflected particularly in the case of rural subjects. There was no topic on which the Party was so sensitive as its agricultural policies. Indeed in this field the fanatical intolerance that was the Party's natural reaction to any hint of criticism had begun to manifest itself even in the 1920s.

In 1924 the Union of Peasant Writers had boasted over 200 members (for comparison, VAPP had over 700, and the Union of Writers, the base of the fellow-travellers, 323). But in the next eighteen months their number grew to over 700.[3] This dramatic increase was not entirely due to an influx of peasant autodidacts; it was considerably assisted by the Party-sponsored entry of writers whose ideology was more attuned to Marxist and proletarian ways of thinking. These effectively took over the Union of Peasant Writers and gradually expelled the better-known peasant writers of the time. Finally, in 1928 they were able to set up a new All-Russian Association of Peasant Writers, whose platform stated:

> 1). . . . Не всякий писатель, пишущий о крестьянстве, является *подлинно* крестьянским писателем. 2). Крестьянскими нужно считать таких писателей, которые на основе пролетарской идеологии, но при помощи свойственных им крестьянских образов в своих художественных произведениях организуют чувство и сознание трудовых слоев крестьянства и всех трудящихся в сторону борьбы с мелко-буржуазной ограниченностью — за коллективизацию быта и психики . . .*[4]

Thus collectivisation, the most important event in the Russian countryside since the Emancipation of the serfs, is hardly reflected at all in Soviet literature of the period. Indeed, in many respects, more has been said about collectivisation in the literature since 1956, notably in Stadnyuk's *People are not Angels* (*Lyudi ne angely*, 1962), than in the 1930s. This was partly because the literature of the peasantry had been suppressed, and literature on the subject was composed by city-based writers, or proletarianised ex-peasants, with their natural sense of superiority to the peasantry. Collectivisation, therefore, appears usually only as an episode in the Soviet novels of the Five-year Plan. The first novel to be devoted to the subject, Panferov's *Bruski* (1928–37), aroused much heated controversy, before being accepted into Soviet literature.

* 1). Not every writer who writes about the peasantry, is truly a peasant writer. 2). Peasant writers are to be considered only those who, on the basis of a proletarian ideology, but with the assistance of the peasant imagery habitual to them, organise the attitudes of the labouring strata of the peasantry and of all workers towards the struggle with petty-bourgeois narrowness – and for the collectivisation of life and psychology. . . .

Uncommitted readers are likely to find it shapeless and almost unreadable.

The most famous work on the subject, however, Sholokhov's *Virgin Soil Upturned* (*Podnyataya tselina*, 1931, sequel in 1960), avoids most of the weaknesses of this kind of literature. The novel deals with the historical events of the climax of collectivisation, from the autumn of 1929 to the spring of 1930. The hero of the novel, Davydov, a sailor from Leningrad totally ignorant of village life and of all agricultural matters, is one of the 25,000 who has been sent out by the Party into the villages. He can rely on only a handful of Communists to support him, and the majority of the peasants, even when they are inclined to collectivisation, are contemptuous of his ignorance. In this aspect of the novel, Sholokhov is remarkably objective. His knowledge of the Cossacks, his ability to create a variety of memorable characters, and his ribald sense of humour are a good match for the irresistible, but impersonal, authority reposed in Davydov.

The propagandist elements come out in the depiction of the 'middle peasants'. There is of course no 'middle' way open to them in the atmosphere of these years, and the need to polarise every character sometimes strains the narrative. For example, it is moving when the model middle peasant, Maydannikov, finds himself able to accept the case for collectivisation intellectually and ideologically, but still remains tormented by his concern for his own animals, now in the collective herd: it becomes slightly absurd when Maydannikov's struggle with his baser instincts so impresses Davydov that he tries to persuade him to join the Party.

The other alternative is shown in the figure of Ostrovnov, a hard-working self-made peasant, who becomes the manager of the collectivised herds. Ostrovnov, however, is deeply shaken by the cruelty shown to the *kulaks*, and he drifts, by the conventional logic of the times, into an anti-Soviet conspiracy. But at this point he suddenly develops a life of his own; he threatens to become a model manager, and for a time, looks like dropping out of the conspiracy altogether. He has to be recalled to his villain's role by some rather forced and melodramatic complications. For all its propagandist intentions, however, the novel is an amusing, convincing, and, at times, moving, account of collectivisation in one fairly representative village. If the horrific experiences of some areas are not to be found in its pages, at least the difficulties and genuine opposition among peasants of all classes are not glossed over. The promise of the first part of *Virgin Soil Upturned* is unfortunately frittered away in the garrulous sequel.

Rather more controversial was the work of Ivan Katayev, whose accounts of collectivisation, though also written from the standpoint of the Party, were riddled with doubts and questions. His story *Milk* (*Moloko,* 1929) is an account of a senior and respected peasant, whose character comes under suspicion during the anti-*kulak* campaign. The local peasants are at first unwilling to condemn him; but when personal tragedy overtakes him (his son is murdered) they at once turn on him, and he is disgraced. The revelation of the petty motives and inconsistent results of dekulakisation, the evident perplexity of the narrator, a loyal but sensitive Party man, make the story one of the most fascinating in Soviet literature. It appeared at the height of the collectivisation campaign and was at once denounced. Katayev's later story *Meeting* (*Vstrecha,* 1933) is built on the contrast between a smug urban Communist, sent out to assist in collectivisation, and the poorest peasant in the village. The Communist gradually accepts the loss of his bourgeois comforts and privileges, as he rises to the challenge. The poor peasant, the victim of a landowner's maltreatment, is a drunkard, and the village butt, until he finally responds to the chance the *kolkhoz* gives him. Even when his daughter dies he finds the spirit to put in an extra day's work before succumbing to one last drunken orgy. It is in this situation that the 'meeting' of the title takes place. The story is told with Katayev's usual honesty, but the moral intentions are all too obtrusive. In the Soviet Union, however, this story is nowadays rated a successful answer to the doubts expressed in *Milk*. Like many other members of the 'Mountain-Pass' group, Ivan Katayev was arrested and executed in 1937.

Nearly all these works reflect the increasingly elitist tendencies of Soviet literature; they are told from the angle of townsmen or Party officials. Even when concentrating on the peasantry, authors found it easier to deal with *kulaks* than with the ordinary men most directly involved. Boris Kornilov produced a handful of propaganda poems on the subject of the *kulak*, but none on the poor peasant. Pavel Vasilyev, in his long narrative poem *Kulaki* (1933–4), obviously relishes the opportunities of depicting hard and unscrupulous men, their terse and allusive language, their ruthless actions and their cunning schemes. By comparison, the forces of progress, the school teacher and the poor peasants, are pale and weakly drawn. Zabolotsky's *Triumph of Agriculture* (*Torzhestvo zemledeliya,* 1930) and Kaverin's *Prologue* (*Prolog,* 1931) are almost unique in sounding a note of irony about the aims and execution of collectivisation.

The most remarkable literature of the peasantry in this period came undoubtedly from Andrey Platonov. In the 1920s he had made his name by stylised accounts of the Civil War, eccentric Russian craftsmen and satires on bureaucrats. In the 1930s, however, when the majority of Soviet artists were occupied with creating model Communists, prominent and heroic leader-figures, Platonov turned to the most insignificant citizens of the Soviet Union, the poor peasantry and the semi-educated urban proletariat. In place of his earlier flamboyant style, he now began to write in a new manner, apparently naive and artless, but in fact a marvellously expressive medium for his compassionate outlook.

Platonov's most characteristic device is his use of 'wrong' words. If in his earlier work the purpose is usually comic, in his works of the 1930s the effect is much more subtle. In the first place, this misuse of words creates an immediate impression of a tongue-tied and uncomprehending narrator; the bureaucratic jargon which confuses the speech and thought of the characters increasingly suggests the dehumanisation of men and their language; but beyond all this Platonov succeeds in conveying a sense of deeper meanings, only dimly glimpsed by his inarticulate heroes. Thus his story *Digging the Foundations* (*Kotlovan,* 1930) begins:

> В день тридцатилетия личной жизни Вощеву дали расчет с небольшого механического завода, где он добывал средства для своего существования. В увольнительном документе ему написали, что он устраняется с производства вследствие роста слабосильности в нем и задумчивости среди общего темпа труда.
>
> Вощев взял на квартире вещи в мешок и вышел наружу, чтобы на воздухе лучше понять свое будущее. Но воздух был

пуст, неподвижные деревья бережно держали жару в листьях, и скучно лежала пыль на безлюдной дороге, — в природе было такое положение.*[5]

This combination of official circumlocutions with everyday syntax, of near-meaningless abstractions with matters of life and death, creates a strange sense of dislocation, a stylistic equivalent for the individual caught in the incomprehensible machinery of a modern state.

In this remarkable story Platonov records his observations of both industrialisation and collectivisation. In both, the foundations are energetically being dug; orders constantly arrive for extending the foundations even more ambitiously; but by the end of the story nothing has been erected on them. In his account of collectivisation Platonov ironically passes judgment on its Utopianism by a poker-faced description of how the horses set up their own collective:

> На дворе лошади открыли рты, пища упала из них в одну среднюю кучу, и тогда обобществленный скот стал вокруг и начал медленно есть, организованно смирившись без заботы человека.†[6]

Two types frequently recur in Platonov's writings: a cripple, hideously mutilated and pathologically embittered as a result of the past; and an innocent orphan-child, equally a victim of the past, but ignorant, trusting and defenceless. The two are thrown together in a half-parental, half-tyrannical relationship; often it ends with the death of the child. Like Mayakovsky, Platonov did not believe that the past could be eradicated so easily; as he saw it, the dead hand of the past still lay over the present. Indeed, this striking image might well serve as an allegory of the premature revolution.

* On the thirtieth anniversary of his personal life Voshchev was sacked from the small mechanical workship where he had been acquiring the means for his existence. In his notice of dismissal they had written that he was being discharged from the works because of his increasing weakness and thoughtfulness amid the general tempo of work.

In his room Voshchev packed his belongings into a sack and went out into the open air, so as to comprehend his future better there. But the air was empty, the motionless trees carefully guarded the warmth in their leaves; the dust lay depressingly on the deserted road – such was the situation in nature.

† In the yard the horses opened their mouths, the food fell out into a single central pile, and then the socialised animals stood around and began to eat slowly, organising and disciplining themselves without any human intervention.

Many of Platonov's works were suppressed, others circulated only in manuscript. He himself was violently attacked in the Soviet press, Stalin wrote 'Scum' over the text of one of his stories, and he was eventually arrested and exiled. He reappeared during the war, continuing to write of the lives of ordinary Russians, but without the piercing intensity of the 1930s. He was denounced again in 1947, and lived in obscurity until his death in 1951. The bulk of his work is still unpublished.

The best-known peasant writer of the 1930s, Mikhail Isakovsky, was the son of a poor peasant from the Smolensk region. His poetry is a good example of the Party's prescription for peasant literature; it is full of the benefits that the Revolution and the city had brought the Russian village; electrification, mechanisation, the radio, etc. No one would deny that this verse expressed the views of many peasants, but this idealised vision of the industrialised countryside is curiously smug. Isakovsky is content to remain within the forms of his peasant predecessors, Koltsov and Surikov, merely injecting a more positive and 'optimistic' content into their familiar metres and stanza forms. There is no fresh vision or turn of phrase to suggest that the countryside is being viewed by a poet as opposed to a lyrical Party spokesman. Isakovsky never contemplates the possibility that some peasants might disagree with him, or even that progress has brought some losses. Isakovsky wrote nothing on collectivisation, except for a short poem *Enemy* (*Vrag*), about a *kulak*, and that only in 1935. The visual equivalent of Isakovsky's verse is Gerasimov's painting *Feast on the kolkhoz* (*Pir na kolkhoze*, 1937).

The best of Isakovsky's disciples, Aleksandr Tvardovsky, was long content to follow in his footsteps. Admittedly, his long poem, *The Land of Muravia* (*Strana Muraviya*, 1936), the story of a peasant's search for the Utopian land of Muravia, which he eventually finds in the *kolkhoz*, is far more ambitious in its scope, and it possesses a sly wit, quite outside Isakovsky's range, but its theme is unmistakably propagandist. With his service in the Army during the war, and the publication of *Vasiliy Terkin* (1941–5) Tvardovsky finally broke away from the constrictions of this narrow genre. Finally, by his work as editor of *Novyy mir* (1950–4 and 1958–70) Tvardovsky was to play a unique role in uncovering the abuses and falsehoods of the Stalinist past, especially as they concerned the peasantry. Thanks to his courage and persistence, interest has revived in the peasantry as a social and literary theme. It is likely that he will be remembered even more as an editor than as a poet. He died in 1971.

5
Boris Pasternak

Unlike the other writers discussed in this book, Pasternak's life and outlook were not disrupted in any obviously dramatic way by the events of 1917. He had broken a leg in childhood, and the resulting lameness rendered him unfit for military service during the Great War; he was a non-combatant in the Civil War too. We know very little of his actions and attitudes during the Revolution, and there are few indications in his works before *Doctor Zhivago*. This detachment from public events has often led to Pasternak's being termed a poets' poet. If this is taken to mean the poet's indifference to the concerns of everyday life, it is hardly fair or accurate; but in the sense that the central theme of all his work is the nature of poetry and the role of the poet, then the description is an apt one.

Pasternak, no less than Mayakovsky, believed that poetry is an essential element in life. But where Mayakovsky sought to transform the world by means of his poetry, Pasternak regarded art as a natural creative force, existing independently of the artist, but channelling its energies through him. Blok had considered the poet's function as listening to the 'music' of inspiration, and trying to find some verbal and formal equivalent, which would convey it to the ear of his readers. But for Pasternak the poet is completely passive, more of a medium than an agent in its composition:

> Поэзия, когда под краном
> Пустой, как цинк ведра, трюизм,
> То и тогда струя сохранна,
> Тетрадь подставлена, — струись!*[1]

* Poetry, when under the tap/there lies a truism like a bucket's zinc,/Then even then the stream's preserved./The paper's underneath – gush forth!

The idea of inspiration as an irresistible stream of creative power, whether of rain or of tap-water, of ink or of tears, runs right through his work, from the first line of the first poem in his first book:

"Февраль. Достать чернил и плакать."*[2]

down to the last poems he wrote in 1958 and 1959.

Pasternak was brought up in a cultivated and artistic family. His father was a well-known painter, while his mother was a concert pianist, until she chose to give up her career for her family. Artists, musicians and writers frequented their home; Lev Tolstoy was a friend of the family, and the composer Skryabin paid occasional visits. Under the spell of his music Pasternak's first ambition was to become a composer, and he relinquished it only because he did not possess perfect pitch. From music he turned to law and then to philosophy; he went abroad to study at the University of Marburg. Here the break-up of his first love affair, and his growing dissatisfaction with his gift for philosophy led him back to the arts, and so to poetry.

Pasternak was later to claim that his belated turn to poetry gave him an advantage, in that his sensations and associations had not been dulled by the familiarity with the conventions and fashionable models that comes of long preparation and study, and often makes it difficult for poets to find their own voice. This may be so, but he was also gifted with an extraordinary ear and eye, which reveal themselves in the astonishing imagery, the energetic rhythms and the unprecedented rhymes, that are features of even his earliest poetry. He was naturally drawn towards Russian Futurism, with which he shared an interest in the purely technical aspects of poetic composition.

His most successful early poems fuse his novel poetic vocabulary with a complex system of syntax and sound-composition that serves to illustrate, or rather to illuminate, the sense.[3] By the use of puns, ambiguities over prepositions and personal pronouns, Pasternak achieves his favourite effect of allowing the poem to speak for itself, as though it had been created not by the poet, but by the idiosyncrasies of the Russian language. In this way he contrives to create a formal equivalent for his conception of poetry and the role of the poet. If the poet's

* February. Get out the ink and weep.

'I' appears in these poems, it is usually only to disappear as Nature and language find that they can express themselves more effectively without his agency; in Pasternak's poetry, it is not the poet, but the rain, which composes acrostics and looks for rhymes.[4] Paradoxically, Pasternak's poetry has often been regarded as the ultimate in subjectivism; rather, however, the poet discovers himself only in abandoning his subjective impressions, and allowing external forces, nature, language, the immediacy of sense impressions to speak through him. Pasternak liked to speak of this quality as 'realism', and he claimed to detect it in the work of all great artists, whether painters, poets or composers.

In all these respects Pasternak stands at the opposite extreme from Mayakovsky, for whom poetry was an imposition of human will and purpose on inert material. Where Mayakovsky is rhetorical and self-orientated, Pasternak is reticent; there are few autobiographical poems in his work. Where Mayakovsky's poems catch the eye by their appearance on the printed page, short broken lines, printed (from 1923 onwards) step-wise across the page, Pasternak's, after some youthful experiments in typographical lay-out, are usually arranged in conventional stanza-forms.

To some extent, his rejection of the Mayakovsky manner was deliberate; he was all too aware of the influence of Mayakovsky, and he had begun to notice similarities in his own style. But the two men also stand for two opposing tendencies within the Russian intelligentsia. Mayakovsky came from a remote Caucasian village; he stormed the capitals from outside, and there is no respect for the past or tradition in his work. Pasternak was born in Moscow, in the heart of the Russian intelligentsia; its traditions and values are felt strongly in all his work; it was natural for him to play down his originality, to dress it in conventional forms. Mayakovsky's surname is a rare one, if not unique; it means 'Lighthouse', as he was well aware. Pasternak's means 'parsnip', and though this word nowhere appears in his works, it is typical of the everyday, humdrum words that he liked to introduce into poetic contexts.

The events of 1917 affected Pasternak as a poet, rather than as a citizen. In an almost Blokian way, the shock waves of the Revolution coincided for him with an outburst of poetic inspiration. He wrote more poetry in this one year than in any other; much of it went into *My Sister Life* (*Sestra moya zhizn*), the book that brought him fame when it was published in 1922. In this book poems about love, reflections on the nature of art and inspiration, and the intoxicated contemplation of nature, coalesce to create an impression of the unparalleled freshness of life, and its limitless potentialities. The book is subtitled 'Summer 1917', and as Pasternak later wrote:

> В это знаменитое лето 1917 года, в промежутке между двумя революционными сроками, казалось, вместе с людьми митинговали и ораторствовали дороги, деревья и звезды. Воздух из конца в конец был охвачен горячим тысячеверстным вдохновеньем и казался личностью с именем, казался ясновидящим и одушевленным.*[5]

Later Pasternak was to give similar sentiments on the atmosphere of the time to Yuriy Zhivago at Melyuzeyevo.

During the years of Civil War Pasternak earned his living by translations for the World Literature Publishing House. His senior in the German division, Blok, did not think highly of these translations, and Pasternak himself was later to disparage them. He next found employment on the fringes of the literary world, as a salesman in a bookshop, as a research assistant in libraries – jobs which left him time for poetry. With the publication of *My Sister Life* and *Themes and Variations* (*Temy i variatsii*, 1923) his poetic reputation was established. The poems in these books were written between 1916 and 1922 and they mark the culmination of Pasternak's early manner.

By 1923, however, this kind of lyrical introspection was regarded as something of a luxury. Pasternak was compared reproachfully with his contemporary Mayakovsky. It may be noted that Mayakovsky did not grudge him his individual road. Indeed it appears that he admired and envied him for it; he is said to have known these two books of Pasternak by heart. But the totally changed situation of the writer in the new society was bound to affect Pasternak's outlook and style, and

* In that famous summer of 1917, in the interval between the two revolutions, it seemed that the roads, the trees and the stars were holding meetings and making speeches alongside the people. The air was possessed from end to end with the hot respiration of thousands of miles: it seemed a personality with its own name, clairvoyant and inspired.

the poet himself seems to have felt the need to bring his poetry closer to the Revolutionary scene.

Between the years 1923 and 1930 he made several attempts to break out of his lyric world into larger forms and more public themes. (This trend was perhaps in part a reflection of the current move away from the short story to the novel.) Equally important was his attempt to simplify his style, and this too accorded with the mood of the times, though greater simplicity is probably a natural accompaniment to an increase in scale. For Pasternak, however, the attempt to communicate more directly with his people was not simply the result of Party pressure; it was to become one of his main concerns in later life.

The first of these more ambitious poems, *The Lofty Ailment* (*Vysokaya bolezn,* 1923, revised 1928), tries to define the place of the poet in great historical events. It opens with an evocation of the Trojan War, known to later generations only through the poems of Homer. Can the poet of today's events hope for similar immortality? Pasternak is not optimistic. After a depiction of the chaos of the preceding years, he goes on to accuse the Russian intelligentsia, who had once worked for the Revolution, of having lost contact with the ordinary working people. He includes himself in this indictment, but recalls that he did at least visit the Ninth Congress of the Soviets in 1921. He remembers his doubts and reservations on the way there, and asserts that he is still shocked by the ideological fanaticism of many Communists. At the end of the poem all these hesitations are finally swept away by the appearance of Lenin and the massive ovation that greets him. For all its good intentions, however, *The Lofty Ailment* is not a successful poem; it is diffuse and clumsily proportioned. But the attempt to strike a public attitude, to find a justification for the poet in the Revolution, makes it an important landmark in Pasternak's development.

After the generalised, philosophical concerns of *The Lofty Ailment*, Pasternak turned to a more factual subject, which would simplify the problems encountered in the earlier poem. In *The Year 1905* (*1905 god*, 1925–6) he tried to give a panoramic picture of the first Russian revolution by depicting several sections of Russian society and some of the historic events of the year. We see the older intelligentsia, the massacre of 9th January, the peasants and factory workers, the naval mutiny in Sevastopol, university students, and finally the Moscow rising of December. The events of the year provide a natural framework for the poem, and, except for a brief introduction, it is written throughout in the same metre, a galloping, breathless five-foot anapaest.

For all its simplicity of design, the poem evidently gave Pasternak considerable trouble. The variants and rejected drafts help to show some of his preoccupations in this work. Above all the poem attempts to rehabilitate the intelligentsia: the fathers are shown as having prepared the revolution, and their children, the students, carry on their good work, and suffer in the cause. The poet himself, as a boy of fifteen, witnesses these events, and his family is emotionally involved in the outcome. Yet it is difficult to feel that the intelligentsia are really with the revolutionary movement in this poem, for each of the sections is self-contained and isolated; the poem remains a collection of vivid scenes, not a unified work of art.

The most successful of these works is undoubtedly *Lieutenant Shmidt* (*Leytenant Shmidt,* 1926–7). Here Pasternak builds his poem on a single incident, the mutiny headed by Lieutenant Shmidt in the autumn of 1905. The naive and impractical character of Shmidt no doubt appealed to Pasternak; he emerges as a distinct individual, perhaps the only one in Pasternak's poetry. Hints at a love affair, and complex family relationships round out his character, while the need to choose between his love for his mistress and his family and his sense of mission provides psychological depth. This concentration gives the work a natural unity, which is unimpaired by the variety of metres and styles, moods and points of view, characteristic of the poem.

The most remarkable feature of *Lieutenant Shmidt,* however, is Pasternak's own Olympian view of events. By a variety of devices, such as the repetition of the word 'October' with its associations of 1917, he forces the reader to look at the poem from a contemporary standpoint, as well as through the eyes of his hero. Shmidt is protesting not merely against the corruption and brutality of the Tsarist regime; he is challenging the whole cycle of rebellion and repression. In describing the courtroom Pasternak observes that the whole scene will sooner or later be repeated, with the prosecutors of today in the dock tomorrow. In another part of the poem he recalls the dialectical process by which yesterday's heresy becomes tomorrow's dogma:

О государства истукан,
Свободы вечное преддверье!
Из клеток крадутся века,
По Колизею бродят звери,
И проповедника рука
Бесстрашно крестит клеть сырую,
Пантеру верой дрессируя,
И вечно делается шаг
От римских цирков к римской церкви,
И мы живем по той же мерке,
Мы люди катакомб и шахт.*[6]

The phonetic similarity between '*tsirkov*' and '*tserkvi*' seems to illustrate the ease with which the persecuted become persecutors in their turn. The repetition of 'we' and the regular use of the present tense culminate in 'We too live . . .' spelling out the implications for Pasternak's contemporaries.

Although the poem is ostensibly about a revolution, Pasternak's view of the individual as a medium for events is still unaltered. Unlike other revolutionary figures of Soviet literature, Shmidt is a passive hero. He offers no ideological justification for his actions; he merely appeals to the elemental will of the Russian people that had mysteriously selected him; he can only co-operate with this power. He does not control or direct events. Indeed he is a contemplative, almost a philosophical figure, an image of the poet himself. In this respect the poem provides a bridge between the early lyrics and the ideas of *Doctor Zhivago*.

The Year 1905 and *Lieutenant Shmidt* are of all Pasternak's works the most acceptable to the Soviet authorities. At the time, however, it was pointed out that although his interest in 1905 was an improvement on his previous position, he had still

* O idol of the state,/the eternal outer door of freedom./The centuries creep out of their cells,/the beasts prowl round the Coliseum,/and the hand of the preacher/fearlessly makes the sign of the cross over the damp cage,/hoping to tame the panther by faith,/and the step from Roman circuses to the Roman church/is endlessly repeated./We too live by the same standard,/we, men of the catacombs and mines.

not come to grips with the subject of 1917. This explanation was disingenuous, for the implications of *Lieutenant Shmidt* were not lost on the Soviet censors: they excised a few short passages from the poem and sixteen lines from Shmidt's last speech.

The final major work of this period is *Spektorsky* (1930), a novel in verse, on which Pasternak had worked for several years. It is closely connected with *Povest* (translated as *The Last Summer*) and probably formed part of a novel which Pasternak was planning at this time. *Spektorsky* is concerned with the same theme as *Lieutenant Shmidt*, the fate of the intellectual in an age of action and violence; but the problem is now seen from the opposite angle. Sergy Spektorsky is a weak drifting hero, who achieves nothing. His flabbiness is emphasised by the energy of the women around him; his sister is active in the social reform movement; of his mistresses, one is a social-revolutionary, and the other later becomes a partisan leader. Spektorsky is unable to commit himself to any cause, or even to love. His leit-motif of 'sleeping by day' emphasises his detachment and inability to act. It is difficult indeed to find any redeeming feature in him.

The most surprising feature of this poem, therefore, is the parallelism between the narrator, the 'I' of the poem, and Spektorsky. They share the same characteristics, and the narrative often switches from one to the other as if to stress that there is no significant difference between them. The narrator introduces himself as:

Привыкши выковыривать изюм
Певучестей из жизни сладкой сайки*[7]

cultivating a dilettante aestheticism like Spektorsky. He treats his task of collecting Leniniana with a flippancy that must be unique in Soviet literature. When, at the end of the poem, Spektorsky seems to have been at least temporarily stirred out of his apathy by the return of Olga, a former mistress of his and now a Party functionary, the narrator is left alone: he has dozed off during their conversation, and 'while I slept, they both had disappeared'.[8]

It is of course dangerous to identify this 'I' with the poet

* Accustomed to winkling out the currants of sweet melody from the sugar-bun of life.

Pasternak, but its use suggests that Pasternak recognised in himself some features of the intelligentsia, which were irrelevant and even absurd in the present age. The length of time during which he worked on the poem and the related works in prose, confirms that this reappraisal of traditional intellectual values was not just a temporary sop to the anti-intellectualism of the RAPP period (1928–32), but the expression of a deep inner concern. Both the rebel-martyr Shmidt and the dissociated remote Spektorsky have left their traces in the character of Doctor Yuriy Zhivago.

Of these works only *Lieutenant Shmidt* can really be considered a success. Pasternak wrote no more poems of these dimensions. But they had helped him to simplify his style, and had given him some practice in working with larger structures; to that extent the experience had been invaluable. Henceforth Pasternak was to devote himself to the lyric forms in which he had made his name, and in which he expressed himself most naturally. But first he was to review his life in the autobiographical *Safe Conduct* (*Okhrannaya gramota,* 1929–31), in which he attempted to trace the evolution of his poetic sensibility. The stages in his personal development correspond to the three main sections of this work: Rilke and Skryabin, Europe, and finally Mayakovsky. The work ends with Mayakovsky's suicide, and the shock-waves it caused.

In speculating on the motives leading up to Mayakovsky's suicide, Pasternak speaks of his running headlong into the opposition of a new, incomprehensible and unsympathetic city, in the face of which Mayakovsky suddenly lost his former assurance:

> Что значит робость отрочества перед уязвимостью этого нового рожденья? . . . Но разве бывает так грустно, когда так радостно? Так это не второе рожденье? Так это смерть?*[9]

The contrast of the 'second birth' with 'death' leads on to the title of Pasternak's next book of poems, *Second Birth* (*Vtoroye rozhdeniye,* 1932), a collection of shorter poems, written in 1931–2. It was as if the death of Mayakovsky had shifted the

* What did the timidity of youth mean in the face of the vulnerability of this new birth? . . . But can it really be so sad, when it is so joyful? So this is not a second birth? So this – is death?

responsibility for Russian literature to Pasternak's shoulders: the alternatives of 'second birth' or 'death' had been divided between them. The same idea can be found in the title *Safe Conduct,* suggesting a mysterious power that was to bring Pasternak unscathed through the troubles and dangers around him – an assurance that was to grow all the stronger during the terrible experiences of the later 1930s.

In the year of Mayakovsky's suicide Pasternak was beset by family troubles. He had left his first wife for the wife of one of his friends and the friction inside the Pasternak circle had become intolerable. For a time he and his new wife were actually homeless. Hearing of his plight, the Georgian poet, Paolo Yashvili, offered him his hospitality in the Caucasus. The summer spent in the South, and the many visits that followed brought a new dimension into Pasternak's life. He declared that if he were ever to bring out a new edition of *Safe Conduct* (the book had been suppressed in the Soviet Union) he would insert a chapter on the Caucasus, as a formative influence on his development, equal to the others described there. In his later *Essay in Autobiography* (*Avtobiograficheskiy ocherk,* 1956–7), Pasternak carried out this promise. It was the last experience in his life that he thought worth commemorating.

The Second Birth, then, marks a new start in Pasternak's career. The book contains a variety of poems, grouped loosely into seven sections. There are love poems, poems about poetry, and a new attempt to define the role of the poet under socialism. It opens with an extended philosophical poem, *The Waves* (*Volny*), in which the poet states his intention of including everything: his past experiences, his present ideals and his aspirations, his place as a poet in Soviet Russia. His love affair with the Caucasus now becomes part of the general fascination the region had always held for Russians, since the time of Pushkin and Lermontov. (Perhaps, too, Pasternak remembered that Mayakovsky was born in Georgia and spoke the language.) Thus Pasternak places himself in a long historical tradition, and suggests his awareness of the historical role that he now felt called upon to play. In Georgia the grim burden of the past, with its countless invasions and devastations, echoed in the barren mountainous scenery of the Northern Caucasus, is inseparable from the fertility of the vineyards and pastures in the South, the natural beauty and vitality of the people and their rich cultural traditions. It is a natural symbol for the synthesis of opposites, man and the elements, the present and the past, the poet in an age of revolution, the creation of a work of art, and in the last resort for the final synthesis of Communism. The poem ends triumphantly with the opening words: 'Here everything will be included', re-interpreted in this light.

Not all the poems, however, share this optimism. In *When I weary of the claptrap of toadies* (*Kogda ya ustayu ot pustozvonstva*) the poet tries to answer the doubts of his friends: politically he may have his reservations over the abuses of the regime, but the same power that inspired both the poet and the revolutionaries in 1917 is too great to be argued with; he and his contemporaries may have been run over and maimed by the new age, but this is a small price to have to pay. Elsewhere, as in *While we clamber over the Caucasus* ('*Poka my po Kavkazu lazayem*'), the idyllic representation of the mountains is darkened by the prophetic images of gas attacks and executions.

Pasternak's new attitude to the role of the poet is expressed most memorably in the short poem: *O, had I known that this is how . . .* (*O, znal by ya, chto tak byvayet . . .*), in which he looks back on his youthful flirtation with poetry, and compares it with his present awareness of its tragic obligations. The poet is now not just a vehicle for art or natural vitality, but of history and fate. The gush of liquid that recurs throughout his work is now not water but blood. The poet is no longer required merely to turn on a tap, but to stake his life.

This new and tragic interpretation of the poet's role owes something, no doubt, to the tragedy of Mayakovsky, and it held out the promise of a new direction for Pasternak's poetry. From 1932, in line with the new policy of encouraging the non-Communist intelligentsia, favourable references to him began to appear in the Soviet press. At this stage Pasternak still imagined that he could reconcile his own individual vision with the requirements of the Party. He therefore resisted pressures to become just another Soviet poet. In the poem *To a Friend* ('*Drugu*', 1931 – the friend was Boris Pilnyak), he expressed his dilemma:

И разве я не мерюсь пятилеткой,
Не падаю, не подымаюсь с ней,

Но как мне быть с моей грудною клеткой,
И с тем, что всякой косности косней?*[10]

The poem goes on to warn that the poet cannot be co-opted so easily into the purposes of the politicians – it is dangerous even to leave a seat for the poet – dangerous not only for the poet, but for the politicians too.

At about this time Pasternak went to the Urals to observe the results of industrialisation. But the contrast between the luxurious treatment that he received and the sight of the ragged starving workers was too much for him and he returned to Moscow before the end of the tour.[11] At the Writers' Congress he was at first carried away by the euphoria of the occasion; he compared it to the language of poetry. But he ended his speech with a prophetic warning of the dangers inherent in the State's monopoly of artistic patronage:

При огромном тепле, которым окружают нас народ и государство, слишком велика опасность стать литературным сановником.†[12]

In the years following *Second Birth* Pasternak wrote virtually no poetry, but selections from his earlier works continued to appear; there were editions in 1933, 1934, 1935, and 1937. During these years he turned instead to translations from the Georgian poets, both classical and contemporary. Pasternak did not know Georgian, and he worked from a literal translation, done by an intermediary; for the atmosphere, he relied on the descriptions of his friends. The translations were a success and led many other Russian poets into this field. It is also possible that they won Pasternak some goodwill in high places, since Stalin, and the later Chief of the Security Police, Beriya, were both Georgians.

Pasternak continued, however, to reflect on his place in Soviet literature. In a speech of 1936 he explained that he

* And don't I measure myself against the Five-year Plan,/Stumble and rise again as it does? But what do I do about my own lungs and heart,/About that which is stubborner than any stubbornness?

† In view of the immense warmth with which the people and the State have surrounded us, the danger of becoming a bureaucrat of literature becomes all the greater.

was trying to evolve a new style, and that:

В течение некоторого времени я буду писать плохо . . . пока не свыкнусь с новизной тем и положений, которых хочу коснуться.*

But he still insisted on preserving a certain amount of artistic individuality:

На эти общие для всех нас темы я буду говорить не общим языком, я не буду повторять вас, товарищи, а буду с вами спорить, и так как вас — большинство, то и на этот раз это будет спор роковой и исход его — в вашу пользу. И хотя я не льщу себя тут никакими надеждами, у меня нет выбора, я живу сейчас всем этим и не могу по-другому.†[13]

Pasternak was referring in particular to two poems in the New Year's number of *Izvestiya*: one of them tries to work the names of Lenin and Stalin into a list of what ought to be included in contemporary poetry. In a letter to a friend he referred to them as 'idiotic verses'.[14] But though unsuccessful, these poems are not insincere or hypocritical; they are just forced.

After these poems there follows another interval of five years, in which he seems to have written no poetry; he published a few more episodes from his projected novel, and devoted himself chiefly to his translations from the Georgian and from German and English lyric poetry; it was at this time that he first tried his hand at translating Shakespeare (*Hamlet*, 1940–1). His next original poems appeared in print only at the beginning of 1941. They reveal a totally new approach to the composition of poetry. They are simple in content and in style, and are the first evidence we have of a profound spiritual experience that Pasternak seems to have gone through in 1940, and which probably made him a Christian.

* For some time I shall be writing badly . . . until I can finally cope with the novelty of the themes and situations that I want to deal with . . .

† I shall speak of those themes that are common to us all in a language that is not common property. I am not going to repeat you, comrades, I am going to argue with you, and since you are in the majority, the argument will be a fateful one, and its outcome – in your favour. And although I do not delude myself with any hopes, I have no choice, my whole life is involved, and I cannot do otherwise.

Pasternak now tries to present himself as an ordinary, typical citizen. Everyday details from his life are introduced not because they are part of the poem and its composition, as in his earlier works, not even because they are glimpses of an unusual man, but because the poet is a man like any other. He is depicted as a simple countryman, engaged in working his garden. The style of this poetry too is deliberately unobtrusive and matter-of-fact:

Я под Москвою эту зиму,
Но в стужу, снег и буревал
Всегда, когда необходимо,
По делу в городе бывал . . .

Обыкновенно у задворок
Меня старался перегнать
Почтовый или номер сорок,
А я шел на шесть двадцать пять.*[15]

These trivial prosaic details seem to break down the barriers between the poet and his fellow-countrymen; he observes the peasants, students, and craftsmen in the train, recognising 'the unique features of Russia', and by the time they reach their destination the poet's 'I' has been absorbed into the collective 'we'.

The device, of course, recalls Mayakovsky's *Good*!, but there are differences between them. Mayakovsky, in merging into the community, does not surrender his individuality, but discovers it refreshed and liberated in a new unashamed 'I' and 'my' in his concluding vision of Communism. Mayakovsky never ceases to be Mayakovsky. Pasternak's absorption into his fellow-passengers and his new prosaic tone seem less persuasive, because a great writer (as Tolstoy discovered) cannot lay aside his individuality so easily. It remains an intellectual and ethical ideal. It was in this spirit that Pasternak later declared that he would not lift a finger to save three quarters of his early works.[16]

The German invasion simplified Pasternak's position. He

* I am living outside Moscow this winter/But in frost, in snow, in blizzards,/ Whenever it has been essential/I have visited the city on my business . . . Often the mail-train or number forty/Would try to overtake me/In the back-alleys/But I was going for the six-twenty-five.

no longer felt the need to demonstrate his oneness with the people either to himself or to the Party; it could be taken for granted. But life in the rear, and later evacuation to Chistopol, tormented him with guilt. Too old for military service, he applied for a post as a war correspondent; after several delays his request was eventually granted in the autumn of 1943; the result, *Trip to the army* (*Poyesdka v armiyu*), is a conventional piece of war reportage, describing the devastation left by the retreating Germans.

His poems of these years are mostly devoted to the war. They achieve the simplicity that Pasternak had sought for so long – but the simplicity is more simplification than new wisdom. The virtues of Russian partisans, the heroism of a wounded sapper, the invincibility of the Red Navy, all these are conventional war poetry themes and Pasternak has nothing to add to them. It is not easy to be objective in time of war, but such sentiments as:

Должны нам заплатить обидчики
Сторицею и чистоганом.*[17]

are far removed from the noble wisdom of *Lieutenant Shmidt* with its warnings of the dangers of continuing the cycle of violence and revenge.

The cultural freeze that ensued in 1946 did not affect Pasternak as drastically as it did Anna Akhmatova and Zoshchenko. He remained a member of the Union of Soviet Writers, and though he was to have no new poetry published until 1954, his translations from the Georgian, of several more plays by Shakespeare, of both parts of Goethe's *Faust*, and the publication of a small selection from his own earlier poetry, continued to provide him with a livelihood. Some of the poems that he composed during these years later found their way into *Doctor Zhivago*.

Although this novel falls outside our period, its subject, the fate of the Russian intelligentsia after the Revolution, might have provided the conclusion for this study. For all Pasternak's high opinion of it, however, the book is a disappointment. In the 1950s it appeared as something of an anachronism – the crushing of the old intelligentsia was a feature of the 1920s

* The offenders must repay us/A hundredfold and in hard currency.

and early 1930s – the post-Stalin period was marked by the emergence of a new Soviet intelligentsia, devoted to the same causes and ideals as its nineteenth-century predecessors. Pasternak's faith in the necessity of art and its redemptive power links him to Blok and Zamyatin, but his later indifference to political and social issues would dismay them; it has little appeal in a country where for the previous twenty-odd years literature had been almost totally divorced from real issues. The character of Zhivago himself, an old man at the age of thirty, prone to self-pity, though in fact enviably well-cushioned against the hardships of his time, with his lofty sentiments all too often betrayed by the bitterness of his speeches and by the pettiness of his actions, holds out no new ideals for Soviet readers. The lyric gift that sustains the poems of Zhivago so magnificently betrays the novel into frequent inconsistencies (notoriously in the account of Zhivago's time among the partisans), into miscalculations of tone and emphasis, and a failure to individualise any of the characters. Even if they are meant to 'symbolise' life or individualism, as is sometimes claimed, surely it is desirable for them to show some of these qualities?

Pasternak's place in Soviet literature is not easy to estimate. Although he is now claimed as a Soviet poet, the fact remains that for several decades he was relegated to the sidelines of official literature, and in his final years he was disgraced and persecuted. For all his lyrical gifts and his many striking poems, he wrote no works which succeed in catching the spirit of an age, or are universally accepted. In this respect he has been unfortunate; Mayakovsky may have tarnished his reputation in the eyes of some critics with a mass of trivia and ephemera, but his major works are proof against contamination. Pasternak tried to move with the times, but he was never quite in step with them. Throughout the 1920s and 1930s his many admirers expected from him a work that would match his abilities with a worthy theme, but when *Doctor Zhivago* finally appeared after Stalin's death, even some of his friends were disappointed.

Pasternak's genius is essentially lyrical; even in music he looked primarily for the lyric element; his favourite composers were Chopin and Skryabin. Between the years 1923 and 1930 he tried his hand at some larger forms, narrative and philosophical poems; but important as these are for his general development they were only an interlude in his work. Early in his career he dreamed of writing a novel: *The Childhood of Lyuvers* (*Detstvo Lyuvers,* 1918) seems to have been intended as the opening chapter, and lengthy excerpts, such as *The Last Summer,* continued to appear right up to the eve of the Second World War. It was in fact only realised with the completion of *Doctor Zhivago*. But just as the poems of Zhivago are the finest part of the novel, so, it seems, will Pasternak's lyric poetry come to outweigh his more ambitious works.

Pasternak's influence on Soviet poetry has been considerable: in the 1920s his unusual imagery and dynamic rhythms appealed to many young poets, and seemed to them to express the mood of the age. In the 1950s his conversational, reasonable tone impressed the new generation of poets who were rebelling against the bombast of most Stalinist verse. His influence as a poet is likely to grow, and perhaps, like Tyutchev and Fet, some of whose techniques and mannerisms he has adopted, his importance will be fully appreciated only many years after his death.

6

Leonid Leonov

Leonid Leonov might seem to be the most conventional of Soviet writers. Of his first two novels one, *The Badgers* (*Barsuki*, 1924), was based on the aftermath of the Civil War, and the other, *The Thief* (*Vor*, 1927), on life in the NEP period. In the 1930s his novel *The River Sot* (*Sot*, 1930) was devoted to industrialisation, another, *Skutarevsky* (1932), to the Sovietisation of the old Russian intelligentsia, and yet another *The Road to Ocean* (*Doroga na okean*, 1935) to the new 'positive hero' of socialist realism. The Second World War drew three more works from him, and the death of Stalin was followed by the last of his novels to date, *The Russian Forest* (*Russkiy les*, 1953), often regarded as the first swallow of the 'thaw'. His work might almost serve as a miniature history of Soviet literature.

This seeming conventionality disappears on closer acquaintance. Of all Soviet novelists Leonov is the most individual; his works are characterised by an elaborate style, a highly personal system of thought and imagery, and they are built on acute philosophical and psychological conflicts. He is interested chiefly in exceptional personalities; whether they are bandits, commissars, or university professors, his heroes are invariably outstanding at their trade. His characteristic themes spring from the moral problems raised by Communist theory and practice, and his works often tend towards a tragic statement, though this is usually muted and superficially resolved in order to comply with the requirements of Soviet literary theory. All these features distinguish his books from those of other Soviet novelists. In the 1920s he enjoyed the reputation of being one of the most promising young Soviet writers, but he was finally accepted by Soviet critics only very late in his career, after the death of Stalin.

Leonov sees himself as a link in a long historical and cultural tradition. His works are frequently built on the continuity of the past and the present; his heroes have almost always matured before 1917, like their creator. So it is natural for him to see the Revolution as a major turning-point in the history of Russia, rather than as a final break with the past, as some early Soviet writers liked to believe. If in the 1920s Leonov adopted this position as a *poputchik* writer, he was gradually driven to find some philosophical justification for it. He found it in the belief that everything in the universe is interconnected and interdependent (the dominant images of his last two novels, the 'ocean' and the 'forest' are natural symbols for this idea); the past and the present, the good and the evil associated with them are eternal and inseparable. For Leonov, art is the supreme method of recording this dialectical process, not just the material, physical details of an age, but its atmosphere, not just the propagandistic elements of 'reality in its revolutionary development', but also those innumerable other ties that link the present to the past and affect it in subtle and incalculable ways.

This sense of life as a meaningful flux is exemplified best of all by Leonov's style. His works are richly allusive, with references to the Bible and the Homeric poems, and more recondite subjects such as horticulture, the history of the popes, and legends of the caliphs. Based on the syntax of classical Russian, his prose is unmistakably that of a Soviet citizen. Modern Russian contractions and acronyms and his own neologisms fit quite naturally into it. He has managed to create, single-handed, his own literary language out of the slowly evolving *lingua franca* of the new Soviet educated classes. Nobody but Leonov could have written a page of his works.

Leonov's own life straddles the two epochs. He was born in 1899 of a middleclass family, and he had completed his formal education by the time of the Revolution. His father, a political exile, was the editor of a local newspaper in Archangel, and the young Leonov's first works, poems and reviews, were published in its pages. After the Revolution he was confined for a while to Archangel by the British intervention, and then volunteered for the Red Army. He saw service in the south of Russia, where he soon found his way on to the staff of an army newspaper. At the end of the Civil War, he applied for entry to Moscow University, intending to study medicine, but he was rejected. He took some work as a plumber, and composed a few stories largely for his own amusement: these attracted the attention of some literary men, and several of them were published. Since then Leonov's biography has been largely that of his books.

His career as a Soviet writer falls into three periods which correspond to the major stages in the history of Soviet Russia. The first of them covers the years 1922–9. For Leonov it was largely a time of experimentation, as it was in Soviet literature generally. It took him some time to find his own voice, and in his early stories he tried out other authors' styles and devices quite openly. This imitativeness certainly weakens his first novel, *The Badgers*, though the scope of the book, the ambitious range of characters and the stylistic virtuosity reveal unmistakably a talented writer. Leonov really found himself only with his second novel, *The Thief*, the work that made him famous.

Dmitriy Vekshin, the 'thief' of the title, had been one of the most brilliant Red commissars of the Civil War; but his mercurial temperament had led him into a grave breach of discipline – he had murdered a prisoner – and he had been expelled from the Party. At the end of the war the traditional difficulties of the demobilised serviceman are only increased by this stigma, and he is further demoralised by the introduction of the NEP, which he regards as a betrayal of all the ideals for which he had just been fighting. He becomes a thief, devoting his ingenuity and courage to undermining a society which he now repudiates. His protest, however, is made in the name of the Revolution, and however low he sinks he always remains loyal to this ideal. Accordingly he is not branded as a traitor; Leonov plays down the criminal and anti-social aspects of his activities. It is rather Communism that is on trial, and its ability to harness and make creative use of Vekshin's boundless energies.

In the key image of the novel Vekshin is compared to a 'planet that has been torn out of its orbit'.[1] Each of the four parts ends with the word 'Sun' as a reminder of the life-giving pull which will eventually reclaim him. Particularly important in this image is the idea of flight, which is to evolve throughout the whole course of Leonov's work. The word carries many overtones: there is the romantic idea of being raised above the rest of humanity, of being conspicuous, of being superior; then again there is the idea of danger and therefore heroism; finally there is the idea of aspiration, the inability to be satisfied with what has been achieved.

Vekshin's career is paralleled in the figure of his sister, Tanya, the trapeze artist. Her star turn, the *shtrabat*, a dangerous leap across the circus, with no safety net below her, provides another version of his 'flight'. Like her brother she takes a pride in constantly inventing new difficulties and overcoming them. But for Tanya the end is tragedy; she misses her footing and falls to her death.[2]

Vekshin's own career is marked by the same urge to self-destruction. His motto is 'upwards and onwards'; he refuses to be satisfied by the achievement of any of his goals. He is horrified to see his former commanding officer now transformed into a sedate Party functionary. Above all he rejects happiness, for that implies a final achievement, or at least a coming-to-terms, and consequently an abrogation of man's duty to aspire 'upwards and onwards'. 'Happiness is always bourgeois; happiness is when there's no further to go',[3] says one of the characters in the novel. On the other hand Vekshin's antithesis, the bureaucrat Chikilev, dreams of the day when men will be happy to order; and even the Communists in the book regard happiness in terms of social and physiological organisation: 'You'll be able to manufacture it like goloshes or light-bulbs.'[4]

In Leonov's scheme of values suffering and tragedy are inseparable from human dignity, from 'flight'. They provide the only evidence of spiritual vitality, evidence that has to be constantly re-asserted by new exploits. Indeed, a tragic outcome is the only really consistent end for Vekshin himself. Leonov, however, holds out a tentative prospect of regeneration for his hero through hard physical labour and education:

> Остальное — как Митя попал к лесорубам, и был бит сперва, а потом обласкан, как работал в их артели, и пьянел от еды, заработанной тяжким трудом шпалотеса, как огрубел, поступил на завод, учился, как приобрел свое утерянное имя — все это остается вне пределов сего повествования.*[5]

* For the rest – how Mitka fell among lumberjacks, how he was beaten at first and then welcomed, how he worked in their artel, and grew drunk on food that he had earned by the heavy labour of a lumber-jack, how he was coarsened, how he went to a factory, studied, how he regained the name that he had lost; all this falls outside the limits of the present narrative.

This ending hardly provides a convincing solution to Vekshin's restless aspirations, but the fact that the reader remains dissatisfied is in itself an indication of how seriously Leonov had treated the conflict between individual conscience and social utility in the rest of the novel.

Leonov's need for an optimistic end to Vekshin's career comes from his belief that the same qualities are inherent in the Bolshevik Revolution. Vekshin cries:

Революция есть прежде всего полет вверх и вперед, вверх и вперед.*[6]

On the other hand the doubters see the Revolution in terms of a brave but essentially earthbound slog. The *déclassé* aristocrat Manyukin writes:

Ты скажешь опять, что еще во мраке туннеля идет поезд, не вырвался еще в голубой просвет по ту сторону горы. Не долог ли туннель? Не безвыходен ли?†[7]

The whole idea of flying is an assertion of the creative leap, the stroke of genius, but it is not surprising if Leonov baulks at associating the tragic overtones of this image with the Revolution. On the other hand the 'tunnel' raises the question: if the Revolution is no more than that, is it worth anything at all?

In many ways *The Thief* was characteristic of its period. The cultivation of the individualist hero, the attempt to reconcile him with a collectivist ideology, and concern over the apparent stagnation of Communism were common themes in Soviet literature of the time. The Soviet writer was still comparatively free, and though the novel received some hostile criticism, it was re-published a few times up to 1936, after which it was effectively suppressed. In other ways *The Thief* points the way to Leonov's later works, not least in his choice of hero, justified in the following words:

Тем и примечательна революция наша, что скинула орнаментум . . . теперь все устанавливается по будничному ранжиру . . . Пропойца пьет, жена дипломата чистит ногти . . . Голый

* The Revolution is first and foremost a flight, upwards and onwards, upwards and onwards.

† Perhaps you'll tell me that the train is still deep in the tunnel, hasn't yet burst out into the blue glimmer at the far end? But hasn't the tunnel gone on rather long? What if there's no way out of it?

человек исчезает из обихода, и в поисках его приходится спускаться на самое дно.*[8]

The upheavals of the Great War, Revolution, Civil War, and the subsequent hardships and privations, had, as it were, torn off the artificialities of custom and civilisation from human nature. Now was the time to find out what man was really like in his natural 'naked' state. This idea is central to Leonov's work, for he is not so much interested in the changes that Communism would bring to human nature, as in the unchanging and eternal essence of mankind. His works imply tacitly that Communism should be made for man, not man for Communism.

With the publication of *The Thief* Leonov won instant recognition as one of the most important Soviet writers. Gorky marked him out for special attention, and his works began to be translated in the West. By 1929 he had been elected first chairman of the new RAPP-controlled Union of Writers. He had arrived. One could guess at this change from Leonov's works alone. From now on his heroes are not underdogs and rebels, but men at the top of the tree, prominent commissars and world-famous scientists. The concern with 'flight' and tragedy, mortality and happiness, however, still remains the dominant motif in the work of Leonov's second period, 1929–36, though these values are now subtly redistributed.

With the end of the NEP and the inauguration of the First Five-year Plan, the cult of individualism, so characteristic of Soviet literature during the 1920s, gave way to the new ideal of collectivism. This convention too is reflected in Leonov's novels of the period. Thus the individualistic scientist Skutarevsky (in the novel of the same name) is finally reconciled with the Party and the labouring masses in the closing pages. On a deeper level the commissar Kurilov, in *The Road to Ocean*, debarred from Party activity by a fatal illness, is amazed to discover that Communism has richly equipped him for human relationships. He makes new friendships and finds himself actually capable of love.

Yet these men are recognisably Leonov heroes. Professor

* That's what's so remarkable about our revolution. It's torn off all the ornaments . . But now everything is returning to its normal round . . . The drunkard drinks and the diplomat's wife cleans her nails . . . The naked man is disappearing from the scene fast; to find him one has to plumb the very depths.

Skutarevsky is working on the wireless transmission of electricity, a new variant of the leap of creative energy. He actually drives his car like an aeroplane, commenting:

Полет, вот естественное состояние человека, все остальное — лишь кощунственное отступление от нормы.*[9]

Kurilov indulges in flights of imagination, dreaming of his Utopia, Ocean, 'the capital of men who fly naturally and effortlessly'.[10] On the other hand flight still retains its tragic associations for Leonov. Even in the Communist Utopia, the possibility of suffering and tragedy is not excluded:

Но хотя все было у них в руках, — хлеб, работа и сама судьба, нам часто попадались люди с озабоченными лицами. Мы поняли, что и у них бывает печаль, что и они знают трагедии, но лишь более достойные высокого звания человека.†[11]

The cosmonauts, envisaged by Kurilov, return from their first space-flight, dead or blinded by their experiences. For Skutarevsky: 'Flight – that's the only way for a man to die',[12] and just at his moment of triumph he recognises the fateful signs of an imminent heart-attack. Kurilov collapses just when love seems to have humanised him conclusively.

For all this, however, the tragic images of Skutarevsky and Kurilov are somewhat muffled. They are sick men, middle-aged, and, ironically, they are even more isolated and conscious of their isolation than the individualist Vekshin had been. They are both aware that the best of life is behind them, and that they will not live to see the glorious future for which they have worked. Their devotion to the cause has left them with no personal interests or private life. This gives them a pathetic, almost sacrificial air, which overshadows their more obviously heroic attributes. Skutarevsky joins the Party only after a series of shattering blows in his private life and his work. But there is no real tragedy here; the safety net of Party membership is waiting for him. As for Kurilov, the act of flying has been suspended and made static: 'he was like a bridge and people passed over him into the future.'[13]

* Flight – that's man's natural state; everything else is just a blasphemous lowering of the norm.

† But even though everything was theirs, – bread, work and fate itself, we often came across people with careworn faces. We realised that they too could be sad and experience tragedies, but tragedies more worthy of man's lofty calling.

These new heroes are loyal, respectable Soviet citizens. They find fulfilment, not in flying in the face of society, but in identifying themselves with it. In *The Thief* the idea of flying had been a condition of life, an expression of the need to intensify experience by danger and courage. It was a symbol of the individual's right to set his own challenges and to seek his own happiness. But in the Russia of the 1930s no such rights could be assumed; they had to be earned and proved. Kurilov tells one of the characters:

—. . . при социализме деятельность каждого будет средством доказать свое право на радость.

— Право на радость или на хлеб?

— Не путайте, заблудитесь. Право на хлеб сейчас дает всякий труд, но только творчество — право на радость, а завтра всякий труд будет творчеством.*[14]

The pedestrian Communists and bureaucrats of *The Thief*, with their desire to regulate human happiness, would have welcomed the suggestion.

The most impressive feature of these novels is their relevance to their times. Leonov is interested not merely in reflecting the official propagandist picture of his age, but in trying to catch something of its darker side. This too is part of the present, and cannot be ignored; it too will have its effect on the character of the future. At its most superficial level this comes out in the references to shoddy standards. In *Skutarevsky*, for example, there is a recurrent complaint: 'They've started putting cigarette ends in the bread again.'[15] Of greater significance are the occasions when Leonov moves beyond the inefficiencies of any modern industrial society to the peculiar hazards of life in the Soviet Union. Telephone-tapping, the interception of letters, informers, the disappearance of friends: all of these come to the surface surprisingly often, and Leonov's characters seem to accept them as all in the natural order of things:

Известие об его аресте было для всех полной неожиданностью, которой, однако, никто почему-то не удивился.†[16]

* ' . . . under socialism each man's activity will be a means of proving his right to joy'. 'His right to joy or to bread?' 'Don't confuse the issue or you'll get lost. Today every kind of labour bestows the right to bread, but only creativity the right to joy, and tomorrow all work will be creative'.

† The news of his arrest was completely unexpected, but for some reason no one was surprised by it.

These tendencies are carried furthest of all in *The Road to Ocean*. The title of the novel is a good example of Leonov's counterpoint of symbols. In its literal sense the 'road' refers to a railway line which is under the supervision of the hero Kurilov. The eventual destination of this line is Shang-hai, here identified as the future capital of world Communism, under the name of Ocean (a significant name when one recalls Russia's traditional struggles to find an outlet to the sea). It is only natural for a Communist writer to think too of the Marxist image of the ocean of Communism into which the rivers of history will flow; accordingly, the victorious general in the last battle against capitalism is called Yang-tse, the river on which Shang-hai stands. At the other end of the scale Ocean is the condition of each of its inhabitants, and so the 'road' is traversed not only by humanity, but by each individual human being.

The novel is sometimes dismissed as a conventional exercise in the creation of a model Communist hero, but this is to miss the point of the opening pages, which, as has been shown, are a false start. Instead Leonov returns to his earlier theme of the 'naked man'. He strips his hero of all his usual activities and attributes in an attempt to discover the essence, not the clichés, of an ideal Communist. Indeed the whole novel is skilfully designed to arouse expectations of a conventional approach in order that Leonov may underline the difference of his treatment.

The figure of Kurilov has already been discussed (see pp. 230–2). His antagonist, Gleb Protoklitov, is an even more fascinating character. It is he who is suspected of the 'sabotage' in the opening pages, and these suspicions are only strengthened when he turns out to be the son of a Tsarist judge (who had once condemned Kurilov to Siberia) and to have fought in the White Guards during the Civil War. Yet no evidence is produced to show that Gleb actually did commit this sabotage (or even that there was any sabotage in the first place). Leonov later points out that Gleb was conscripted into the White Guards against his will; in any case he is hardly to blame for his parentage. Thus Leonov contrives to suggest that Gleb may be an implacable enemy of the Soviet regime, while at the same time providing a perfectly satisfactory answer to all these imputations. This double focus is to be sustained throughout the novel.

On the evidence that we are given Gleb is not necessarily a

traitor. His tragedy springs from his decision to remain in Russia after the defeat of the Whites and to try to make a new life for himself. Inevitably, this involves a good deal of concealment and even falsification, but Gleb seems to have succeeded; he becomes an engineer and makes his way to the top; he becomes a member of the Party. Even his unsympathetic brother Ilya recognises him as a 'persevering man, uncomplainingly earning the right to live and have his mistakes forgotten'.[17]

By a strange coincidence Ilya is also the surgeon who is to operate on Kurilov, and Gleb hints to him that, with Kurilov's suspicions now aroused, the family would be safer with him out of the way. Ilya's first reaction is to call another surgeon to take his place; but, in a remarkable throwaway sentence, very typical of his work, Leonov observes:

> Он вернулся с полдороги вовсе не потому, что было поздно, и коллега, который мог заменить его на операции, уже находился в кровати.*[18]

Kurilov dies under the operation, and Ilya then denounces Gleb to the Komsomol.

In the traditional Soviet interpretation Gleb is represented as an unrepentant White officer, whose aim is to attain a position from which he can conduct his sabotage more effectively; his hatred of Kurilov is taken to be conclusive proof of his anti-Soviet intentions. Ilya, on the other hand, is made out to be a loyal, though misguided, intellectual who unmasks his brother as soon as he understands his wicked intentions. But there is another equally valid interpretation. As far as we know, Gleb has served the Party irreproachably. Ilya is far more bourgeois in his habits (his collecting mania is a recurring symbol in Leonov's works, and in Soviet literature generally, for a bourgeois and therefore anti-Soviet outlook); his relationship with Gleb he regards with distaste and embarrassment. And yet, even though Kurilov dies so conveniently for him after the operation, Ilya is automatically given the benefit of the doubt; although he too has denied his origins and falsified his past his belated denunciation of his brother is accepted unhesitatingly as evidence of a change of heart – that very change of heart which

* Halfway there he turned back, but not at all because it was too late and the colleague who could have taken his place at the operation was already in bed.

Gleb is continually denied. In such a context the phrase 'uncomplainingly earning the right to have his mistakes forgotten' acquires a profound irony.

So the tables have been turned. At first Gleb's falsehoods are presumed to indicate his guilt. In fact he was merely trying to lead an honest life; how in the conditions of the time could he tell the truth without disaster ensuing? His falsehoods only mirror those of his society. In reality, as in this novel, it was the honest men, not the cynics, who had most to fear. This is borne out by the reactions of Soviet readers. Accustomed to believe the worst about the Whites and their relatives they have read very much more into the text than has been put there by the author. In this way they too bear unconscious witness to the moral confusion of the time and, unwittingly, reinforce the book's relevance to the years of the great purges.

In the tragic character of Gleb Protoklitov and his hopeless situation (for his ultimate ruin is never in doubt) Leonov discovers unsuspected riches. Even in the horrific scene where Gleb attempts to murder one of his old comrades now blackmailing him, he obstinately retains the reader's sympathy, and the author's too. Not only are the men who hunt and betray him infinitely more repulsive (significantly, Kurilov's illness and inactivity enable him to escape this taint) than Gleb himself, but his situation and response to it remind Leonov of an earlier ideal. It is actually Kurilov who observes that Gleb 'would make a good airman',[19] and Gleb really does recall Leonov's flying heroes. His life represents a new variation on theirs. Like Vekshin he too is a 'naked man' with none of the defences or camouflages of normal men. Faced with the prospect of annihilation he refuses to come to terms. He exists in defiance of the abyss.

With this figure Leonov also provides a brilliant solution to one of the thorniest problems facing the Soviet novelist; Gleb Protoklitov is both literarily viable and a characteristic figure of his times. He is the 'villain', but he provides no opposition and no threat. Politically he is passive; his main crime is that he is on the run, struggling to create an identity. In this all too typical situation Leonov discovers a psychological goldmine. It was to provide him with an anti-hero and a conflict (none the less real for being only the shadow of a conflict) which recur in varying forms throughout the rest of his work.

The Road to Ocean is Leonov's most ambitious novel, both in its formal experimentation and in the importance of the issues it raises. However, after initial approval it ran into vicious and Philistine criticism, largely because it did not develop into the conventional Soviet novel that its beginning had seemed to portend. Within a year of its first publication it had been virtually suppressed. Leonov must have felt this painfully, for after producing five novels in the twelve years, 1924–35, he was to wait another eighteen before publishing his next, *The Russian Forest*. In the meantime he turned to the stage.

The change in Leonov's fortunes was caused, at least in part, by a spiteful campaign which had been running for several years. It took various forms: semi-political provocations of the usual Soviet kind, distortions of the content and meaning of his works and, more insidiously, suppression of everything he had written up to 1936. Altogether some forty editions of his novels had appeared by this date; none was to be reissued again until 1947, one of them, *Skutarevsky*, only after Stalin's death, while another, *The Thief*, has never been re-published in its original form. This campaign continued with a series of vicious attacks on Leonov's plays of 1937–40, culminating in violent denunciations of *The Snowstorm* (*Metel*, 1940), a play which had already been performed successfully in the provinces and was currently undergoing rehearsals at the Maly theatre. The play compares two brothers, one a corrupt Soviet bureaucrat, the other a conscience-stricken *émigré*, to the advantage of the latter. The play was immediately suppressed, and Leonov himself disgraced. It seems likely that he was only saved by the war.

Leonov's fall was almost as meteoric as his rise. In 1929 he was standing at the top of the tree. A personal friend of Gorky, Chairman of the Union of Writers, and with an international reputation as a novelist, he seemed unchallengeably secure. Yet within a few years he had lost the friendship of Gorky, his books had been virtually suppressed, and after Gorky's death he does not seem to have been considered even as a candidate for any important post in the Union.

These changes are inevitably reflected in his works. His new heroes are no longer men at the hub of affairs, but provincial figures, in agriculture, industry, or local administration. They lack the flamboyance of Leonov's earlier heroes; the accent is on modesty, efficiency, unobtrusiveness; one of these plays is actually called *An Ordinary Man* (*Obyknovenny chelovek*, 1942), and the characters in it drink a toast to 'heroic ordinariness.'[20] Many of these men are engaged in 'creative' work, but they are no longer associated with images of flight. Like Kurilov they are at best 'bridges'. Professor Skutarevsky had driven his car as if it was an aeroplane; Professor Vikhrov, the hero of *The Russian Forest*, prefers to go on foot.

Leonov's heroes are almost always older than himself. None of them has found personal happiness; each of them is sadly aware that he will not live to see the entry into the Promised Land, whose prospect has dominated and given meaning to his life. Inevitably it seems to them that their successors will enjoy the final triumph too easily, without having shared in the efforts and sacrifices that made it possible; they look for some evidence that their children appreciate their work and will be worthy of inheriting it. Leonov himself perhaps shared the feelings of his ageing heroes, for from 1936 onwards he begins to depict the younger generation.

It is here that the image of 'flying' re-appears. These younger heroes – or more often heroines – are often associated with gliding or parachute-jumping; sometimes, by extension, they serve in submarines or tanks. These militaristic images reflect, of course, the atmosphere of the years in which these works were written; but these demonstrations of courage and heroism, while seeming to echo the Vekshins' self-destructive challenge to the void beneath, are no longer pursued for their own sake, but serve as demonstrations that these boys and girls are 'entitled to happiness'. Where the Vekshins had been testing their potentialities to their furthest limits, these new heroes are simply undergoing initiation, or rather confirmation, ceremonies, which they invariably complete successfully.

Leonov was able to contribute some deeply-felt, but not very original works to the war effort, which did something to restore his reputation; for one of them, the play *Invasion* (*Nashestviye*, 1941–2), he was awarded a Stalin prize. It is typical of Leonov that the theme of the play, the return of a man from the labour-camps and his evolution into a Soviet hero, should be only a transparent variation on the theme of *The Snowstorm* which had so nearly destroyed him. His most ambitious work on a war theme is the play *The Golden Coach* (*Zolotaya kareta,* 1946), which came out in the year after the end of the war.

Like most of Leonov's works it is constructed on the interplay of past and present. Some twenty-six years before the play opens, a young penniless schoolmaster, Nikolay Karev, had proposed to Masha Poroshina, only for her parents to forbid him ever to see her again, until he could provide a golden coach for her. Karev left the district and eventually became an outstanding geologist. In the meantime Masha Poroshina, or Marya Sergeyevna, as she has now become, has also risen in the world; she has for many years been mayor of the town. When the play opens, Karev has just returned home for the first time in twenty-six years. He is a widower now, with a grown son, Yakov, only just demobilised from the army. The older people discover that they are still in love with one another, but Marya Sergeyevna is married (as it happens, to a worthless man, a coward and a black-marketeer). Instead, therefore they pin their hopes on a match between their children.

In the language of the play's imagery, Karev may seem to have returned home with his 'golden coach'. But things are not so simple. Marya Sergeyevna's daughter Marka loves and is loved by the soldier Timosha. The situation begins to bear an uncanny resemblance to that of their parents twenty-six years earlier, with the all-important difference that it is now Timosha who is in the position of the former schoolmaster Karev, while Karev and his son are identified with the image of the 'golden coach'. The tension of the play is built around the two alternatives; will the children make up for their parents' broken happiness, which in these circumstances would be to repeat their mistake? Or will they defy their wishes and so avoid their errors? The tension is not finally resolved until the last scene of the play when Marka elects to marry Yakov Karev. The children have repeated their parents' mistakes and will have to pay the same penalties. The power of the 'golden coach' is as irresistible as ever.

This unromantic story is reflected in the physical setting of the play. The action takes place in the immediate aftermath of the war. It is autumn and the prevailing mood is one of hardship and stoicism. The provincial town has been devastated by bombs and shells; many of the characters have been bereaved, one has been blinded, another shell-shocked. It is also frankly recognised that not all Russians have been heroes; there have been cowards and black-marketeers as well. If this was Mayakovsky the play would signify nothing but the complete victory of the past. The interest of Leonov's play, however, lies in his attempt to find some prospects of regeneration in the cheerless present.

On this deeper level, *The Golden Coach* is probably the most affirmative work that Leonov has yet written. It tells of human failures, but it tells too of human responses to those failures. Karev and Marya Sergeyevna, thanks to their earlier misfortunes, have achieved positions that they had never dreamed of. Although they cannot repair the mistakes of the past, cannot even avoid imposing them on their children, they are at least to be admired for the positive results that their lives have achieved. This is to be projected on to the younger generation – and we are to believe that their mistakes and disappointments will similarly spur them on to greater achievements. And beyond this Leonov holds out the hope of transforming the sufferings of Russia, devastated twice within quarter of a century, into something creative and affirmative.

Thus, in spite of the austerity and suffering that mark every page of *The Golden Coach*, the work contrives to be both realistic and optimistic (one of the ideals of socialist realism). Unfortunately none of these virtues were visible to the play's first critics in 1946. Zhdanov objected, and the play was suppressed so effectively that few even of Leonov's admirers know of its existence; it has never been staged, and it survives only in a wretchedly printed edition of 500 copies. Leonov did not attempt to publish another artistic work until after Stalin's death, seven years later. But this time he was not disgraced; journalism of the Soviet novelist's kind, praises to Stalin, denunciations of the West, routine articles on literary matters, continued to flow from his pen; these years also saw the birth of his best known outside interest – forestry.

The Golden Coach marks the end of a period in Leonov's development. For almost twenty years, since the composition of *The Thief*, he had prided himself on his depiction of the contemporary scene; his works abound in topical references, often more than was healthy; even when he switched to drama in 1936, he still emphasised that the plays were set 'in our times'. But since the rejection of *The Golden Coach* in 1946, he has never again attempted to deal with contemporary Soviet reality. *The Russian Forest* deals with the events of 1941–2, and his only other new imaginative work, the film scenario *The Flight of Mr McKinley* (*Begstvo mistera Mak-kinli*, 1960), is set in a very hypothetical future.

The Russian Forest continues Leonov's revelations of the darker side of Soviet reality begun in *The Road to Ocean*. The plot is built round the rivalry of two professors of forestry. The hero, Vikhrov, favours a carefully regulated equilibrium between felling and planting. His opponent, Gratsiansky, concedes that this is desirable in theory, but calls it impracticable at the present time of economic and political strain; while these difficulties last, the infinite resources of the Russian forests should be exploited wholesale; there will always be plenty of time to restock them once Communism has been attained. The principles behind this debate, the relationship of ends to means, of theory to practice, are of course among the central philosophical issues of Russian Communism. Leonov's treatment was particularly controversial, since the forestry practice of the Soviet Government had been closer to Gratsiansky's position than to Vikhrov's. Indeed the rapid industrialisation of the country had been financed largely by the export of timber supplied by the notorious labour camps. The serious consequences of this policy for the environment were already making themselves felt in Stalin's last years.

Leonov, of course, is not interested only in the scientific and economic sides to the controversy, but in its human and social effects. Throughout the novel the Russian forest and the Russian people are regularly bracketed in a single phrase; often one is used as a symbol or a simile for the other; various characters are compared to trees, while the forest actually 'looked like people'. The novel is about the people of Russia, and the issues involved, for all their scientific packaging, are worked out in terms of individual Russians. Looked at in this light the cynical attitude of Gratsiansky to the trees of the forests becomes more than just bad husbandry. Like *The Road to Ocean*, *The Russian*

Forest is concerned with the purges and labour camps of Stalinist Russia.

Leonov now carries the ambiguity of Gleb Protoklitov a stage further. For the first half of the book, the reader is uncertain which of the two protagonists is the hero and which the villain. But gradually it becomes plain that it is Vikhrov who is the loyal Soviet scientist and Gratsiansky who is just the opposite. Indeed so monstrous are the eventual revelations of Gratsiansky's past treacheries, from his collaboration with the Tsarist Okhrana to his spying for the enemy in the Second World War, that the reader may well ask how it was that Gratsiansky should have survived so long and even flourished in a period when all secret dissenters, saboteurs and counter-revolutionaries were being ruthlessly exterminated.

The question has been foreseen and indeed suggested by Leonov, and his answer is that there is a natural logic in this – that it is the unscrupulous Gratsianskys of the world who are best fitted to survive in Soviet conditions; while the honest men suffer, the Vikhrovs (there are clear autobiographical elements in Leonov's account of his life), who are so busy getting on with their work that they have neither time nor inclination to defend themselves. Gratsiansky's glib mastery of Marxist jargon gives Leonov unlimited scope for revealing the cynical uses to which these abstract phrases could be put in Soviet practice. Vikhrov is actually brought to trial in the 1930s, though, admittedly, he is eventually acquitted.

Here Leonov might have seemed to shirk the issue by brushing it aside with a facile happy ending. But his introduction of the issue was still courageous and well ahead of the times. Even if it was too early in 1953 to show how innocent and loyal Soviet citizens could be condemned on trumped-up charges, Leonov was still prepared to admit, well before de-Stalinisation, that people had at least been accused unjustly; his readers could be relied on to judge for themselves how often justice actually prevailed. Here too he brings his readers back to the labour camps.

Leonov may well claim to have been the major novelist of the Stalin period. He is unique among Soviet writers in having tried to work within the limitations of the censorship, without totally sacrificing his integrity or retreating into silence (at least before

1946). His achievement has been sadly underlined in the years since *The Russian Forest*. It was widely hoped that the 'thaw' would release a new stream of works from him, but, apart from the unworthy *The Flight of Mr McKinley*, he has devoted himself to revising the most controversial of his early works. These revisions have added no new laurels to Leonov's name. Undertaken at a time when other Soviet writers were trying to 'unrevise' their mutilated works, his have moved in the direction of greater conventionality (only in *Invasion*, revised in 1964, have the implications of Fedor's imprisonment been spelt out). *The Golden Coach* (revised in 1955) has been re-written to provide a happy ending (this is the version which is generally known, and the one staged by the Moscow Arts Theatre), but only at the expense of discrediting all the major characters. In 1964 Leonov revised the work yet again; this time he returned to the 1946 solution, but the 1955 characterisation is left essentially unaltered, and the combination of discredited characters and the original ending makes the play more pessimistic than any of the earlier versions. In the new *The Thief* (1956–9) Leonov strips his hero of all his former glamour; he sees him now simply as a thief, and pours scorn on his own earlier suggestions of his eventual redemption. Even the one apparently new story, *Evgenia Ivanovna* (1963), proves to be only a revised version of a work first composed in 1938, but not published.

It may be that Leonov's creative springs have dried up, but it is also possible that Leonov, after evolving a method of writing serious works under Stalinism, found, once Stalin was dead and the terror relaxed, that he could not write outside this situation. But the habit of writing was too strong to be broken and so he turned to his earlier works, in the hope of reminding Soviet readers of his past achievements, already obscured by the more sensational poems, plays and stories of the early 'thaw'. The re-publication of his most controversial works, even though heavily revised, is a silent testimony to the terrible times that he witnessed and tried to record.

Leonov's position in the Soviet literary world today is not an enviable one. Despised by those who preferred silence to compromise and by those for whom Stalin's reign is past history, distrusted by those timeservers for whom the Stalin era provided unprecedented opportunities for careerism and by those who regard all its survivors as irreparably compromised, he is today largely ignored and forgotten by the Soviet reading public. Too adventurous for the critics of the 1930s and 1940s, his novels have come to seem all too conventional for those Russians who are only now discovering the achievements of the Western novel in this century, and the new possibilities open to their own literature. Yet Leonov's relevance to the Soviet scene, his superb sense of style, the individuality of his heroes and villains, and the tragic implications of his work as a whole, suggest that this period of neglect is only temporary, and that a revaluation of his achievement is inevitable.

Conclusions

It is always presumptuous to attempt a cultural survey of a period so close to one's own. It is probable – indeed it is virtually certain – that the picture will look quite different in fifty years' time. The mainstream of a national culture sometimes follows subterranean channels, and few people would chart its course in any country in this century with much confidence.

In the case of modern Russia these difficulties are further compounded by the continuing world-wide controversy over Russian 'socialism'. To most Soviet readers the account given in this book will seem grotesquely distorted, with discussions of Zamyatin, Klyuyev and Pasternak, and an emphasis on Leonov to the virtual exclusion of Demyan Bednyy, Aleksey Tolstoy, Sholokhov and a host of worthy socialist-realist writers who have acquired an ephemeral fame and wealth by avoiding any hint of relevance to the actual concerns of either reader or artist. On the other hand it may well come to seem that the omission of Khlebnikov, Andrey Belyy, Mandelshtam and Akhmatova, and *émigré* writers, artists and composers (such as Stravinsky) from the foreground of such a book is tantamount to writing of Russian culture in the nineteenth century with only passing references to Pushkin, Gogol, Tyutchev and Turgenev. It is far too early yet to write such a book. For better or worse this study is concerned with the Soviet, rather than the Russian, cultural scene.

One of the effects of Stalinism was to drive creative literature underground and keep it there. The poetry and prose of some of the greatest Russian writers of the period 1890–1930 was totally suppressed; even Dostoyevsky was taboo for many years. The resulting distortions of Russian cultural history have been reflected unconsciously in many non-Soviet studies. But at least the works of these authors had once been published, and the books existed in libraries somewhere; readers in the West were not bound by the literary canons of Soviet Russia. For artists living under Stalin the situation was different; with no hope of publication, and with few friends who could be relied on, they could write only for themselves and their desks. Works of the class of Bulgakov's *The Master and Margarita* are only just beginning to emerge from this limbo. Nobody can say how many more such works there are to follow, or how profoundly they will affect our understanding of the Soviet cultural scene.

In many ways, however, it is easier for a Western student of modern Russian literature than it is for his Soviet counterpart. He enjoys easy access not only to works published in the Soviet Union, but also to much literature that has been suppressed or circulates there only clandestinely. Thanks to the endeavours of Professor Gleb Struve and Boris Filippov, scholarly editions of major poets such as Gumilev, Mandelshtam, Akhmatova and Klyuyev, to which there is nothing remotely comparable in the Soviet Union, are now available in the West. More recently Wilhelm Fink Verlag of Munich has re-issued the prose of Belyy, the complete works of Khlebnikov, and important Formalist studies, in photographic reprints. With this wealth of material to hand, and more promised, the Western student is in a far better position to chart the course of Soviet culture than all but a handful of Soviet scholars.

This paradox brings us to the central contradiction of the Soviet period. It is undeniable that the cultural policies of the Communist Party have achieved much in the way of general education: universal literacy, easy access to museums and libraries, art galleries and concert halls, and in the sciences, a solid base of theoretical research and technological application that have made the USSR the second power in the world. Immense sums of money have been and are spent in supporting and subsidising these activities. This achievement cannot be denied. But this generosity has extended only to officially approved aspects of culture. The other side of the coin is a Philistine intolerance of all cultural novelty and experiment. The hostility which the Party showed to the Proletkult, LEF, the Formalists (to name only the movements that have figured in this book) led inexorably to the slaughterhouse of the great purges and the Arakcheyevian regimentation of Stalin's last years.

It is sometimes argued in mitigation that 'at least the Communists take culture seriously'; by the same logic it could be argued that Lysenko took genetics seriously. In fact culture in the USSR is assessed on the most crudely utilitarian principles. For this reason the arts have always fitted rather awkwardly into Soviet Marxism. From Trotsky to Gorky and Stalin, and even to Khrushchev and the present rulers, the Russian Communist leaders have regularly reproached their artists for lagging behind the times; at the same time socialist realism has ensured that they shall not do anything else. Those few artists or works of art that have tried to reflect the present or run ahead of it have been consistently denounced, though in some cases, notably Mayakovsky's, after a decent lapse of time, they have been accepted.

Thus, paradoxically, the first State to be founded on Marxist principles is in many ways a standing refutation of them. The role of such personalities as Lenin, Stalin, and Gorky has profoundly, and most un-Marxianly, affected the course of Russian social, economic and cultural history. At the same time, the legacy of the nineteenth century has not succumbed so easily to the creation of a 'socialist culture'. The spiritual and aesthetic values asserted by the great Russian writers from Pushkin to Blok, and, more surprisingly, the *engagé* 'critical realism' tradition, have continued to subvert the one true course of socialist realism ever since its inception. Conversely, the Communist Party may claim to have successfully mastered Marx's teachings and applied them, but the fact remains that Soviet Russia is more vulnerable to Marxist criticism than any bourgeois State. Nowhere else in the world are philosophy, art and science, the whole superstructure of the underlying socio-economic realities, manipulated so thoroughly in the interests of the ruling class.

The explanation of these paradoxes would seem to lie in the central paradox of the premature Marxist revolution. Its consequences, from Brest-Litovsk, through the NEP, socialism in one country, the First Five-year Plan, socialist realism, the great purges, Lysenkoism, the Second World War, are still with us today.

Nineteenth-century Russia has been immortalised not by its rulers but by its poets, novelists, composers and scientists. In spite of the many compromises and capitulations of Russian intellectuals in the twentieth century, the Soviet era will surely be remembered in a similar way; as the age of Pavlov, Vavilov, Kapitsa and Sakharov, of Blok, Mayakovsky, Meierhold and Solzhenitsyn, to whose names Marx and Stalin will be little more than footnotes.

Notes

Part I

Chapter 1 MARXISM AND THE BOLSHEVIKS

1 *Essential Writings of Karl Marx,* selected by David Caute (London 1967), p. 49.
2 In his book *Imperializm, kak vysshaya stadiya kapitalizma* (*Imperialism as the Highest Stage of Capitalism,* 1916).
3 Karl Marx, Friedrich Engels, *Manifesto of the Communist Party* (Moscow n.d.), p. 114.
4 *Essential Writings of Karl Marx,* p. 231.
5 *Ibid.*, p. 43.
6 Friedrich Engels, *Anti-Dühring: Herr Eugen Dühring's Revolution in Science* (Moscow 1963), p. 157.
7 See, for example, his *Preface to the Russian edition of the Communist Manifesto in 1882* in Karl Marx and Friedrich Engels, *Selected Works in Two Volumes* (Moscow 1958), I, pp. 22–4.

Chapter 2 TWO WRITERS

1 Ye. Zamyatin, *My* (New York 1952), p. 5.
2 *Ibid.*, p. 7.
3 Ye. Zamyatin, *Litsa* (New York 1965), p. 190.
4 A. A. Blok, *Sobraniye sochineniy* (1960–3), III, p. 27.
5 *Ibid.*, III, p. 274.
6 *Ibid.*, VII, pp. 294–5.
7 A. A. Blok, *Zapisnyye knizhki* (1965), p. 387.
8 A. A. Blok, *Sobraniye sochineniy*, VII, p. 330.
9 A. A. Blok, *Zapisnyye knizhki*, p. 377.
10 A. A. Blok, *Sobraniye sochineniy*, VII, p. 367.
11 V. V. Mayakovsky, *Polnoye sobraniye sochineniy* (1955–61), VIII, p. 266.
12 A. A. Blok, *Zapisnyye knizhki*, p. 441.
13 A. A. Blok, *Sobraniye sochineniy*, VII, p. 350.
14 Korney Chukovsky, *Sobraniye sochineniy* (1965–9), II, p. 312.
15 *Blokovskiy sbornik*, (Tartu 1964), p. 452.

16 A. A. Blok, *Sobraniye sochineniy*, VII, p. 403.
17 *Ibid.*, VI, p. 164.
18 *Ibid.*, VI, p. 165.
19 *Ibid.*, VI, pp. 166–7.
20 *Ibid.*, VIII, p. 539.
21 *Ibid.*, VII, p. 422.

Chapter 3 POLITICAL AND SOCIAL HISTORY

1 This theory is discussed at length in I. Deutscher, *The Prophet Armed* (Oxford 1954), pp. 149–62.
2 V. V. Mayakovsky, *Polnoye sobraniye sochineniy* (1955–61), IX, p. 548.
3 V. I. Lenin, *Sochineniya* (1941–67), XXXII, pp. 272–6.
4 For an account of Soviet laws of property and inheritance see S. Kucherov, 'Sobstvennost v Sovetskom Soyuze', *Grani,* No. 57, pp. 182–203.
5 In fact preparations for the reform of the alphabet had begun under Nicholas II.
6 M. Gorky, *Sobraniye sochineniy* (1949–55), XXVII, p. 322.
7 These examples have been taken from Donald Treadgold, *Twentieth Century Russia*, p. 258.
8 See V. V. Mayakovsky, *Polnoye sobraniye sochineniy* (1934–8), VI, p. 233.
9 The full story is well told in Adam Ulam, *The Bolsheviks*, pp. 571–4.
10 I. Deutscher, *Stalin*, p. 317.

Chapter 4 INTELLECTUAL LIFE

1 See David Joravsky, *Dialectical Materialism and Soviet Marxism*, pp. 4–5.
2 These paragraphs are based on Paul S. Epstein, 'Diamat and Modern Science', *Bulletin of the Atomic Scientists,* (August 1952), pp. 190–4.
3 Joravsky, *op. cit.*, p. 13.
4 This section is based on *Death of a Science in Russia*, ed. Conrad Zirkle.
5 Loren Graham, *The Soviet Academy of Sciences and the Communist Party,* p. 88.

Chapter 5 THE LITERARY SCENE

1 V. I. Lenin, *O literature i iskusstve* (Moscow 1957), pp. 383–4.
2 Karl Marx, Friedrich Engels, *Literature and Art, Selections from their Writings* (New York 1947), p. 19.
3 *Ibid.*, pp. 19–20.

4 Compare Lenin's comments on Beethoven's *Appassionata:* 'I know nothing better than the *Appassionata,* I could listen to it every day. Amazing, superhuman music. I always think with pride, naively perhaps, what miracles man can work ... But I can't listen to music often, it affects my nerves, makes me want to say silly compliments, stroke people on the head for living in this filthy hell and creating such beauty. But nowadays one mustn't stroke anybody on the head, or they'll bite your hand off; you must beat them over the heads, beat them without any mercy, though, in principle, we're against using violence on people.' (M. Gorky *Sobraniye sochineniy* (1949–55), XV, pp. 39–40).

5 'Once when the conversation turned to the problem of what to substitute for religion, which must inevitably disappear from the consciousness of the labouring masses, he [Lenin] observed that apart from the theatre, i.e. art, there was not a single institution, "not a single organ which we could substitute for religion"'. Vyacheslav Polonsky, *Ocherki literaturnogo dvizheniya revolyutsionnoy epokhi* (Moscow 1929), pp. 82–3.

6 Quoted from V. V. Mayakovsky, *Polnoye sobraniye sochineniy* (1955–61), XII, p. 621.

7 For a more detailed account of Gorky's activities in the years 1917–21, see Bertram Wolfe, *The Bridge and the Abyss,* pp. 77–133.

8 For precise figures see Robert Maguire, *Red Virgin Soil,* pp. 6–7.

9 Vladimir Kirillov, *Stikhotvoreniya i poemy* (Moscow 1970), p. 35.

10 M. Gerasimov, *Stikhotvoreniya* (Moscow 1959), pp. 55–7.

11 A. Gastev, *Poeziya rabochego udara* (Moscow 1964), p. 98.

12 Leonid Leonov, *Sobraniye sochineniy* (1960–2), II, p. 140.

13 Robert Maguire, *Red Virgin Soil,* p. 169.

14 See Vyacheslav Polonsky, *Ocherki literaturnogo dvizheniya revolyutsionnoy epokhi,* pp. 77–112. The article may be found in English translation in Max Eastman, *Artists in Uniform,* pp. 217–52.

15 A. Fadeyev, *Razgrom* (Moscow 1969), p. 41.

16 *Ibid.,* p. 86.

17 *Ibid.,* p. 159.

18 Quoted from V. V. Mayakovsky, *op. cit.,* XII, pp. 150–1.

19 *Ibid.,* XII, p. 327.

20 *Ibid.,* XII, p. 65.

21 *Ibid.,* XII, p. 268.

22 Yu. Olesha, *Povesti i rasskazy* (Moscow 1966), p. 120.

23 See *Istoriya russkoy sovetskoy literatury* (Moscow, Leningrad 1958–61), I, p. 658.

Chapter 6 DRAMA AND CINEMA

1 For more details of this performance see Yuriy Annenkov, *Dnevnik moikh vstrech,* II, pp. 118–26.

2 It has been suggested that Kerzhentsev, the chief organiser of these spectacles, may have borrowed the idea from open-air productions that he had witnessed during his visits to the USA and England. See Spencer Roberts, *Soviet Historical Drama*, p. 29.
3 See V. V. Mayakovsky, *Polnoye sobraniye sochineniy*, XII, pp. 304, 631.
4 Yu. Yelagin, *Temnyy geniy* (New York 1955), p. 264.
5 G. Boltyansky, *Lenin i kino* (Moscow, Leningrad 1925), p. 19.
6 These figures are taken from J. Leyda, *Kino*, p. 169, and Dwight Macdonald, 'The Soviet Cinema', *Problems of Communism*, 1954, No. 6, p. 38.

Chapter 7 THE PEASANTRY

1 Adam Ulam, *The Bolsheviks*, p. 457.
2 For more details see Bertram Wolfe, *The Bridge and the Abyss*, pp. 108–18.
3 P. Sorlin, *The Soviet People and Their Society*, pp. 84–7.
4 L. Schapiro, *The Communist Party of the Soviet Union*, p. 336.
5 *Ibid.*, pp. 321–2.
6 *Ibid.*, pp. 336–7.
7 Leonid Leonov, *Sobraniye sochineniy*, II, p. 182.
8 *Ibid.*, p. 343.
9 Nikolay Klyuyev, *Sochineniya* (Neimanis 1969), I, p. 494.
10 *Ibid.*, I, pp. 502–3
11 Sergey Yesenin, *Sobraniye sochineniy* (Moscow 1961–2), V, p. 140.

Chapter 8 VLADIMIR MAYAKOVSKY

1 V. V. Mayakovsky, *Polnoye sobraniye sochineniy* (1955–61), XII, p. 99.
2 *Ibid.*, I, p. 185.
3 *Ibid.*, XII, p. 7.
4 *Ibid.*, I, p. 249.
5 *Ibid.*, I, pp. 126–7.
6 *Ibid.*, I, p. 136.
7 *Ibid.*, I, p. 25.
8 *Ibid.*, II, pp. 16–7.
9 *Ibid.*, II, pp. 18–9.
10 *Ibid.*, II, p. 211.
11 Mayakovsky was not actually billed to take the part. He took it when the original actor dropped out.

12 *Ibid.*, II, p. 115.
13 *Ibid.*, III, p. 365.
14 *Ibid.*, IV, p. 11–2.
15 *Ibid.*, IV, p. 101.
16 *Ibid.*, IV, p. 103.
17 *Ibid.*, XII, p. 261.
18 *Ibid.*, IV, pp. 171–2.
19 *Ibid.*, XII, pp. 38–9.
20 *Ibid.*, VII, p. 115.
21 See *Litso klassovogo vraga* (The Face of a Class Enemy), *ibid.*, IX, pp. 45–55.
22 V. I. Lenin, *Sochineniya* (1941–67), XXV, p. 87.
23 See V. V. Mayakovsky, *Polnoye sobraniye sochineniy*, XII, p. 559.
24 *Vospominaniya o Mayakovskom* (Moscow 1963), pp. 592–610.
25 V. V. Mayakovsky, *Polnoye sobraniye sochineniy*, VI, p. 304.
26 *Ibid.*, VI, p. 306.
27 *Ibid.*, VIII, pp. 322–3.
28 *Ibid.*, VII, p. 87.
29 *Ibid.*, X, p. 20.
30 *Vospominaniya o Mayakovskom*, pp. 523–4.
31 V. V. Mayakovsky, *Polnoye sobraniye sochineniy*, X, p. 284.
32 *Ibid.*, X, pp 280–1
33 *Ibid.*, XIII, pp. 120-1.
34 *Pravda*, 5 December 1935.

Part II

Chapter 1 SOCIAL AND POLITICAL HISTORY

1 For further discussion of this point see Donald Treadgold, *Twentieth Century Russia*, pp. 263–4.
2 *Soviet Society*, ed. A. Inkeles and K. Geiger (Boston 1961), pp. 69–70.
3 *Constitution* (*Fundamental Law*) *of the Union of Soviet Socialist Republics*, Article 125 (Washington 1945), p. 26.
4 Robert Conquest, *The Great Terror*, p. 28.
5 This theme and its ramifications is the main subject of Leonid Leonov's last novel *The Russian Forest* (*Russkiy les* 1953).
6 A. Pobozhiy, 'Mertvaya doroga', *Novyy mir* (1964), No. 8, pp. 89–181.
7 Robert Conquest, *The Great Terror*, pp. 525–35.
8 *Novyy zhurnal*, 1970, No. 96, p. 241.
9 This account of the opening campaign is based on A. Nekrich, *1941 22 iyunya*, (Moscow 1963), and P. Grigorenko, 'Sokrytiye istoricheskoy pravdy', *Novyy zhurnal*, 1970, No. 96, pp. 223–63.
10 P. Sorlin, *The Soviet People and Their Society*, p. 197, estimates war losses at 18 million.

Chapter 2 MAKSIM GORKY

1 M. Gorky, *Sobraniye sochineniy* (1949–55), II, p. 7.
2 Bertram Wolfe, *The Bridge and the Abyss*, p. 15.
3 M. Gorky, *Sobraniye sochineniy*, VI, p. 166.
4 *Ibid.*, VI, p. 170.
5 *Ibid.*, XVIII, p. 281.
6 V. I. Lenin, *Sochineniya*, 1941–67, XVI, p. 186.
7 *Na literaturnom postu*, 1927, No. 20, pp. 53-4.
8 M. Gorky, *Sobraniye sochineniy*, XXX, p. 27.
9 *Pravda*, 29 March 1928.
10 *Arkhiv A. M. Gorkogo*, X, Book 2, p. 193.
11 M. Gorky, *Sobraniye sochineniy*, XXIV, p. 368.
12 *Ibid.*, XVII, p. 212.
13 *Ibid.*, XXV, pp. 124–5.
14 *Ibid.*, XXIV, p. 447.
15 *Ibid.*, XXV, p. 183.
16 *Arkhiv A. M. Gorkogo*, X. Book 2, pp. 400, 402.
17 See for example, M. Gorky, *op. cit.*, XXVI, p. 46, and *Arkhiv A. M. Gorkogo*, X, Book 1, p. 261.
18 M. Gorky, *Sobraniye sochineniy*, XXV, p. 400.
19 *Ibid.*, XXVII, p. 47.
20 *Ibid.*, XXVII, p. 156.
21 *Ibid.*, XXX, p. 126.
22 *Ibid.*, XXX, p. 295–6.
23 *Ibid.*, XXX, p. 283.
24 Maxim Gorky, *Untimely Thoughts*, tr. H. Ermolaev (New York 1968), p. 19.
25 M. Gorky, *Sobraniye sochineniy*, XXVI, p. 238.
26 *Ibid.*, XXVI, p. 55.
27 *Ibid.*, XXVI, p. 31.
28 *Arkhiv A. M. Gorkogo*, X, Book 2, p. 420.
29 *Arkhiv A. M. Gorkogo*, X, Book 1, p. 386.
30 M. Gorky, *Sobraniye sochineniy*, XXX, p. 277.
31 *Ibid.*, XVII, p. 273, and XXVII, p. 259.
32 D. Shub, 'Maksim Gorky i kommunisticheskaya diktatura', *Mosty* I (1958), p. 248.
33 *Arkhiv A. M. Gorkogo*, X Book 1, p. 278.
34 D. Shub, 'Maksim Gorky i kommunisticheskaya diktatura', *Mosty* I (1958), pp. 251–2.
35 *Arkhiv A. M. Gorkogo*, X, Book 1, p. 213.
36 *Ibid.*, XXX, p. 334.
37 *Ibid.*, XXX, p. 372.
38 See Pavel Vasilyev, *Stikhotvoreniya i poemy* (Leningrad 1968), p. 27.
39 I. Shkapa, *Sem let s Gorkim* (Moscow 1964), pp. 379–80.

Chapter 3 THE CULTURAL SCENE

1 Quoted from D. Joravsky, *Soviet Marxism and Natural Science*, p. 264.
2 V. I. Lenin, *Sochineniya* 1941–67, p. 29.
3 Quoted from Bertram Wolfe, *Communist Totalitarianism* p. 109.
4 This account is based on J. Kucera, 'Soviet Nationality Policy: The Linguistic Controversy', *Problems of Communism*, 1954, No. 2, pp. 24–9.
5 *Soviet Science*, ed. Ruth Christman (Washington 1952), p. 94.
6 N. A. Gorchakov, *Istoriya sovetskogo teatra* (New York 1956), p. 277.
7 Leonid Leonov, *Sobraniye sochineniy*, 1960–2, V, p. 283.
8 R. A. Bauer, *The New Man in Soviet Psychology*, p. 99.
9 L. Schapiro, *History of the Communist Party of the Soviet Union*, p. 410.
10 The book has now been published in the West, *The Rise and Fall of T. D. Lysenko*, tr. I. M. Lerner (New York 1969).
11 For a fuller account see M. Hayward, 'Pilnyak and Zamyatin: Two Tragedies of the Twenties', *Survey*, No. 36 (April–June 1961), pp. 85–91.
12 *Novyy mir*, 1930, No. 5, p. 36.
13 Leonid Leonov, *Sobraniye sochineniy*, IV, p. 332.
14 Ilya Erenburg, *Sobraniye sochineniy* (Moscow 1962–7), VII, pp. 609–11.
15 For an extended analysis of the part played by the literary views of social critics in the nineteenth century, see Rufus Mathewson, *The Positive Hero in Russian Literature*, (New York 1958).
16 *Pervyy vsesoyuznyy syezd sovetskikh pisateley*, Stenograficheskiy otchet, (Moscow 1934), p. 4.
17 Leonid Leonov, *Sobraniye sochineniy*, VI, p. 7.
18 *Ibid.*, VI, p. 416.
19 I. Vinogradov, 'Za sovetskuyu klassiku', *Literaturnyy sovremennik*, 1936, No. 5.
20 *Survey*, No. 64 (July 1967), p. 179.
21 A. Solzhenitsyn, *V kruge pervom* (New York 1968), p. 68.
22 B. Pasternak, *Doktor Zhivago* (Milan), p. 519.
23 N. A. Gorchakov, *Istoriya sovetskogo teatra*, p. 265.
24 *Ibid.*, p. 404.
25 J. Leyda, *Kino*, p. 274.
26 *Ibid.*, p. 340.
27 *Ibid.*, p. 361.
28 Z. Ben Shlomo, 'The Soviet Cinema', *Soviet Survey*, No. 29, 1959, p. 70.

Chapter 4 THE PEASANTRY

1 W. S. Churchill, *The Hinge of Fate* (Boston 1950), p. 498.
2 P. Sorlin, *The Soviet People and their Society*, p. 151.

3 R. A. Maguire, *Red Virgin Soil*, p. 392.
4 *Chitatel i pisatel*, 7 July 1928.
5 *Grani*, No. 70 (1969), p. 3.
6 *Ibid.*, p. 67.

Chapter 5 BORIS PASTERNAK

1 B. Pasternak, *Stikhi i poemy 1912–1932* (Ann Arbor 1961), p. 101.
2 *Ibid.*, p. 177.
3 This aspect of Pasternak's early poetry is well analysed in D. L. Plank, *Pasternak's Lyric* (Mouton, The Hague, 1966).
4 B. Pasternak, *Stikhi i poemy 1912–1932*, p. 101.
5 Quoted from B. Pasternak, *Stikhotvoreniya i poemy* (Moscow 1965), p. 631.
6 B. Pasternak, *Stikhi i poemy 1912–1932* (Ann Arbor), pp. 145–6.
7 *Ibid.*, p. 275.
8 *Ibid.*, p. 316.
9 B. Pasternak, *Proza* (Ann Arbor), pp. 287, 288.
10 B. Pasternak, *Stikhi i poemy*, p. 223.
11 Yu. Krotkov, 'Pasternaki', *Grani*, No. 60, 1966, pp. 69–70.
12 B. Pasternak, *Stikhi, 1936–59* (Ann Arbor), p. 218.
13 *Ibid.*, p. 222.
14 B. Pasternak, *Letters to Georgian Friends*, transl. D. Magarshack (London 1968), p. 66.
15 B. Pasternak, *Stikhi 1936–59*, p. 28.
16 B. Pasternak, *Proza*, p. 352.
17 B. Pasternak, *Stikhi 1936–59*, p. 49.

Chapter 6 LEONID LEONOV

1 L. Leonov, *Vor* (Moscow 1928), p. 154.
2 The importance of this episode has been remarked by Helen Muchnic in *From Gorky to Pasternak* (New York 1961), pp. 283–5.
3 L. Leonov, *Vor*, p. 395.
4 *Ibid.*, p. 195.
5 *Ibid.*, p. 540.
6 *Ibid.*, p. 408.
7 *Ibid.*, p. 174.
8 *Ibid.*, pp. 40–1.
9 L. Leonov, *Sobraniye sochineniy* (Moscow 1960–2), V, p. 110.
10 *Ibid.*, VI, p. 132.
11 *Ibid.*, VI, p. 418.
12 *Ibid.*, V, p. 110.

13 *Ibid.*, VI, p. 416.
14 *Ibid.*, VI, p. 320.
15 *Ibid.*, V, p. 10.
16 *Ibid.*, V, p. 271.
17 *Ibid.*, VI, p. 506.
18 *Ibid.*, VI, p. 535.
19 *Ibid.*, VI, p. 51.
20 *Ibid.*, VII, p. 346.

Bibliography

A vast number of books have been devoted to Soviet Russia, and they would by themselves stock a large library. The following bibliography is, therefore, necessarily a select one. It consists of books which proved particularly useful in compiling the present study and which can be recommended for further reading. Most of these books contain substantial bibliographies of their own. By no means all books and articles referred to in the text are included in this bibliography.

It should also be observed that this bibliography lists mainly Western sources. Soviet historical, social and cultural studies are of course essential reading for any serious student of Soviet affairs, but since about 1930 they have owed more to the current political line than to the despised ideal of 'bourgeois objectivity'. Very few Soviet works can therefore be recommended in an elementary bibliography of this nature.

Bibliographies

HORECKY, PAUL L., *Basic Russian Publications. An annotated Bibliography on Russia and the Soviet Union,* (Chicago 1962).

HORECKY, PAUL L., *Russia and the Soviet Union. A Bibliographic Guide to Western-Language Publications,* (Chicago 1965).

Marxism

BERLIN, ISAIAH, *Karl Marx: His Life and Environment,* (Oxford 1963).

CAREW-HUNT, R. N., *The Theory and Practice of Communism,* (London 1950).

MEYER, ALFRED G., *Leninism,* (Harvard 1957).

WETTER, G. A., *Dialectical Materialism: A Historical and Systematic Survey of Philosophy in the Soviet Union*, (London 1959).

History

CARR, E. H., *The Bolshevik Revolution 1917–1923*, Vols. I, II, III, (London 1950–3).
The Interregnum 1923–1924, (London 1954).
Socialism in One Country 1924–1926, Vols. I, II, III, (London 1958–64).
CARR, E. H., and DAVIES, R. W., *Foundations of a Planned Economy 1926–1929*, Vols. I, II, (London 1969).
CHAMBERLIN, W. F., *The Russian Revolution 1917–1921*, Vols. I, II, (New York 1935).
CONQUEST, R., *The Great Terror*, (London 1968).
DANIELS, ROBERT V., *Red October*, (New York 1967).
DEUTSCHER, ISAAC, *The Prophet Armed: Trotsky 1879–1921*, (Oxford 1954).
The Prophet Unarmed: Trotsky 1921–1928, (Oxford, 1959).
The Prophet Outcast: Trotsky 1928–1941, (Oxford 1963).
Stalin: A Political Biography, (Oxford, 1949).
FAINSOD, MERLE, *How Russia is Ruled*, (Harvard 1953).
INKELES, ALEX, and GEIGER, KURT, eds., *Soviet Society: A Book of Readings*, (Boston 1961).
LEWIN, MOSHE, *Lenin's Last Struggle*, (New York 1968).
NEKRICH, A., *1941 22 iyunya*, (Moscow 1963).
NETTL, J. P., *The Soviet Achievement*, (London 1967).
SCHAPIRO, LEONARD, *The Communist Party of the Soviet Union*, (London 1960).
SORLIN, PIERRE, *The Soviet People and Their Society*, (New York 1968).
SOUVARINE, B., *Stalin: A Critical Survey of Bolshevism*, (New York 1939).
TREADGOLD, D. W., *Twentieth Century Russia*, (Chicago 1959).
ULAM, ADAM B., *The Bolsheviks*, (New York 1965).

Science

BAUER, R. A., *The New Man in Soviet Psychology*, (Harvard 1952).

CHRISTMAN, RUTH, ed., *Soviet Science,* (Washington 1952).
EPSTEIN, PAUL S., 'Diamat and Modern Science', *Bulletin of the Atomic Scientists,* August 1952, pp. 190–4.
GRAHAM, LOREN, *The Soviet Academy of Sciences and the Communist Party,* (Princeton 1967).
JORAVSKY, DAVID, *Soviet Marxism and Natural Science 1917–1932,* (New York 1961).
MEDVEDEV, ZHORES, *The Rise and Fall of T. D. Lysenko,* tr. I. M. LERNER, (New York 1969).
ZIRKLE, CONWAY, ed., *Death of a Science in Russia,* (Philadelphia 1949).

The Arts

ALEXANDROVA, V., *A History of Soviet Literature,* (New York 1964).
BROWN, EDWARD J., *The Proletarian Episode in Russian Literature 1928–1934,* (New York 1953).
Russian Literature Since the Revolution, (New York 1963).
VAN DER ENG-LIEDMEIER, A. M., *Soviet Literary Characters,* (The Hague 1959).
ERMOLAEV, HERMAN, *Soviet Literary Theories 1917–1934,* (Berkeley 1963).
GASIOROWSKA, XENIA, *Women in Soviet Fiction,* (Madison 1968).
GIBIAN, G., *Soviet Russian Literature in English: A Check-List Bibliography,* (Cornell 1967).
GORCHAKOV, N. A., *Istoriya sovetskogo teatra,* (New York 1956).
GRAY, CAMILLA, *The Great Experiment: Russian Art 1863–1922,* (London 1962).
HAYWARD, MAX, and LABEDZ, L., eds., *Literature and Revolution in Soviet Russia,* (Oxford 1963).
LEYDA, JAY, *Kino: A History of the Russian and Soviet Film,* (London 1960).
LONDON, KURT, *The Seven Soviet Arts,* (London 1937).
MAGUIRE, R. A., *Red Virgin Soil: Soviet Literature in the 1920s,* (Princeton 1968).
MATHEWSON, RUFUS A., *The Positive Hero in Russian Literature,* (New York 1958).

MIKULASEK, MIROSLAV, *Puti razvitiya sovetskoy komedii 1925–34 godov,* (Prague 1962).

ROBERTS, SPENCER E., *Soviet Historical Drama: Its Role in the Development of a National Mythology,* (The Hague 1965).

SINYAVSKY, A., and MENSHUTIN, A., *Poeziya pervykh let revolyutsii,* (Moscow 1964).

STRUVE, GLEB, *Russian Literature under Lenin and Stalin 1917–53,* (Oklahoma 1971).

TAMASHIN, L., *Sovetskaya dramaturgiya v gody grazhdanskoy voyny,* (Moscow 1961).

TROTSKY, L., *Literatura i revolyutsiya,* (Moscow 1924).

YELAGIN, YURIY, *Ukroshcheniye iskusstv,* (New York 1952).

ZAVALISHIN, VYACHESLAV, *Early Soviet Writers,* (New York 1958).

Index

Index

Index

Index

Index

Index